A Handbook
for *Social Science*
Field Research
Essays & Bibliographic Sources
on Research Design and Methods

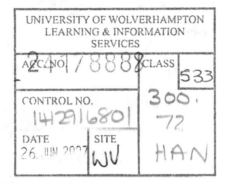
Edited by

Ellen Perecman *Council for Canadian-American Relations*
Sara R. Curran *University of Washington*

SAGE Publications
Thousand Oaks ▪ London ▪ New Delhi

For information:

Sage Publications, Inc.
2455 Teller Road
Thousand Oaks, California 91320
E-mail: order@sagepub.com

Sage Publications Ltd.
1 Oliver's Yard
55 City Road
London EC1Y 1SP
United Kingdom

Sage Publications India Pvt. Ltd.
B-42, Panchsheel Enclave
Post Box 4109
New Delhi 110 017 India

Printed in the United States of America

Library of Congress Cataloging-in-Publication Data

A handbook for social science field research: Essays & bibliographic sources
on research design and methods / edited by Ellen Perecman and Sara R. Curran.
    p. cm.
Includes bibliographical references and index.
ISBN 1-4129-1680-1 (cloth)
ISBN 1-4129-1681-X (pbk.)
   1. Social sciences—Field work. 2. Social sciences—Research.
3. Social sciences—Methodology. I. Perecman, Ellen. II. Curran, Sara R.
H62.H24528 2006
300′.72′3—dc22

                      2005022714

This book is printed on acid-free paper.

06   07   10 9 8 7 6 5 4 3 2 1

Acquiring Editor:	Lisa Cuevas Shaw
Editorial Assistant:	Karen Gia Wong
Production Editors:	Diana E. Axelsen and Denise Santoyo
Copy Editor:	Bonnie Freeman
Typesetter:	C&M Digitals (P) Ltd.
Indexer:	Kathy Paparchontis
Cover Designer:	Edgar Abarca

Contents

Acknowledgments

We would like to express our gratitude to the people who provided the foundation stones for the bibliographical content in this volume: Brad Barham, Agricultural and Applied Economics, University of Wisconsin—Madison; William Beeman, Anthropology, Brown University; David William Cohen, History/Anthropology, University of Michigan; David Collier, Political Science, UC Berkeley; Albert Fishlow, International and Public Affairs, Columbia University; Barbara Geddes, Political Science, University of California, Los Angeles; Bryna Goodman, History, University of Oregon; Emily Hannum, Sociology, University of Pennsylvania; Janet Hart, Political Science, University of Michigan; Gail Henderson, Sociology, University of North Carolina School of Medicine; Dennis Hogan, Demography, Brown University; John Knodel, Sociology, University of Michigan; Larissa Adler Lomnitz, Anthropology, Universidad Nacional Autonoma de Mexico; Andrew Orta, Anthropology, University of Illinois; Alberto Palloni, Demography, University of Wisconsin; Joseph Potter, Demography, University of Texas; Lakshmi K. Raut, Economics, University of Hawaii; Michele Shedlin, Sociomedical Sciences, Sociomedical Resource Associates; Thomas Spear, History, University of Wisconsin; and Luise White, History, University of Florida.

Among the contributors to this volume, Alma Gottlieb, Steve Harrell, Albert Park, Andrew Schrank, Bob Vitalis, and Michael Watts also provided foundational material for the bibliographies. We are grateful to them for that as well as for helping us shape the final bibliographies and bring them up to date. But none of that could have been accomplished without the invaluable assistance of Elizabeth Armstrong, Sociology and Public Affairs, Princeton University; Maria Patricia Fernandez-Kelly, Sociology, Princeton University; Tamara Giles-Vernick, History, University of Minnesota; Carolyn Rouse, Anthropology, Princeton University; Mario Small, Sociology, Princeton University; and Ashley Timmer, formerly with the Social Science Research Council (SSRC).

Special thanks to David Featherman, former president of the SSRC, for suggesting to Ellen Perecman long ago that it would be useful to begin compiling a bibliography of research methods for International Predissertation

Fellows; to Sheila Biddle for coming up with the idea for the International Predissertation Fellowship Program in the first place; to former program assistants at SSRC Lisa Angus, Sara Defeo, Alexa Dietrich, and Asia Sherman and former SSRC program coordinator Leila Kazemi; to Melanie Adams and Sarah Martin at Princeton University for assisting with the editing, organization, and production of the endless iterations of this manuscript; and to the Ford Foundation.

Extra special thank-yous are in order for Adam Perecman Frankel, Steve Harrell, Andrew Schrank, Tom Spear, and Michael Watts for going beyond the call of duty on more than one occasion and to Lisa Cuevas Shaw at Sage for sharing our faith in this project.

Finally, thank you to the hundreds of IPFP fellows whose experiences made us realize just how badly a book like this was needed. We hope it meets with your approval.

About the Authors

Sara Curran is Associate Professor of International Studies, Public Affairs, and Sociology at the University of Washington. Her interests include gender, demography, development and globalization, and environment. She is currently completing a manuscript titled *Shifting Boundaries, Transforming Lives: Globalization, Gender and Family Dynamics in Thailand.* She has published articles in *Ambio, Demography, Journal of International Women's Studies, Journal of Marriage and the Family, Population and Development Review, Rural Sociology, Social Science Research,* and *Teaching Sociology.* She was the recipient of the 2001 Sociologists for Women in Society Mentoring Award. She received her Ph.D. in sociology from the University of North Carolina in 1994.

David L. Featherman is Professor of Sociology and Psychology at the University of Michigan and founding director of the Center for Advancing Research and Solutions for Society. He studies aging and life course, social stratification, social psychology, social mobility, human development, and gerontology. His publications include *Social Science and Policymaking: A Search for Relevance in the Twentieth Century* (2001), "Social Self Efficacy and Short-Term Variability in Social Relationships: The MacArthur Successful Aging Studies" (1997), *Life-Span Development and Behavior* (1991), "Class and the Socialization of Children: Constancy, Change or Irrelevance?" (1988), "Ontogenesis and Sociogenesis: Problematics for Theory and Research About Development and Socialization Across the Life-Span" (1985), and "Opportunity and Change" (1978). He received a Ph.D. in social psychology from the University of Michigan in 1969.

Tamara Giles-Vernick is Associate Professor of History at the University of Minnesota. She studies African and environmental history and has published a book, *Cutting the Vines of the Past: Environmental Histories of the Central African Rainforest,* and articles in publications including the *Journal of African History, Environmental History,* and *Ethnohistory.* She is working on a book, preliminarily titled *Of Birds, Bugs, and Fevers: Malaria,*

Environment, and Public Health in French Soudan, 1900–1960, which explores an intellectual history of malaria among Bambara people in Mali, and an edited collection that analyzes the convergences of environmental history and the history of public health in the imperial world. She earned her Ph.D. in history from Johns Hopkins University in 1996.

Alma Gottlieb is Professor of Anthropology at the University of Illinois, where she also holds appointments in the Women's Studies Program and the Center for African Studies. Her research interests include the ethics and epistemology of fieldwork, gender systems and ideologies, indigenous religious traditions, African family structures, social and feminist theory, and the craft of writing anthropology. Her current research is focused on infants and infant care in anthropological perspective. Her publications include an award-winning coauthored memoir of fieldwork, *Parallel Worlds: An Anthropologist and a Writer Encounter Africa* (with Philip Graham, 1994), as well as *The Afterlife Is Where We Come From: The Culture of Infancy in West Africa* (2004), *A World of Babies: Imagined Childcare Guides for Seven Societies* (with Judy DeLoache, 2000), *Under the Kapok Tree: Identity and Difference in Beng Thought* (1996), *Beng-English Dictionary* (with Lynne Murphy, 1995), and *Blood Magic: The Anthropology of Menstruation* (with Thomas Buckley, 1988). She received her Ph.D. in cultural anthropology from the University of Virginia in 1983.

Stevan Harrell is Professor of Anthropology at the University of Washington and Curator of Asian Ethnology at the Burke Museum of Natural History and Culture. His studies include demography, family, ecology, education, ethnicity, and material culture in China and Taiwan. He is interested in the politics of translation between Chinese- and English-language anthropology, collaborative research and field narratives, the environment and society around Yangjuan Primary School in Southwest China, and the reconstruction of fertility in historical populations from genealogical records. His recent publications include "The History of the History of the Yi, Part II" (*Modern China*, 2003), *Ways of Being Ethnic in Southwest China* (2001), and *Perspectives on the Yi of Southwest China* (2001). He earned a Ph.D. in anthropology from Stanford University in 1974.

Albert Park is Associate Chair and Associate Professor of Economics and Associate Director and Faculty Associate of the Center for Chinese Studies at the University of Michigan and Faculty Affiliate of the Population Studies Center (Institute of Social Research), also at the University of Michigan. He also has affiliations with the Population Studies Center and William Davidson Institute of the University of Michigan. His research interests are in development, transition, labor, applied microeconomics, and the Chinese economy. He has supervised several collaborative survey research projects in urban and rural China. His recent publications include "Economic Returns to Schooling in Urban China, 1988 to 2001" (forthcoming), "How Has Economic Restructuring Affected China's Urban Workers?" (forthcoming), "What Is China's True Unemployment Rate?" (2005), "Are China's Financial Reforms Leaving the Poor Behind?" (forthcoming), "Joint Liability Lending and the Rise and Fall of China's Township and Village Enterprises" (2003), "Competition Under Credit Rationing: Theory and Evidence From Rural China" (2003), "Education and Poverty in Rural China" (2002), and "Regional Poverty Targeting in China" (2002). He received his Ph.D. in economics from Stanford University in 1996.

Ellen Perecman is Executive Director of the Council for Canadian-American Relations in New York City as well as founder and Executive Director of New Worlds Theatre Project. She has published numerous articles, book chapters, and edited volumes in the field of neurolinguistics and behavioral neurology, including *Cognitive Processing in the Right Hemisphere* (1983), *The Frontal Lobes Revisited* (1987), and *Integrating Theory and Practice in Clinical Neuropsychology* (1989). A professional actress, Perecman trained with Julie Bovasso and Vivian Matalon and has appeared on the New York stage most recently in staged readings of classic Yiddish plays. Perecman received her Ph.D. in linguistics from the Graduate Center, City University of New York, in 1980.

Michael J. Piore is a David W. Skinner Professor of Political Economy and Associate Director of the Center for Technology Policy and Industrial Development at the Massachusetts Institute of Technology. He is a labor economist interested in the broad interplay between economics, politics, and society. He has worked on a number of labor market and industrial relations problems, including low income labor markets, the impact of technology on work, migration, labor market segmentation, and the relationship among the labor market, business strategy, and industrial organization. His most recent book is *Innovation –The Missing Dimension* (2004). Other publications include *Beyond Individualism* (1995), *The Second Industrial Divide* (1984), *Dualism and Discontinuity in Economic Life* (1980), *Bird of Passage* (1979), *Unemployment and Inflation, Institutionalist and Structuralist Views* (1979), and *Internal Labor Markets and Manpower Analysis* (1969). Piore received his Ph.D. in economics from Harvard University in 1996.

Andrew Schrank is Assistant Professor of Sociology at the University of New Mexico. He works on the sources and consequences of foreign investment, local entrepreneurship, and economic transformation in the Third World. His most recent publications include "Ready-to-Wear Development: Foreign

Investment, Technology Transfer, and Learning-by-Watching in the Apparel Trade" (*Social Forces*, 2004) and "Entrepreneurship, Export Diversification, and Economic Reform: The Birth of a 'Developmental Community' in the Dominican Republic" (*Comparative Politics*, forthcoming). He is also completing a book manuscript on the social foundations of economic diversification in the Caribbean basin. He earned his Ph.D. in sociology from the University of Wisconsin—Madison in 2000.

Susan E. Short is Associate Professor of Sociology at Brown University. Her current research, which draws on survey as well as ethnographic data, focuses on social welfare and its articulation with social change. Her published work includes articles on fertility and reproductive health, household economic processes, women's work and child care, child well-being, and mixed-methods research. Recent publications include "Use of Maternal Health Services in Rural China" (*Population Studies*, 2004, with Fengyu Zhang) and "Second Births and the Second Shift: A Research Note on Gender Equity and Fertility" (*Population and Development Review*, 2004, with Berna Miller Torr). She holds a Ph.D. in sociology from the University of North Carolina at Chapel Hill.

Robert Vitalis is Director of the Middle East Center at the University of Pennsylvania. His research interests include state and market formation in Saudi Arabia, the political and cultural economy of the world oil industry, American expansionism, history of international relations and development studies, and race and American international relations theory. He is working on two books, *America's Kingdom*, about Saudi Arabia, and *North Versus Black Atlantic*, about the origins of international relations and development studies in the United States. His recent publications include "International Studies in America" (2002), "War, Keynesianism and Colonialism: Explaining State-Market Relations in the Post-War Middle East" (2000), "American Ambassador in Technicolor and Cinemascope: Hollywood and Revolution on the Nile" (2000), "The Graceful and Generous Liberal Gesture: Making Racism Invisible in American International Relations" (2000), and *When Capitalists Collide: Business Conflict and the End of Empire in Egypt* (1995). He received his Ph.D. in political science from the Massachusetts Institute of Technology in 1989.

Michael Watts is Chancellor's Professor of Geography and Director of African Studies at the University of California, Berkeley, and was a Fellow at the Center for the Advanced Behavioral Sciences at Stanford University, 2004–2005. He established the Berkeley Working Group on Environmental Politics in 1994 and was the Director of the Instituite of International Studies, 1994–2004. He currently directs the undergraduate Development

Studies Program. His research interests are political economy, political ecology, Africa, South Asia, economic development, peasant societies, social and cultural theory, U.S. agriculture, and the world oil industry. His publications include *Globalizing Agro-Food* (1997), *Liberation Ecologies* ([1995] 2004), *Geographies of Global Change* ([1995] 2002), *Reworking Modernity* (1992), and *Silent Violence* (1983). He is currently working on a book about oil and empire. He received his Ph.D. from the University of Michigan in 1979.

Foreword

E very human successfully negotiates daily life as an unwitting but naïve
behavioral scientist. Only with the benefit of dozens of at least tacit
models of mind (e.g., self-expression, intentions, emotions, decision strategies), real and imagined social relationships (e.g., cooperation, conflict,
negotiation), and how they are combined into complex institutions like
families, firms, neighborhoods, and nations are we capable of creating order
out of complexity—if not chaos—each day. What separates this naïve but
necessary and pragmatic representation of mind, selves, and society from the
enterprise called analytical social science are forms of mental discipline—
that is, analytical observation, thinking, and evidence-based reasoning about
social experience. That discipline is just as pragmatic as the naïve social
science that allows us to navigate our way through life each day, testing
our tacit models of what we expect to happen against what does happen
by assessing our misjudgments and mistakes. So analytical social science
and naïve social science are equally pragmatic—that is, drawn from the real
world and reformulated as experience requires, so as to make our lives
livable and comprehensible among kith and kin, insofar as we are able.

But the mental discipline of analytical social science that raises its
enterprise above the naïve is not easy work. And it requires tools to assist
analytical observation, thinking, and reasoning. It requires still other tools
to extract observations—the data of social science—from ongoing thoughts,
social relationships, and institutional practices, for example. After all, the
conduct of social science is nearly always embedded within the everyday
realities of social relationships and personal mental life, the tacit stuff that
can "bias" what we as social scientists see and interpret as empirical reality.
Thus, truly analytical social science demands still other tools to organize and
interpret these observations, these data, in ways that become credible and
useful well beyond what is tacitly useful from our naïve models of social
realities. And finally, the burdens of being a social scientist require more
than the rigorous discipline of analytical observing and reasoning; there are
special ethical burdens as well. Scientists who conduct their research in
others' homes or communities or who seek their life stories as data have

obligations to protect confidentiality and anonymity. In addition, the standards for truthfulness and authenticity owed to one's fellow scientists impose a high bar for research integrity. So being a social scientist is not for the faint of heart or the social gadfly.

A Handbook for Social Science Field Research provides a tool kit that will equip advanced undergraduates and graduate students, even early career social scientists with narrow disciplinary training, for ever more sophisticated, analytical, self-conscious, and ethical social science. What is so unusual about this collection of essays and bibliographies—this tool kit of best practices—is what it explicitly takes for granted as the fundamental task of doing analytical social science and therefore what practices are essential.

One foundational assumption is that the empirical or phenomenal social world is complex. However, every tool we would use to analyze that complexity—literally to take it apart and examine interrelationships, whether observations, interviews, or archived documents, for example—has its limitations. And therefore the very complexity of what we seek to understand requires multiple methods or analytical tools, one to supplement the other's strengths and compensate for its shortcomings. For too long, social scientists were trained within deep methodological wells, as for example anthropologists within the ethnographic traditions of participant observation or sociologists within survey research questionnaires and samples of populations. What they each saw was the sky from the bottom of their respective wells and rarely, if ever, the horizon's scope. To the credit of *A Handbook for Social Science Field Research,* the association of a preferred methodology with a discipline is severed, and all who would do social science are urged to find and use various methods that add to their grasp of complexity—to their scope or field of vision—and to the sense they can make of it.

A second assumption is that social complexity consists, at least in part, of local differences in customs, tacit cultural assumptions, and institutions that nonetheless may manifest some greater or lesser similarity from place to place. This assumption underlies the whole rationale for fieldwork, that is, taking social science questions or hypothetical propositions constructed about one societal or cultural setting into another. Are the answers the same? Do the propositions hold with equal force? And just as important, how would I know? The classical rationale for fieldwork was to elicit a systematic understanding of the lived world of some "foreign" people or place as a taken-for-granted reality that was different—at least in some ways—from one's home base as a reference point. Of course, fieldwork in contemporary terms begins by recognizing that self and other can (and must) be distinguished only with great analytical care, as noted in this book. And doing fieldwork in the 21st century does not require literally going abroad, especially in heterogeneous, pluralistic societies with Internet connectivity, in order to analyze or construct patterns of similarity and difference in human behavior and institutions. In fact, while this book was intended primarily as preparation for those going abroad to do social science, it serves equally well those who seek to capture and characterize diversity and global connectivity within their own societal context.

A third assumption is that the present is but a point in time and that history, like place, is part of social complexity—part of the dynamic of social complexity in the here and now. This is not the same as saying that the present is merely the realization of the past and that therefore one can deeply comprehend the present only by beginning at the beginning, as a historian in the archives. But a strong case is made that those who would capture social life as it is unfolding, for example in differential equations capturing time-sensitive rates of change or adaptation (such as the diffusion of HIV/AIDS among rural married women in South Africa) might also want to plumb the archives for information about four decades of apartheid to put the contemporary coefficients into context. This idea—and the wise guidance of this book—corrects another regrettable distinction or false methodological division within the human sciences—the distinction between qualitative and quantitative analysis. While the historian and the epidemiologist or demographer may tend to begin with different methods—the former qualitative and the latter quantitative—both use their tools analytically against standards of evidence, argument, and logic, as social scientists. Again, A Handbook for Social Science Field Research would have the social scientist—whether economist or historian, demographer or anthropologist—reach across the quantitative-versus-qualitative divide for quantitative and qualitative methods that in their complementarity help find order in the complexity.

Which brings me finally to the history of the International Predissertation Fellowship Program at the Social Science Research Council (SSRC) during the course of my presidency in the 1990s. This book grows out of that program, as noted by its coeditors Ellen Perecman and Sara Curran. The Program was the brainchild of at least two colleagues at the Ford Foundation, Sheila Biddle and Peter Stanley. Sheila and Peter sought the advice of the SSRC and its collaborator, the American Council of Learned Societies (ACLS), as well as the guidance of many university-based scholars around the country as to how best to prepare a new generation of social scientists and humanists seeking to study the world outside the United States. Foreign area studies, as it was called just after World War II, was created as a means of ensuring a solid base of ongoing advanced study and also of wider cultural sophistication in a nation too often ignorant of the world beyond its shores. In the late 1980s and early 1990s, the Ford Foundation, the chief nongovernmental supporter of such scholarship and education, sought new ways to infuse more social science capacity and methodological diversity into these fields more often dominated by humanistic and linguistic approaches. So the collaboration between the SSRC (mostly social science) and the ACLS (mostly the humanities) seemed a natural one for the Foundation to explore as a means of cross-fertilizing ways to globalize the local (the wont of social science) and localize the global (the wont of the humanities). The IPFP was a means to that cross-fertilization. The Program recruited social scientists (mainly from the core social science disciplines) and provided preparations (linguistic and other) for dissertation work in the field, that is, outside the United States. Later, the Program recruited as well from graduate students already predisposed to research abroad, sometimes with a comparative idea in mind, and with formal preparation for work in one regional setting but needing preparation for comparative work in a second.

It is important at this point to emphasize that neither the IPFP nor the multi-method case made by this book implies that a single social scientist should master all methods so as to be equipped for all circumstances. In fact, while the various authors of the reflective chapters of this book have shared the personal, intellectual benefits of using multiple approaches, that practice is both difficult and very demanding to command at a high level of expertise. It takes nothing from the conviction of these narratives or from the book's foundational and correct message to students to note a different but complementary approach: namely, collaboration among those whose methodological expertise is complementary. In fact, much of contemporary social science stems from collaborations rather than from scholars working alone. Indeed, one of the legacies of the IPFP is sets of awardees, now former fellows, who discovered each other as research partners and now collaborate, combining their respective methodological as well as substantive strengths.

Thus, *A Handbook for Social Science Field Research* reflects only a part, but a wonderfully illustrative one, of the great human productivity of the Ford Foundation's investment, of the two councils' stewardship of their commission under the IPFP grant from Ford, of the many distinguished faculty mentors who guided the Program and its awardees during their projects, and of course of the Program's staff. David Szanton, then at the SSRC, worked closely with Biddle and Stanley at Ford and the Councils' two presidents in shaping the original program objectives. But it was Ellen Perecman, over a dozen years, who provided senior staff leadership, liaised with Sheila Biddle and the faculty advisors, and assisted with student recruitment; she made the program work and adapted it to its changing context and student needs. This book, a tribute to the Program, is also a tribute to Ellen and to the shared vision she and Sara Curran possessed to make it a reality. As former president of the SSRC, I am both pleased and proud of their collective achievement on behalf of a new generation of social scientists.

—*David L. Featherman*
University of Michigan

Introduction

At the beginning of our own research careers, one over a quarter of a century ago and the other ten years ago, each of us had the good fortune to work as part of a team with researchers more seasoned than we who showed us how to apply what we had learned as graduate students to our experiences in "the field." For one of us (SC), "the field" was Thailand. For the other (EP), it was the human brain, a "field" in only a nontraditional sense of the term. Despite the fact that our backgrounds as researchers could not be more different, there is a memory we share: the anguished moment when we realized that our best-laid research plans had failed miserably in the real world.

Fortunately for both of us, our senior colleagues were always there to cushion the fall. They reminded us that we were not failures; they pointed us to books and articles that provided us with the knowledge we needed to understand why our research plans had failed. They were there to assure us that the most important lesson we could learn about conducting research in "the field" was to be flexible, to be ready to shift gears at any moment, and that we were not expected to have all the answers.

Fast-forward to 1999. One of us (SC) was now a member of the faculty at Princeton University, the other (EP) a program director at the Social Science Research Council (SSRC). By now each of us independently had learned the three cardinal tenets of field research:

1. Every research question—regardless of field or discipline—is uniquely defined by a specific set of circumstances.

2. There can be no attempt to answer a question without deep knowledge of the specific contextual parameters defining those circumstances.

3. Such deep knowledge comes only to those who have paid their dues.

Our paths converged in the context of a fellowship program administered by the SSRC and the American Council of Learned Societies (ACLS): the International Predissertation Fellowship Program (IPFP). Developed and administered from 1990 to 2002 by Ellen Perecman, with the intellectual support of ACLS's Stephen Wheatley and with funding from the Ford Foundation, the IPFP was designed to compensate for the frequent failure of graduate training programs in the social sciences to devote sufficient attention to the full range of methods available for research, to counteract the tendency for social science disciplines to rely on some methods to the exclusion of others, and to ameliorate a situation in which students of the individual disciplines are rarely taught field research methods or sufficiently briefed on a host of practical issues concerning the conduct of field research.

The hallmark of the IPFP was the annual training conference and regional workshop series designed to bring young researchers together with seasoned ones to explore issues of research design from a cross-disciplinary and cross-regional perspective. Those conferences and workshops became the impetus for this volume, as year in and year out we watched how, through the interaction between more and less experienced students and between students and faculty, students' research design skills were sharpened, their thinking about how to conduct social science research was broadened, and they became more self-conscious about the implications of each and every choice they would make in their research. Students were encouraged to retain for future use a specially prepared bibliography of materials addressing or illustrating methods, tools, and practices of social science field research, which was updated annually. Over the life of the IPFP and through the largesse of conference faculty, the bibliography grew.

As each of us watched students and faculty learn from each other how best to take advantage of the research practices of different disciplinary traditions, as we watched them engage with one another with absolute intellectual abandon, we learned what young researchers wanted to know and what they needed to know. We learned how important—and comforting—it is for them to rediscover that university professors were also once clueless graduate students. We were reminded, on the one hand, how generous and humble seasoned researchers can be when asked to reflect on the lessons they have learned in the course of earning their stripes and, on the other hand, how grateful young researchers are for the opportunity to benefit from their seniors' mistakes. It became clear to us that there was a long-standing and growing demand in the social sciences for innovative approaches to international field research on the pressing questions of our day that reflect a convergence of methods and concepts from across the disciplines and that are based as much on science as on common sense.

Students were disarmed by the accessibility and honesty of conference and workshop faculty, by the idiosyncrasy of many of the messages, and by the irreverence with which those messages were often conveyed: Irreverence toward the academy; irreverence toward the hierarchy within the academy; and irreverence toward "the rules of the game."

As students wrestled intellectually with faculty over beers in hotel bars and faculty shared their most embarrassing moments in the field between laps in the pool, we decided it was our duty to try to bottle this experience to the extent possible—complete with its intimate feel and its irreverent attitude—so that its benefits might be shared by future generations of students as well. *A Handbook for Social Science Field Research* is our attempt to do that.

Each of the two parts in the book has two principal components: contemplative essays on the conduct of social science research are followed by bibliographies containing a unique and substantial collection of references bearing on issues in and around that essay. Essays by leading social scientists in an array of disciplines address research design, specific research methods, the value of combining methods and tools to strengthen research design, and research ethics. The essays speak to methodological issues authors feel were neglected in their own graduate careers and should be included in the training protocols of graduate students and junior researchers today. They offer perspectives on the value of a given research method from scholars within and outside the discipline most strongly associated with the method—perspectives readers are unlikely to have gotten in their graduate training programs.

Throughout the essays in this volume, we have worked to maintain the sense of irreverence and commitment to honesty that pervaded the IPFP conferences. An important ethical message shines through for readers about the essential requirement that research be conducted with as much transparency as possible. Throughout these essays, authors hammer home the importance, whether in the reading of texts or during an interview, of publicly acknowledging skepticism, double-checking, triangulating, reflecting on how one's own emotions might be affecting interpretations, or revisiting questions and earlier answers. The authors make the case for demystifying the fieldwork experience and advancing fieldwork methods for the next generation of scholars by revealing the thoughts, emotions, decisions, and reactions they experienced in the course of their fieldwork.

The book begins in Part I with essays and tools for their purpose that take readers through the process of choosing the most effective research tools: archives (Robert Vitalis); the case study method (Andrew Schrank); ethnographic approaches (Alma Gottlieb); oral histories (Tamara Giles-Vernick); focus groups (Susan Short); surveys and secondary data sources (Albert Park); and combining qualitative and quantitative tools (Michael Piore). Part II includes reflections on essential background reading for fieldwork by Stevan

Harrell and Andrew Schrank and discussions of the process of designing a research project (Michael Watts), carrying it out ethically (Sara Curran), and reworking it when the realities of the field confront the blueprint for the project (Andrew Schrank).

Insofar as the essays here provide multiple perspectives, they show how a wide range of methods, tools, and practices can enhance research by broadening the approach—and the set of skills—brought to it. Alma Gottlieb uses the playful image of a seesaw as a metaphor for the relationship between quantitative and qualitative research methods: "As if attached by a fulcrum, they form part of a single dynamic system, but at any given moment they produce two different, indeed sometimes incommensurable forms of knowledge." Authors identify advantages—and pitfalls—of using a particular tool or method and provide criteria for deciding whether that tool or method is the optimal one for answering a given set of research questions.

Our contributing authors work within disciplines, but they do not pretend to speak for or represent those disciplines. When they speak, they speak from the heart with a candor that is wonderfully refreshing in a literature of carefully chosen words and politically correct positions. In the authentic voices of some of the most experienced and well-respected American social science researchers engaged in international research today, these essays reflect lessons learned—and wisdom gained—from years of conducting social science research. Michael Watts tells us with brutal honesty that "graduate training can sometimes appear like permanent crisis management." Michael Piore reveals that he "stumbled into" his research approach and then "continued doing it because it was interesting and fun and seemed to yield insights into problems I considered it important, socially and morally, to solve. Miraculously, what I was doing attracted enough interest and attention that I got tenure anyway, despite my research approach." Albert Park admits that "one of my goals [in the essay] is to provide advice I wish I had been given at an earlier stage in my career." Bob Vitalis boasts that "I still have an incomplete in multivariate statistics on the books . . . and so you won't find me writing models."

One is caught off guard when Andrew Schrank tells us that he gets insights from "the acknowledgments, prefaces, introductions, and appendices to my favorite books . . . [into] how they were written. . . . To whom did the author talk? When? Why? At whose prompting? With what results?" Or when Alma Gottlieb writes that "as you collect data, your understanding of the local situation *should* keep changing, and attending to your own changing understandings may well suggest reorienting your original focus" and that "it is important to think about how your own emotional biography may shape your research agenda."

And one is completely disarmed by Steve Harrell's statement: "I suspect that the number of pints drained in this exercise [of comparing your own ethnographic experiences to those of others] has not diminished as the amount of ink spilt has increased." Or by Michael Watts's advice on writing a proposal: "To stand a chance, your proposal must not simply be solid; it must jump out of the pile. . . . There are several ways in which a proposal can achieve this distinctiveness. One is to have three typos in the first line." Or by Michael Piore's view that "In interpreting interviews, I do not think sufficient attention is ever given to the possibility that the world is really chaotic."

Although the book does not cover all social science disciplines or all issues concerning field methods in the social sciences, the slices we have chosen to cover are those we and our authors consider most relevant. We decided that the issue of ethics and fieldwork deserved a stand-alone essay even though the topic is addressed throughout the book. For, as Alma Gottlieb reminds us so poignantly: "Ethical issues pervade every decision, great and small, that one makes. . . . Should you put your own position at risk and help your long-time informant when he finds himself on the wrong side of the law? . . . Is it better to expend a large proportion of your scarce research funds trying to save the life of a gravely sick infant . . . or to save the funds for others with a greater likelihood of recovery?" And as Tamara Giles-Vernick points out, deciding what to write about can present an ethical problem since it is sometimes necessary to "distinguish carefully . . . between writing *about* sensitive or confidential concerns and divulging these concerns."

Sara Curran's essay takes an in-depth look at how our usual forays into the field frequently begin with a nod toward the regulated aspects of ethical concerns via our applications to institutional review boards (IRBs). But a researcher soon realizes that ethical concerns reach well beyond the regulations precisely because successful fieldwork necessarily involves social relationships that are imbued with differential power and potential conflicts of interest. Negotiating these relationships ensures access to the field and "data" but can also be fraught with ethical compromises.

The book contains a number of invaluable bibliographies: Archives, Case Studies, Ethnography, Oral History, Focus Groups, Surveys and Secondary Data Sources, Study Design and Quantitative Methods, and Research Ethics and Other Essential Reading. Within the individual bibliographies, subsections often address specific areas of focus. These carefully constructed bibliographies constitute a rich source of materials—both in print and on the Web—that address or illustrate a range of quantitative and qualitative research methods, tools, and practices and that have relevance for a wide range of quantitative and qualitative research methods and tools. All are publications and websites that we consider important as one prepares to do fieldwork in the developing world for the first time—or for the fiftieth time.

Each of the bibliographies represents a collaboration between the editors of this volume and their consultants, on the one hand, and the original architects of the lists of reference materials that served as the foundation for these bibliographies—some of whom are essay authors—on the other. The bibliographies also include a section on the ethics of field research, a topic rarely given the attention it deserves. The bibliographies are organized topically; subheadings have been created to highlight the different kinds of materials available within each category of methods or tools (e.g., archives, case studies), as well as to make it easy for readers to find the references they will find most useful. While the bibliographies are intended to reflect a sampling of key references in each area, the citations that appear at the end of individual essays under the heading *Supplemental References* will provide a richer exposure to a field.

This book, like the conferences and workshops that inspired it, is intended to help new researchers understand how to choose the research methods, tools, and practices that will best address the questions they are trying to answer—regardless of whether the choices meet departmental regulations for Ph.D. theses. And like those gatherings, its aim is to provide an opportunity for researchers to step back and reflect on the strengths and limitations of their disciplines and to broaden the scope of their thinking about the methodological options available to them as social scientists. It invites them to consider ways in which research methods and perspectives from across the social science disciplines might advance their research goals. In short, its aim is to reinvent what it means to do good research and what it means to be prepared for it.

—*Ellen Perecman and Sara R. Curran*

PART I

Selecting the Right Tools

The essays to follow in Part I offer reflections from a variety of authorities in the fields of anthropology, economics, history, political science, and sociology. The authors of these essays provide readers with insight and perspective about how different methodological approaches enhance understanding of a context and enrich knowledge within and across disciplines. Each essay reflects the author's efforts to build a stronger social scientific understanding of people, events, history, and social change by breaching the discipline's methodological boundaries. Some authors write from the vantage point of their own discipline's methods in an attempt to reach out to members of other disciplines. Others write about how their work has been enriched by methods they have drawn from outside their own disciplines (e.g., the Vitalis and Piore essays). In each case, readers are given a taste of the author's nitty-gritty personal experiences, of basic guidelines for taking a particular methodological approach, and of epistemological insights into how a method relates to theory, knowledge, and disciplinary boundaries.

Essay authors provide perspectives on how to think about their respective methods of observation and analysis, where to begin and what to consider when employing that method, and how the experience of going into the field armed with a particular methodological approach is met with unanticipated opportunities and constraints, often requiring alternative or additional methodological tools. Each essay is paired with a bibliography of relevant references.

Robert Vitalis provides a political scientist's perspective on archival methods. His very personal account of how he stumbled into doing archival research in the mid-1980s provides a telling story of how the case, the field experience, and most important, who you are as a researcher can dictate the methodological approach. He describes his approach to political institutions and questions as "reverse engineering of particular processes of myth making" through systematic collection and analysis of archival documents. He describes his approach and archival methods generally and also debunks disciplinary stereotypes and myths in history and political science, alleviating any potential unease on the part of nonhistorians about employing archival research methods.

Andrew Schrank's essay on case-based research defines case study research and argues for its relevance as a source of causal inference, providing guidelines for how to do a case study, and giving a justification for how case-based research can be used to uncover causal mechanisms. Along the way, Schrank highlights classic studies using case-based research as touchstone references for theory and substantive insight.

In a detailed and wide-reaching essay, Alma Gottlieb provides well-developed examples of ethnography and how it complements other social science field research methods. She argues that minimal fluency in a local language, proper note-taking skills, and knowledge of hermeneutics are critical tools for ethnographic fieldwork. Gottlieb concludes her essay by outlining the guideposts for future methodological developments in the field of ethnography. Her very practical essay pairs nicely with Stevan Harrell's insights about the history and development of the ethnographic method in Part II of this volume.

Tamara Giles-Vernick provides a nuanced essay on the strengths and weaknesses of oral historical methods. She alerts readers to the pitfalls associated with oral accounts and the hermeneutical intricacies of situating oneself, the teller, and the historical moment, and she provides guidance on how to avoid those pitfalls by integrating oral historic accounts with other sources of information. She sensitizes the reader to the ethical dilemmas of collecting, caring for, and writing about oral historical accounts, including discussions about the construction of trust with informants, objective and subjective interpretations of falsehoods, awareness of selective accounts, and the political consequences of publishing particular accounts.

Focus group interviews are frequently critiqued but provide useful insights for researchers employing mixed-method approaches. Susan Short's essay provides a balanced and comprehensive perspective on focus groups, offering advice on when they can be used best and when they are not appropriate. Her essay offers useful techniques for conducting and analyzing focus group interviews. And, finally, she considers the ethical constraints inherent in focus group interviewing.

Albert Park begins his essay on survey methodology by explaining what surveys can and cannot do and how they complement qualitative research methods. The remainder of his essay discusses various types of surveys, the advantages of using extant surveys, and the factors to consider when deciding to conduct one's own survey or collaborate with others. His essay elaborates on key elements of survey research, including sampling issues, questionnaire design, data collection management, and analysis of survey data. He then addresses the pitfalls and opportunities of using surveys cross-culturally and in developing countries. Park ends his essay with thoughts and references on how to analyze survey data.

In the second of two essays in which authors discuss their experiences breaching the methodological conventions of their own disciplines, Michael Piore explores how qualitative methods have informed his study of economic processes. His account provides valuable insights for economists going into the field, as well as for noneconomists interested in engaging with economic theories and methods. Like Vitalis, Piore demonstrates how he allowed himself to be led by his intuition and, further, allowed his field observations to challenge economic theory. Also like Vitalis, Piore demonstrates how both the theory and his intuition spurred a systematic collection and analysis of open-ended interviews to better understand the motivations and behaviors of economic actors. Piore concludes by providing a brief methodological exercise showing how narratives can be used systematically in economic analyses.

1

Archives

The Past Is Another Country[1]

Robert Vitalis

I.

The basic point of this chapter is a simple one. If you are a social scientist and you plan to write about the past—for example, about the ending of the Cold War or the vicissitudes of the Venezuelan oil industry or the twisting course of democracy promotion in the Philippines or in Haiti—then you will have to adopt the method of historians.[2] That is, you will have to go to the archives. Virtually all social scientists preparing to write a dissertation in international or comparative or area studies today take it for granted that they will be conducting research abroad, in the field, for 1 or 3 or 6 or 12 months, perhaps in Cairo or Jakarta, Maracaibo or Baku, Paris or Chiapas. Much of their training before and after taking general exams or writing qualifying papers is geared (we hope) toward developing the skills and techniques necessary for this fieldwork: studying Tagalog or Farsi or Spanish, designing appropriate survey instruments, making contacts with research institutions and scholars, taking classes in and practicing ethnographic methods, figuring out where to find data sets that they need or how to build their own, and the like. Virtually no one successfully obtains funding and begins a project away from home without first demonstrating some degree of sophistication and rigor about place and about method.

Writing seriously about a place in a time other than one's own demands a similar degree of rigor and methodological self-consciousness. The past is another country in which researchers must demonstrate their minimal competence before setting out, and about which, by journey's end, they ought to tell us something new and significant. To write a history or historical case (or even to write *the* history chapter) without undertaking original research in primary sources is akin to surveying a population while ignoring protocols about random sampling, to testing a model but forgetting about the problem of multicollinearity, or to spending 6 months at a site as a participant-observer without ever taking field notes.

As you will see, taking the archival turn is less daunting than it might first appear. Even if it were not the case, there is no getting around the issue, assuming that you value rigor and reliability in your scholarship.

Since 1984, all the research and writing I have done as a political scientist have involved working with primary sources of one kind or another—State Department record sets, the files of the Ministry of Housing and Reconstruction in Cairo, the private papers of a Saudi dissident, and the private papers of American political scientists. Each of the projects was involved primarily with theoretical debates within parts of political science. On conventional maps of the discipline, these projects would be located in regions known as comparative politics, political economy of development, and international relations. But I have also published my work in history journals.

I took this archival turn in my work entirely by accident. In May 1984, I was at the Massachusetts Institute of Technology (MIT), preparing to go to Cairo for a year to research a dissertation on multinational corporations in construction and infrastructure development. It was the beginning of the wave of expansion in U.S. services overseas that would make firms like Halliburton and Bechtel into household names. Given the close relationship to state building, studying the engineering industries made sense. Egypt was then an emerging market of the first rank because of the millions of dollars in U.S. aid flowing there as a result of the American-brokered Camp David agreement. In Cairo, the construction sector had served as a redoubt for local capital during the experiment in Arab socialism. The dawn of economic liberalization in Egypt seemed, above all, to be about private sector building in both senses of the term.

One day I corralled a member of the MIT faculty, Thomas Ferguson, and described the project to him. Ferguson, at the time the political economy editor of the *Nation,* possesses encyclopedic knowledge of business and politics in New Deal America. Theda Skocpol once pinned the label "Beardsian" on him in a footnote war the two were waging, and Ferguson wore it as a badge of honor, as well he should have. Charles Beard (1874–1948) was the great Progressive Era historian most famous for advancing economic interpretations of American politics. He served as president of the American Political

Science Association in 1926 and the American Historical Association in 1933. I tell you this so that you will better understand Ferguson's basic response to my short disquisition, which was a characteristic quip: "You got to get the docs on these guys," by which he meant the "documents," that is, the paper trail left by oilmen, bankers, and other investors in the competitive conflicts that he argues are central to understanding the course of American policy at any particular time.

I had no idea what this piece of advice entailed in practice, but I tried to find its relevance in enhancing my project. Ferguson must have given me some minimal direction—it is a little hazy now—because one of his own favored haunts, the business school's Baker Library at Harvard, was the first place I visited. The Baker Library had a copy of the original Arthur D. Little industrial development program designed for the Egyptian military junta in 1954–1955 by Harvard development economist Edward Mason back in the day when the U.S. Agency for International Development was promoting import substitution industries and land reform in the Third World. The real payoff came, however, when I went to Washington and spent a week in the declassified State Department records. It was as if a window had opened to the political economy of a time and place that no one knew about, to judge from the existing literature in Arabic and English. I worked nonstop again that week, reading embassy telegrams, dispatches, and memoranda of conversations.

Once in Egypt, I abandoned the idea of mapping the business groups and conflicts of the moment and instead worked backward in time to trace the course of the business groups and investment conflicts that had shaped the landscape of the 1920s through the 1950s. My research strategy also changed, and I spent more time scouring libraries in ministries and elsewhere around the city than interviewing. I found old newspaper morgues, worked in the Egyptian National Archive (*dar al-watha'iq*) and National Library (*dar al-kutub*), cajoled private papers and documents from a set of remarkably generous engineers and business families, and spent months more in collections in Kew and Oxford in the United Kingdom; Independence, Missouri; Abilene, Texas; MIT; and the U.S. State Department and Agency for International Development.[3]

Two points stand out about my trespassing in the research domain of historians and learning on the run that year. One point, and it is important enough to raise here and take it up again below, is the need for precise and consistent citing of records in order to satisfy the norms of transparency and verifiability. Will someone who follows your trail be able to quickly identify, locate, and assess the documents you used? The other point is about a particular kind of competence that seems to matter to the goal of discovering new materials and producing original insights. Among a set of source-based skills that good historians possess in abundance, I saw the importance of reading clues in sources that would point me to others, ones I had not known or thought about at first. Ludmilla Jordanova, in *History in Practice*, calls this skill "thinking laterally": "Deciding which sources are 'relevant' is rarely straight-forward, and often it is a question of thinking laterally, even of finding oblique sources that provide unexpected insights into a problem" (Jordanova 2000, p. 184).

The book I wrote based on this research, *When Capitalists Collide* (1995), challenged a familiar model of the business community. Egypt and other countries are often described as rent by conflict between archetypal, nationally oriented businessmen, or "class fraction," determined to break the bounds of dependency, and their opponents, an antinational, or "com-prador fraction," acting as a handmaiden of the world market.[4] Young American academics had turned to this kind of dependency-informed sociology of Egypt in the 1970s and 1980s, while Egyptians themselves have been writing in this vein since the 1950s.[5] We called what we were writing "political economy." Our theories indeed seemed robust. Plenty of books in Arabic and French included accounts of Egypt that fit as surprisingly well as they fit Brazil, Kenya, India, and China. We ignored the critics, in particular those among the senior faculty where we trained, whose days in the sun as modernization theorists had passed. By the time I was through with my research, however, things had begun to look different.[6]

Many scholars had been raising questions similar to the ones I was asking while trying to make sense of the records I had found of business conflicts in Egypt between the 1920s and 1950s, before the state nationalized most large (and not-so-large) local and foreign-owned enterprises. For example, political economists working on Africa in the early 1980s contested the nature of local capital in the course of something called the Kenya Debate. Gavin Kitching summed up the issues at stake and resolved much of the confusion surrounding them in the following passage:

> The point, then, is that on both sides in the Kenya debate a great deal of dubi-ous inference from highly partial information is being dignified as theory(ies) of the state and made to stand in place of the sort of knowledge of political processes and struggle which academics do not have and cannot get. My own guess, for what it is worth, is that every businessman in Kenya and every state official from a lower-middle level upward could be categorized as a "national bourgeois" from some points of view, and with reference to some of his/her activities and aspirations, and as a "comprador" from others. They enter into conjunctural alliances around particular struggles and issues which could be categorized as in the interests of transnational capital sometimes in some respects, and as hostile to those interests and nationalist in thrust at other

times and in other respects. Such alliances at times give parts of the state apparatus . . . one coloration and at times another. Similarly "transnational capital" (or particular representatives of particular parts of it) is in there too, making alliances, trying to use people who are trying to use it, at times succeeding, at times failing wholly or partly. (Kitching 1985: p. 31).[7]

In short, it is all very complex and shifting, and a great deal of it social scientists never see and cannot see.

I concluded that Kitching had been too pessimistic. By turning to the kinds of primary sources I had mined over the past few years, social scientists, I felt, indeed seemed to have a way to view these "complex and shifting" maneuvers, at least for some places and some times. It just took a lot of work.

Back then, I thought of political economy as a kind of excavation project of material lying beneath the surface of ideology and culture. Today, I tend to use a different metaphor for work I am finishing on business and politics in the oil industry, on the one hand, and work I am beginning on race and international relations, on the other. I think more in terms of reverse engineering of particular processes of mythmaking.[8] I have tenure. I work on what I like. There is also no denying that I do what I think I am good at. After struggling for years to learn Arabic, I knew better than to pursue the kinds of ethnographic projects undertaken by political scientists like, say, Diane Singerman (1995), Lisa Wedeen (1999), or Janet Roitman (2004). I still have an incomplete in multivariate statistics on the books, so you will not in this colloquial sentence find me writing models. Like many modelers and ethnographers I know, however, I do the work I do because I get great pleasure from it.

Imagine that you see yourself occupying a position on a two-dimensional scale farthest from where you might place me: Vitalis, toward the interdisciplinary (or antidisciplinary) left edge of the x-axis and down at the bottom of the y-axis among the many other essayists and social and literary and style and music critics. You see yourself closer to the right edge of the x-axis, where Joanne Gowa, the William P. Boswell Professor of World Politics of Peace and War at Princeton, and many other border guards are keen to specify what is and is not a proper international relations or comparative politics or American politics question, and who is and is not a real political scientist. You are up high, too, on the y-axis, nearer the prophets who each generation foresee the coming of a real science of politics.

If you locate yourself up in that northeast quadrant of the grid or you are drifting toward the northwest, and you plan to write history or do what, I am sad to report, some now call process tracing, then all the more reason for you to consider that historical research raises a type of internal validity problem for which historians have worked out a reasonably reliable solution: the archives.

II.

Political scientists have a way of caricaturing historians, typically when the point is to put maximum distance between Them and Us. Historians are atheoretical, more intent on telling stories than on constructing explanatory and analytical narratives. A more complex stereotype is that most historians are epistemologically naïve. They are the men and women who tend to believe that facts speak for themselves and whose goal is to write without allowing presuppositions, social values, biases, or theory to interfere. The observation that younger and more politically left-leaning historians have said the same thing each decade since the 1920s about their older and more conservative colleagues would seem to support my point that it is misleading (Novick 1988). It is also the case that historians often draw cartoons of traditional social scientists, but that is a matter for historians to reflect on at some other time.

The influence of Marxism on the history profession speaks directly to the question of the profession's alleged distance from or resistance to theory or theoretical frameworks. My guess is that Marxism mattered more in history than inside other social sciences, certainly inside political science. If you tended to read across these disciplines at the time—Marxist historiography, historical sociology, and political economy—you would have found the approaches, arguments, and debates hard to tell apart.

Where this convergence is even acknowledged, it is also likely to be presented as something new and unique to the 1960s, while older research traditions and scholars fade into, well, history. It is a mistake to do so, because in earlier eras a similar convergence across disciplines was evident in progressive social science and the "new" social history, to cite one example. There is no point in the 20th century where the border guards of the day kept men and, later, women from crossing disciplinary boundaries. I document the common interpretive frameworks across disciplines at great length for the fields we now call international studies, area studies, and development studies, and it is not hard to see convergence. The convergence of debates is easy to see more generally in historians' studies of the social sciences in the United States (Vitalis 2002). Unfortunately, few social scientists have read Peter Novick or Dorothy Ross, who have written histories of the historical profession and the social sciences. For the rest of us, our knowledge of ourselves instead tends to begin at the point where our own professors' careers were blooming, when we joined the profession.

The idea that the historical profession was, back in some simpler time and place, a community that believed facts speak for themselves, let alone that anyone writing history today would describe his own views on the objectivity question this way, is more wrong than right. Competing accounts, rival interpretations, and controversies over what constituted the facts in a case marked the modern profession from the start. Professing your own disinterest while attacking a rival's ideological biases got you only so far. Judgments and debate turned on evidence from the records of the time and how those records—of slave revolts in Haiti or Virginia, of the Versailles Peace Conference, or of social policy making through the New Deal—could be understood.

In a standard first-year-graduate-student class on social scientific method, we learn about the problem of internal validity, or how to reduce the chance that the causal relationship we have posited is a spurious one and that we have missed the factor or variable that actually matters. Historians depend on evidence from archival sources to rule out rival explanations and to increase confidence in their own account. There are plenty of other things historians may do in the course of their careers, certainly, and no one would confuse writing a history of the civil rights movement with running an experiment, even if social scientists who write history try to disguise this at times. To deny the relationship between archives and explanation in historical analysis would be foolish, however. It would be just as foolish to deny the close resemblance at any particular time between what historians call historiographical controversies and what social scientists call theoretical disagreements among those writing on similar problems, cases, and time periods. The fact that these disagreements among the rival accounts of historians and among the rival explanatory frameworks of social scientists mirror one another so closely allows what is sometimes called historical-comparative theory in political science and sociology to be produced. There is only one problem. If historians rest their case for the validity of their own causal accounts on archival research, what is the equivalent internal validity test for all those other social scientists who do not?

My favorite example of the problem these days is Jack Snyder's *Myths of Empire,* published in 1991, although many other books and articles might be used instead of this one. Snyder, who teaches international relations at Columbia University, uses the cases of Great Britain, Germany, Japan, the Soviet Union, and the United States to show how realist theories that stress balance of power cannot explain the puzzle of repeated instances of imperial or superpower overexpansion. Expansionist states seem to pursue "irrational" policies that lead rival powers to form effective counterbalancing coalitions, or, as in the case of the United States in Vietnam, that cost more than they return in benefits. Yet realist theories of statecraft predict that states will act cautiously, not recklessly. So why are the rules of realpolitik often overridden?

Snyder argues that expansionism is fundamentally a process driven by domestic interest groups. In the course of building and sustaining proexpansionist coalitions, rationales have to be put forward that disguise the narrow interests benefiting inordinately from expansion and that persuade others to bear the brunt of the costs. These rationales are what Snyder calls the myths of empire, for instance, ideas about military preparedness, domino theories, and other strategic concepts that function as ideology in the contemporary era. The myths come to be believed over time by some of those groups that benefit from them, as well as by politicians and wider segments of the public, leading states to roads down which they otherwise might not go.

Snyder offers no original evidence to support his major claims about interest coalition behavior and state policy. Rather, he repeatedly asserts that his model works, while referencing scholars who advance "domestic" or "interest-based" or "social" explanations (different traditions use different terms) that are compatible in the very broadest terms with his. To put it slightly differently, Snyder takes historical international relations theory of the early 1990s down a road well traveled by dozens of historians—a road strewn with the wreckage of battles fought for and against this approach—each decade of the 20th century.

A recent dissertation by Jon Isacoff looks carefully at Snyder's use of historians' work in writing about the synthetic treatment of the Vietnam War. Snyder calls Vietnam an exemplary case of strategic overextension. Isacoff shows that in all the studies to which Snyder refers, there is no evidence for the core claim of the book, and he goes on to say,

> the conclusion that Snyder logically draws from the evidence he cites is not the one for which he ostensibly argues. . . . Where was the foreign policy "logroll" in the development of Vietnam policy? The answer seems to be that it is indeed missing from the sources Snyder had at his disposal when he wrote Myths of Empire. (Isacoff 2002, pp. 163–179)

In going back over the sources, Isacoff finds that the main works Snyder referenced tend to prove the opposite of what Snyder asserts. Congress was actually an impediment, not a catalyst of overexpansion (Isacoff 2002).

What I am suggesting is that there tends to be little real value added to knowledge of the past when social scientists "synthesize" published works and call the synthesis historical-comparative theory. If anything, a negative value is added, to the extent that scholars are dispensing with historians' customary tests of validity and reliability. Among historians, learning what others have written about the course of the Vietnam War would be considered a preliminary step in developing analytical competence to deal with the history themselves. It is familiarity with the primary sources and the use of them in producing a historical narrative that historians use as a reliability test.

One possible self-defense is that nonhistorians are bringing theory to the ongoing interdisciplinary seminar, thus buying freedom from history's norms of rigor and reliability. This defense depends, however, on the myth that historians do not think theoretically and that historiographical disputation and argument are matters of taste and preference, a world apart from the analytical puzzles that drive historically oriented inquiries by nonhistorians. Yet making this argument requires one to ignore the remarkable affinity between Snyder's *innenpolitik*, or domestic politics, approach and the school of revisionist histories of Vietnam and Fareed Zakaria's institutionalist-oriented explanation (1998) for 19th-century expansion and the dozens of books and articles by historians who showed that in each of the cases of expansion, it was the leader or the state or politics and not societal interests that drove empire forward.

Not for the first time, social scientists have confused issues of taste, style, and genre conventions with rigor. We have come to think that a theory chapter coming before "the case," the adoption of in-text references, and a preference for parsimony somehow make history writing by nonhistorians more scientific and, hence, more reliable than history writing that "merely" tells stories about the past. It is clear why this happens, given the need to secure jobs, build our careers, climb the promotion ladder, and defend our scholarship to others in our own disciplines who are likely to prefer another model builder to another historical-comparative theorist sitting in the office next to theirs and teaching the graduate course on method next September.

Rigor and reliability are values that are important to all scholars, and if I am correct, then the already embattled interpretivist-identified researchers who are struggling to demonstrate competency with qualitative methods have just been presented with a dilemma. There is a serious flaw in the way they plan their process-tracing exercise. The method to be adopted bears an uncomfortable resemblance to the one undergraduates use when pulling an all-nighter to complete a research paper on the Cuban missile crisis or the first Gulf War or the Cold War's impact on the civil rights movement in the United States. Yet Ph.D. candidates are also likely to get away with it. What do they do?

One might respond, "Wait. What if I make a systematic effort to comprehend the full range of debates in the existing literature? Surely this will reassure my eventual readers of the validity of the historical evidence gathered from secondary sources?" Yet this is no solution at all. Rather, it is what any historian assumes to be the minimum *preliminary* work one does before heading to the archives. It makes the dilemma more, not less, obvious.

III.

Those who choose to take the archival turn have their work cut out for them. But there are steps to take to reduce anxiety, increase efficiency, and make the learning curve less steep. First, it is important to recognize that when you enter a collection and find yourself at a loss for what to do next, you will not be alone. Doctoral programs in history emphasize the existing literature and its flaws, how to read it, and how to critique it. Few social science courses—or history courses for that matter—teach students about archives or what to do there. If you do not believe me, ask the history Ph.D. student sitting next to you in the archive.

There are certain trade-offs after the first year of courses. The historian takes more classes and reads more extensively, not only on nationalism in Egypt, but also on Egyptian intellectual life, the history of Cairo, and the labor movement. The political science student may have read less on Egypt and more on nationalism outside the Middle East and may need more familiarity with the secondary literature on the time and place of his research. Yet, as my first political science professor, Milton Lodge, told me, "You are always playing catch up" in reading specialized literatures, and many researchers have reaped windfalls precisely by bringing the sensibility of one discipline more centrally into the other, as in the cases of the historians Marc Trachtenberg in international relations and Elizabeth Perry in the political economy of China, among many others. Read Tom Ferguson (1995) and Peter Trubowitz (1998) if you want to see exemplary works by historically oriented political scientists who have forced historians to think harder about their fields.

The one advantage that your colleague in history may possess is self-consciousness about the limitations of archival records and thus some understanding about the need to interrogate these records rather than read them naïvely. It is not hard to find primers on these matters, however. See the Archives bibliography that follows this chapter for references, starting with Ludmilla Jordanova. Or search on the Web for the reading lists in graduate seminars. Or ask historians you know.

Interrogating archives did not begin with the linguistic turn in history and what social scientists call poststructuralism or postpositivism or constructivism. The question about privileging archival sources is now routinely subsumed under these rubrics, however. By now, people training as historians or other flavor of social scientist have made a choice either to engage with these issues or else to act as if these issues have no role to play in their work. I might prefer that you work harder and engage questions in the philosophy of knowledge, but it does not matter. Most historians I know who have made the linguistic turn still consider immersion in primary sources to be fundamental to history writing, even if the kind of history they choose to write or what they believe it means to write history has changed.

I have a few practical suggestions to make. I have already stressed the need to develop a system of precise and consistent record keeping in order to begin to satisfy the norms of transparency and verifiability. These norms are crucial to research of all types, of course, not just archival work. If you are unfamiliar with the organization of an archive and want to make it easier for others and yourself to identify in the future the sources you use, I propose that you take a few days to learn the protocols now, well before you are in the field. Once in the field, your time will be short, and mistakes might be costly. The most accessible archive for anyone in a research institution is your university's own archives and special collections. You will find a guide to citing the records kept there. You will also learn how collections are filed and what aids exist to make it easier to use the record sets. Read the papers of a professor in your discipline. Learn something about what scholars in your discipline did in the past and how the department evolved. You may be surprised.

Nonhistorians, you might want to talk about the relevant archival collections with a historian who works in the place and time you are interested in. Where are they located? What will you find there? What does it mean generally to work at those sites? Are officials who will help you, such as the head of the archive, stationed on-site? Are there printed guides that you can consult in advance of your trip to Dakar or Beirut or London? No question is too basic or unimportant, especially what to expect in terms of making photocopies or using your laptop. The information and experience others have accumulated is invaluable, and not only because you will need to include a discussion of the records you intend to use in your proposal for funding. The point is not to learn the hard way but to make the best possible use of your time and your funder's money.

You will nonetheless make mistakes along the way. I would argue that you should make some of them now rather than after you reach the field or when you are writing your dissertation. My last suggestion, therefore, is that you use primary sources in the next paper you write. What you work on will depend on where you are, what kinds of records you have access to, what questions you are interested in, and who is willing to work with you.

Not all social scientists take a historical approach or write about the past. Those who do ought to undertake this approach with an awareness of and facility with the methods used by those who developed them. We ask at least as much from and on behalf of modelers, ethnographers, and survey researchers.

Notes

1. This essay is informed by conversations over the years with friends and colleagues, starting at MIT. They include Catherine Boone, Jason Brownlee, Joshua Cohen, Eric Deveraux, David Gibbs, Ellis Goldberg, Janette Greenwood, Jim Henson, Jon Isacoff, Gregory Nowell, Gretchen Ritter, Janet Roitman, Marc Steinberg, and Peter Trubowitz. Critics at the various Social Science Research Council International Predissertation Fellowship Program conferences and workshops have made a difference too. Thanks to David Collier, Charles Hirschmann, Sara Curran, Alma Gottlieb, and above all Ellen Perecman. I cannot resist: I finished this essay at the Villa Serbelloni, although it is not what the Rockefeller Foundation invited me for, so *grazie* to Gianna Celli and all her bosses. I would like to dedicate this chapter to Tom Ferguson, a small token of thanks for making a difference that matters.

2. History is treated as a social science in some circles and on some campuses and as a humanities discipline elsewhere. In this essay, history is treated as one of the humanities.

3. AID records were still in the National Archives in Washington when I was writing my dissertation; they are now at the University of Maryland in College Park.

4. Berkeley: University of California Press. Electronic edition available at ark.cdlib.org/ark:/13030/ft7f59p188/

5. Mitchell, Timothy. (2003). "The Middle East in the Past and Future of Social Science." In *The Politics of Knowledge: Area Studies and the Disciplines,* vol. 3, edited by D. L. Szanton. University of California Press/University of California International and Area Studies Digital Collection. Retrieved August 10, 2005, from repositories.cdlib.org/uciaspubs/editedvolumes/3/3/

6. For a longer account, see Vitalis, Robert. (1996). "The End of Third Worldism in Egypt Studies." *Arab Studies Journal* 4(1), 13–33.

7. Kitching, Gavin. (1985). "Method and Evidence in the 'Kenya Debate.'" In *Contradictions of Accumulation in Africa,* edited by H. Bernstein and B. K. Campbell. Beverly Hills, CA: Sage.

8. In the American social science tradition with which I identify, theory is something that makes criticism possible, a practice that is undertaken through interpretations of texts in some cases or of events in other cases. W. E. B. DuBois was an exemplar of the tradition, but so were one-time American Political Science Association presidents Charles Beard and Ralph Bunche (who in his younger days wrote the remarkable *World View of Race*).

Supplemental References

Isacoff, Jonathan B. (2002). "The Historical Problem in International Relations." Ph.D. dissertation, University of Pennsylvania.

Kitching, Gavin. (1985). "Method and Evidence in the 'Kenya Debate.'" In *Contradictions of Accumulation in Africa,* edited by H. Bernstein and B. K. Campbell. Beverly Hills, CA: Sage.

Lindblom, Charles. (1998). "Political Science in the 1940s and 1950s." In *American Academic Culture in Transformation*, edited by T. Bender and C. Schorske. Princeton, NJ: Princeton University Press.

Mitchell, Timothy. (2003). "The Middle East in the Past and Future of Social Science." In *The Politics of Knowledge: Area Studies and the Disciplines*, vol. 3, edited by D. L. Szanton. Retrieved August 23, 2005, from University of California Press/University of California International and Area Studies Digital Collection website: repositories.cdlib.org/uciaspubs/editedvolumes/3/3

Roitman, Janet. (2004). *Fiscal Disobedience: An Anthropology of Economic Regulation in Central Africa*. Princeton, NJ: Princeton University Press.

Singerman, Diane. (1995). *Avenues of Participation*. Princeton, NJ: Princeton University Press.

Snyder, Jack. (1991). *Myths of Empire*. Ithaca, NY: Cornell University Press.

Trubowitz, Peter. (1998). *Defining the National Interest: Conflict and Change in American Foreign Policy*. Chicago, IL: University of Chicago Press.

Vitalis, Robert. (1996). "The End of Third Worldism in Egypt Studies." *Arab Studies Journal* 4(1), 13–33.

———. (2002). "International Studies in America." *Social Science Research Council, Items and Issues* 3(3–4). Retrieved August 23, 2005, from www.ssrc .org/programs/publications_editors/publications/items/Items3.3_4.pdf

Wedeen, Lisa. (1999). *Ambiguities of Domination*. Chicago, IL: University of Chicago Press.

Zakaria, Fareed. (1998). *From Wealth to Power*. Princeton, NJ: Princeton University Press.

Bibliography on Archives

1. General References

Abbott, Andrew. (1991). "A History and Sociology: The Lost Synthesis." *Social Science History* 15(2), 201–238.

Adams, Julia, Elisabeth Clemens, and Ann Shola Orloff. (November 2004). "Social Theory, Modernity, and the Three Waves of Historical Sociology." In *Remaking Modernity: Politics, History and Sociology,* edited by J. Adams, E. Clemens, and A. S. Orloff. Durham, NC: Duke University Press.

Bonnell, Victoria. (1990). "The Uses of Theory, Concepts and Comparison in Historical Sociology." *Comparative Studies in Society and History* 22(2), 156–173.

Ferguson, Thomas. (1995). *Golden Rule: The Investment Theory of Party Competition and the Logic of Money-Driven Political Systems.* Chicago, IL: University of Chicago Press.

Gibbs, David. (1994). "Taking the State Back Out: Reflections on a Tautology." *Contentions* 3(3), 115–137.

Hall, John. (1992). "Where History and Sociology Meet: Forms of Discourse and Sociohistorical Inquiry." *Sociological Theory* 10(2), 164–193.

Jordanova, Ludmilla. (2000). *History in Practice.* London, UK: Arnold.

Lloyd, Christopher. (1986). *Explanation in Social History.* Oxford, UK: Basil Blackwell.

Lustick, Ian. (1996). "History, Historiography, and Political Science: Making Use of History in the Absence of a Historical Record." *American Political Science Review* 90(3), 605–618.

Novick, Peter. (1988). *That Noble Dream: The "Objectivity Question" and the American Historical Profession.* Cambridge, UK: Cambridge University Press.

Nowell, Gregory P. (1994). *Mercantile States and the World Oil Cartel 1900–1939.* Ithaca, NY: Cornell University Press.

Ross, Dorothy. (1991). *The Origins of American Social Science.* Cambridge, UK: Cambridge University Press.

Skocpol, Theda. (1984). *Vision and Method in Historical Sociology.* Cambridge, UK: Cambridge University Press.

Skocpol, Theda and Margaret Somers. (1980). "The Uses of Comparative History in Macrosocial Inquiry." *Comparative Studies in Society and History* 22(2), 174–197.

Vitalis, Robert. (1995). *When Capitalists Collide: Business Conflict and the End of Empire in Egypt.* Berkeley: University of California Press.

———. (2002). "International Studies in America." *Social Science Research Council, Items and Issues* 3(3–4). Retrieved August 23, 2005, from www.ssrc.org/programs/publications_editors/publications/items/Items3.3_4.pdf

2. Missionary Archives

Alpers, Edward A. (1983). "The Story of Swema: Female Vulnerability in 19th Century East Africa." In *Women and Slavery in Africa,* edited by C. Robertson and M. A. Klein. Madison: University of Wisconsin Press.

Ranger, Terence. (1981). "Godly Medicine: The Ambiguities of Medical Missions in Southeast Tanzania, 1900–1945." *Social Science and Medicine* 15B(3), 261–277.

3. Law Cases, Commissions, and Inquiries

Chanock, Martin. (1982). "Making Customary Law: Men, Women, and Courts in Colonial Northern Rhodesia." In *African Women and the Law: Historical Perspectives,* edited by M. J. Hay and M. Wright. Boston, MA: Boston University, African Studies Center.

Cooper, Frederick. (1987). "Dockwork and Disorder, 1934–1947." In *On the African Waterfront: Urban Disorder and the Transformation of Work in Colonial Mombasa.* New Haven, CT: Yale University Press. See especially pp. 88–111 on use of archival material.

Davis, Natalie. (1987). *Fiction in the Archives: Pardon Tales and Their Tellers in Sixteenth-Century France.* Stanford, CA: Stanford University Press.

Mann, Kristin. (1991). "The Rise of Taiwo Olowo: Law Accumulation, and Modilibyt in Early Colonial Lagos." In *Law in Colonial Africa,* edited by K. Mann and R. Roberts. Portsmouth, NH: Heinemann Educational Books.

4. Medical Reports

Dawson, Marc. (1987). "The 1920s Anti-Yaws Campaigns and Colonial Medical Policy in Kenya." *International Journal of African Historical Studies* 20(3), 417–435.

Packard, Randall M. (1989). "Urban Growth, 'Consumption,' and the 'Dressed Native,' 1870–1914." In *White Plague, Black Labor: Tuberculosis and the Political Economy of Health and Disease in South Africa.* Berkeley: University of California Press.

5. Personal Papers and Private Correspondence

Kennedy, Dane. (1987). *Islands of White: Settler Society and Culture in Kenya, 1890–1939.* Durham, NC: Duke University Press.

Bibliography: Archives

Marks, Shula. (1989). *Not Either an Experimental Doll*. Bloomington: Indiana University Press.

Vaughan, Megan. (1991). "The Great Dispensary in the Sky: Missionary Medicine." In *Curing Their Ills: Colonial Power and African Illness*. Stanford, CA: Stanford University Press.

6. National and Regional Archives

Barnett, Michael. (1990). "High Politics Is Low Politics: The Domestic and Systemic Sources of Israeli Security Policy, 1967–1977." *World Politics* 42(4), 529–562.

Musambachime, Mwelwa. (1988). "The Impact of Rumor: The Case of Banyama (Vampire-Men) in Northern Rhodesia, 1930–64." *International Journal of African Historical Studies* 21(2), 201–215.

Phimister, Ian. (1986). "Discourse and the Discipline of Historical Context: Conservation and Ideas about Development in Southern Rhodesia, 1930–1950." *Journal of Southern African Studies* 12(1), 263–275.

Vail, Leroy. (1977). "Ecology and History: The Example of Eastern Zambia." *Journal of Southern African Studies* 3(2), 129–155.

Wa, Ye and Joseph Esherick. (1996). *Chinese Archives: An Introductory Guide*. Berkeley, CA: Institute of East Asian Studies.

Waller, Richard. (1990). "Tsetse Fly in Western Narok, Kenya." *Journal of African History* 31(1), 81–101.

7. Urban Archives

Pederson, Susan. (1991). "National Bodies, Unspeakable Acts: The Sexual Politics of Colonial Policy-Making." *Journal of Modern History* 63(4), 647–680.

Summers, Carol. (1991). "Intimate Colonialism: The Imperial Production of Reproduction in Uganda, 1907–1925." *Signs: Journal of Women in Culture and Society* 16(4), 787–807.

8. Newspapers

Van Onselen, Charles. (1982). "Randlords and Rotgut, 1886–1903: The Role of Alcohol in the Development of European Imperialism and South African Capitalism." In *Studies in the Social and Economic History of the Witwatersrand, 1886–1914*. Harlow, Essex, UK: Longman.

———. (1982). *New Babylon*. London: Longman. See especially pp. 44–102.

2

Case Studies

Case-Based Research

Andrew Schrank

W hat is a case study? The *International Encyclopedia of the Social and Behavioral Sciences* offers two distinct and seemingly contradictory answers. While Anthony Orum limits his definition of the case study to an intensive examination of "a single case of a particular phenomenon" (Orum 2001, p. 1509), Andrew Bennett expands the term's purview to "include both within-case analysis of single cases and comparisons between or among a small number of cases" (Bennett 2001, p. 1513). The definitional differences need not detain us for more than a moment, however, for the one-shot case study discussed by Orum and the more explicitly comparative approaches reviewed by Bennett have at least three important characteristics in common. First, the authors agree that the case study is a research design rather than an approach to the collection or analysis of data, and case studies must involve utilization of a wide array of different data sources and a number of different analytic strategies. Second, they agree that the case study examines units of analysis that are not drawn from a well-demarcated population, and that case study authors must therefore be prepared to ask themselves, "What is my case a case of?" and to use their answers to advance their broader theoretical agendas (Ragin & Becker 1992). And finally, both authors agree that case studies are at the center of a storm of controversy in a number of the social sciences, and their authors must therefore be prepared to defend their methods against the slings and arrows of their critics.

Because the merits of case-based methods are discussed in my essay in Part II of this volume and the presumption of the volume is that social scientists are looking for ways to use and combine different methodological approaches, the present chapter has three principal goals. First, it highlights an alternative, problem-oriented approach to case-based research that under-scores the importance of concept formation. Second, it offers a perspective on how case-based research can be used for discovering causal mechanisms. And third, it offers practitioners of case-based research a number of prescriptive rules of the road.

Case-Based Research and Concept Formation

Quantitative social scientists tend to analyze large samples of allegedly representative cases drawn from broader populations of interest. Qualitative social scientists tend to study small samples of purposively chosen cases of a given event or process. Since the letter "n" is generally used to represent the size of a scholar's sample, I follow standard practice and refer to quantitative research as "large-n" research and qualitative research as "small-n" research.[1]

Large-n researchers typically use a variant of regression analysis. They collect data on a representative sample of a well-defined population, regress the dependent variable on a vector of independent and control variables, and assess the absolute size and relative magnitude of the estimated regression coefficients. If the sample is truly representative of the broader population, the variables are measured correctly, the model is properly specified, and the individual regression coefficients are at least twice the size of their respective standard errors, large-n researchers will assume that the sample relationship approximates the "true" (i.e., population) relationship—within a known margin of error—and that the dependent variable is indeed a product of the posited independent variables.

Large-n fundamentalists tend to assume, not only that their inferential statistical methods are inherently superior to the case-based comparative methods I have described, but that small-n researchers can adopt—or at least mimic—their preferred mode of analysis by examining ever larger samples of cases. Thus, they advise small-n researchers to "maximize leverage" by increasing the number of cases at their disposal (King, Keohane, & Verba 1994, chap. 6).[2] While maximizing leverage is often a good idea, it is by no means a universal solution because a paucity of cases (i.e., of degrees of freedom) is only one of the problems confronted by small-n researchers. They are often unsure of what their cases are cases of—that is, of the broader population parameters—until their research is well under way, and they would therefore be unable to choose comparable cases or to guarantee the representativeness of their admittedly larger samples in the first place. Ragin and Becker's 1992 book *What Is a Case?* contains a number of invaluable discussions of the logic behind case-based research.

In fact, the plea for larger sample sizes derives from—and perhaps more important, reinforces—a fundamental misunderstanding of the goals of case-based research. Case-based researchers are frequently engaged, not in a misguided effort to use inappropriate methods to make invalid causal inferences, as their critics would have us believe, but in a preinferential attempt to develop the conceptual underpinnings of future social scientific inquiry. After all, modern social science's most enduring contributions have been concepts rather than causal inferences, and the most fecund concepts have originated in case-based rather than variable-oriented research. Laitin (1995) and Caporaso (1995) make this point in their respective reviews of King, Keohane, and Verba's 1994 book, *Designing Social Inquiry.*

Consider, for example, Chalmers Johnson's *MITI and the Japanese Miracle,* where we discovered "developmental states," "soft authoritarian" regimes, and the differences between "plan rational," "plan ideological," and "regulatory" political economies (Johnson 1982). Or Jeffery Paige's *Coffee and Power,* where we learned to distinguish the "agricultural" and "agroindustrial" fractions of the agrarian elite and to recognize the unique attributes of "democratization through socialist revolution from below" (Paige 1997).

What do these concepts have in common? I would propose a threefold answer. First, they were not available to be operationalized until their authors had thought long and hard about what the cases in question—MITI, Nicaragua, and so forth—were cases of, and they were therefore produced—rather than tested—by the authors of their respective case studies. Second, they are still difficult to operationalize or measure, and they have therefore had their greatest impact in the qualitative rather than the quantitative literature. And third, they have nonetheless been extraordinarily and justifiably influential.

Unmasking the Japanese Miracle With the MITI Case

Johnson's classic account of "the growth of industrial policy" in 20th-century Japan is most assuredly not, as Meredith Woo-Cumings has observed, "a deductive political science study, using Japan as a 'country case' in comparative politics" (Woo-Cumings 1999, p. 25). On the contrary, it is a veteran observer's painstaking effort to account for Japan's unanticipated, unambiguous, and unbelievably rapid recovery from defeat in the Pacific War—something that was so difficult to reconcile with contemporary economic theory that it was widely portrayed as a "miracle" at the time. According to Johnson, however, there was nothing otherworldly about it. Japan's recovery was in large measure the product of an industrial policy designed and implemented by elite bureaucrats associated with the Ministry of International Trade and Industry (MITI), and his task was to unearth their "hidden history" (Johnson 1999, p. 42).

Johnson's historical methodology was dictated not by his discipline—he was, in point of fact, a political scientist and not a historian by training and inclination—but by the paucity of applicable theoretical approaches and conceptual tools available to him when he began to examine MITI in the early 1970s. After all, Japan was neither a "market rational" society, like the United States and Great Britain, nor a "plan ideological" society, like the Soviet Union and China, and Johnson therefore had "no set of theoretical works, no locus classicus such as Adam Smith or V. I. Lenin with which to start" (Johnson 1982, p. 32; see Dahrendorf 1968 on market versus plan rationality).

What, then, was Johnson to do? While his predecessors had almost invariably accounted for the miracle by portraying Japan as "a 'variant' of something other than what it is," Johnson found neither their methods nor their answers satisfactory, and he therefore decided to work inductively by immersing himself in documentary sources on MITI—and the Japanese bureaucracy more generally—in an ambitious effort to understand the origins and consequences of industrial policy (Johnson 1982, p. 17, 1999, p. 42, 2000, pp. xvii-xviii).

Johnson's task would be anything but easy, however, for he was dealing with a less-than-cooperative subject. While MITI's efforts were an open secret among the cognoscenti in Tokyo in the early 1970s, they were nonetheless shrouded in secrecy. "All books that do mention MITI," wrote Johnson in a letter to his editor, "do nothing more than that—because nobody knows anything about it, and the ministry—like all bureaucracies—prefers to remain confidential" (Johnson 1999, p. 42, 2000, p. xviii). Thus, by writing a "one-shot case study" of MITI, Johnson would not only expose the inner workings of the agency responsible for "the care and feeding of the economic miracle itself" but would also undermine a conspiracy of silence that had long united Western observers, who preferred self-serving—if perhaps inaccurate—interpretations of Japanese economic success, and the bureaucrats associated with MITI, who were more than happy to fly under the Western radar (Johnson 1982, p. 10, 1987, pp. 137–138).

The results of his efforts are by now well-known. *MITI and the Japanese Miracle* not only recast the debate over Japan's postwar recovery but also opened the door to a powerful revisionist critique of the prevailing neoclassical development orthodoxy. According to Johnson, the Japanese discovered "a third way between the socialist displacement of the market advocated by Soviet theorists and an uncritical reliance on the market advocated by American theorists" (Johnson 2000, p. 183). They established neither a plan ideological "command economy" nor a market rational "regulatory state" but, on the contrary, a "developmental, plan-rational state," which was in many ways sui generis (Johnson 1982, pp. 19–20). Further, Johnson argues not only that the Japanese miracle was rooted in a particular state-and-private-sector model of development but also that it was historically contingent and therefore difficult to generalize or replicate in other settings. Specifically, Japan in the early 1940s was characterized by an egalitarian social structure, expansive time horizons, and extreme nationalism, which fed naturally into its particularistic developmental state form after World War II. And the wartime mobilization and the institutional infrastructure (which was never dismantled after the war) are the economic miracle's institutional predecessors (e.g., MITI is an organizational descendant of the imperial Ministry of Munitions [Johnson 2000, p. 184, 1999, p. 41, 1982, pp. 239–241, 314]).

Is the developmental state a historically specific or a potentially general concept? Johnson ultimately suggests that it "actually exists in time and space in East Asia and also exists as an abstract generalization about the essence of the East Asian examples" (Johnson 1999, p. 43; see Woo-Cumings 1999, p. 10, for an extension of this point). His many emulators and students would agree. But they should bear in mind that the very notion of the developmental state would in all likelihood never have emerged without a strong dose of inductive research.

"Democratization From Below" in Central America

Paige's analysis of democratic transitions in Central America is another example of how a case-based approach has proved profoundly influential in shifting explanations of social change. Paige's story is revealed in his subtitle: "Revolution and the Rise of Democracy in Central America." Revolution is the *explanans*, or independent variable. Democracy is the *explanandum*, or dependent variable. And Costa Rica, El Salvador, and Nicaragua are the cases. In all three countries, albeit at different times, Paige argues, traditional elites have beaten back the forces of revolutionary socialism—and thereby maintained their class privilege—by offering the masses a series of liberal democratic reforms. Thus, Paige offers an account of democratization "through socialist revolution from below" (Paige 1997, p. 332).

At first glance, Paige's book might appear to be a straightforward application of Mill's method of agreement (see Ragin 1987 as well as my essay in Part II of this volume for a definition). After all, he introduces his cases by noting that in the early 1980s, "it would have been difficult to find anywhere in the world three political systems as different as those of El Salvador, Costa Rica, and Nicaragua." El Salvador was under the control of a military junta, overrun by death squads, and embroiled in civil war. Costa Rica was home to Latin America's oldest stable democracy and Central America's only viable welfare state. And Nicaragua was at the time a revolutionary socialist outpost under constant assault from North America. In fact, in the early 1980s, Central America featured all three of Barrington Moore Jr.'s "political routes into the modern world: through revolution from above and conservative authoritarianism (what he calls 'fascism'), through revolutionary socialism, and through democracy" (Paige 1997, pp. 5–6; Moore 1966). A decade later, however, all three countries had begun to embrace liberal democracy and neoliberal economic reform. What had changed? According to Paige, the revolutions of the 1980s had decoupled the potentially progressive "agroindustrial" members of the Central American bourgeoisie (i.e., processors and commercial agents) from their labor-repressive, and therefore inherently antidemocratic, "agrarian" (i.e., estate-owning) counterparts, and had thereby opened the door to democratization. Although Central American landlords had traditionally been involved in a zero-sum conflict with their semiservile laborers and had therefore been hostile toward democracy, their agroindustrial associates occupied a more productive, and therefore profitable, node in the coffee commodity chain and could afford to offer concessions. As the civil wars of the 1980s raged on, therefore, and the agroindustrial elites came to be disillusioned with—and in some cases disgusted by—their retrograde allies, the prospects for democratization brightened. "The entirely unexpected and, from the point of view of the left, unintended consequence of the failed socialist revolutions in Central America in the 1980s (and the successful social democratic revolution in Costa Rica in 1948)," therefore, "was the triumph of electoral democracy and neoliberalism" (Paige 1997, p. 332). While revolutionary forces had been unable to assume or retain political power in El Salvador or Nicaragua, they had at least been able to divide—and thus win concessions from—the traditional elite and had thereby secured, relatively free and fair elections, if not necessarily the victory of their own preferred candidates, in all cases.

Table 2.1   Method of Agreement Applied to Central America in *Coffee and Power* (Paige 1997)

Case	Outcome	Revolution	Land Tenure	Productivity
Costa Rica, 1940s	Democracy	Yes	Relatively equitable	Medium
El Salvador, 1990s	Democracy	Yes	Highly inequitable	High
Nicaragua, 1990s	Democracy	Yes	Inequitable/ variable	Low

Viewed as an application of Mill's method of agreement, therefore, Paige's story would look something like this:

Democratization is the dependent variable. Revolution is the independent variable. And the outbreak of conflict between traditional agrarian elites and their agroindustrial counterparts, provoked at least in part by their differential responses to the revolutionary upsurge from below, is a crucial intervening variable (not shown in the table).

In short, we can interpret *Coffee and Power* as a straightforward application of Mill's method of agreement. But should we? I don't think so. For Paige began to study Central America in the early 1980s—long before El Salvador and Nicaragua had embarked on their democratic transitions—and published a number of articles purporting to account for regime variation in the region against the backdrop of "the Moore thesis" (i.e., "no bourgeoisie, no democracy") in the late 1980s and early 1990s (Paige 1987, 1990; Moore 1966, p. 414).

In other words, Paige embarked on his project with a different question, a different research design, and a different hypothesis. On the one hand, he set out to address the growth of authoritarianism in El Salvador, democracy in Costa Rica, and socialism in Nicaragua, and he therefore implicitly invoked a variant of Mill's method of difference. On the other hand, he portrayed revolution from below as an impediment—rather than a prelude—to democratization, and therefore characterized Central America's future as a struggle between socialism and authoritarianism rather than authoritarianism and liberal democracy.

If Moore viewed the "making of the modern world" as a struggle between liberal democracy and authoritarianisms of both the right and the left, Paige viewed the making of modern Central America as a struggle between socialism and neofascism. While Moore had portrayed the bourgeoisie as the progenitor of liberal democracy, Paige came to view it as a threat, and he therefore placed his hopes in an alliance of workers, farmers, and middle-class intellectuals. After all, Costa Rica's democratic reforms had been ushered in not by a

Table 2.2   Method of Difference Applied to Central America in
Paige's Earlier Work (Late 1980s)

Case	Outcome	Revolution	Land Tenure	Productivity
Costa Rica, 1940s	Democracy	Yes	Relatively equitable (Small farmers and urban middle classes provide democratic counterweight to dominant class.)	Medium
El Salvador, 1990s	Authoritarianism	Yes	Highly inequitable (No petit-bourgeois or middle-class counterweight to dominant class.)	High
Nicaragua, 1990s	Socialism	Yes	Inequitable/variable (No petit-bourgeois or middle-class counterweight to corrupt and divided dominant class.)	Low

progressive bourgeoisie—on the contrary, the Costa Rican bourgeoisie had been anything but progressive in 1948—but by pressure from industrial workers, the absence of a powerful, landed aristocracy, and the presence and foresight of a reform-minded middle class. The Sandinistas in Nicaragua had garnered the support of a rapidly growing informal and rural proletariat and had thereby overthrown a corrupt regime backed by reactionary—but increasingly divided—landed allies. And the military in El Salvador had assumed power to "put down a militant, organized proletariat" on behalf of a competitive agrarian bourgeoisie. The Salvadoran case therefore raised "the possibility that a bourgeoisie, agrarian or industrial, supports democracy only when it is not faced with a revolutionary challenge from below" (Paige 1990, p. 40).

In short, Paige treats socialist revolution from below as an impediment to democracy in his articles and as the spur to democracy in his 1997 book. While his accounts of divergence and convergence would appear to be contradictory, Paige could easily have reconciled the two accounts by retroactively downplaying the strength of the revolutionary impulse in late 20th-century Central America. If the revolutionary tide of the 1980s had been seriously eroded by the 1990s, for example, democratization would not have been so surprising in light of his earlier theory, and his accounts of divergence and subsequent convergence would arguably have been rendered consistent with one another over time.

But Paige pursued a different, less consistent, and ultimately more ambitious agenda: He abandoned his earlier account and instead argued that social revolution had divided the forward-looking, agroindustrial elements of the elite from their reactionary agrarian counterparts and was therefore a necessary condition for—rather than an insurmountable obstacle to—democratization in all three cases. Costa Rica's agroindustrial elite had deflected a revolution from below by reluctantly embracing democratization and social reform in 1948. El Salvador's agroindustrialists had realized that eternal civil war—with its incalculable attendant costs—was too high a price to pay for their traditional alliance with the landed wing of the aristocracy in the early 1990s. And Nicaragua's agroindustrialists had worked with the Sandinistas in the struggle against Somoza in the 1970s and against the Sandinistas in the counterrevolution sponsored by the United States in the 1980s. In each case, however, the agroindustrial elites had abandoned their landed counterparts and thereby opened the door to democratization, in response to an upsurge from below.

What had happened in Central America in the 1980s? And why did Paige change his mind regarding the unity of the upper class? While democratic transitions answer the first question, extensive field research answers the second. After all, by the late 1990s Paige had interviewed dozens of leading representatives of the agrarian and agroindustrial elites in all three countries and had reconsidered—and therefore revised—his hypotheses in light of their stories of elite conflict. Defenders of traditional, large-n approaches would dismiss his strategy as curve fitting and would simply counsel the rejection of the Moore thesis. But Paige's book has garnered awards, influenced scholars, and transformed the way we think about democratic transitions, not only in Central America, but also in the developing world more generally. It offers a historical explanation of an important political process, a conditional theory of democratization from below, and a number of new concepts that are almost certainly applicable beyond the confines of Central America. It has therefore made a decidedly important contribution regardless of whether it has lived up to the expectations of the large-n fundamentalists (Kurtz 1999; Topik 2000; Wood 2000; Yashar 2002).

Industrial Downgrading in the Middle American Garment Trade

A final example of case-based concept formation comes from my own work on the garment industry in the Caribbean Basin. The assembly of basic garments from imported materials would appear to constitute the lowest wrung on the—admittedly metaphorical—ladder of industrial development. Countries like Korea, Taiwan, and Hong Kong allegedly gained entry into the industrialized world by importing textiles, fabric, and even cut parts of clothing, stitching them together into finished goods, and then exporting the finished goods to industrial and commercial buyers in developed countries. They subsequently "upgraded" their production profiles by learning not only to cut, dye, purchase, and eventually make their own fabric but to design, package, and even market their own garments. In other words, they gradually moved from the less remunerative assembly node of the apparel commodity chain to the more remunerative production of full packages of clothing for foreign buyers and then to the truly profitable design and marketing of their own brands of clothing for foreign consumers (Gereffi 1999).

A number of analysts have observed what appears to be a similar process of industrial upgrading under way in contemporary Mexico (see, e.g., Bair & Gereffi 2001). The North American Free Trade Agreement, they argue, lured foreign buyers—who might otherwise have gone to East Asia—south of the border, where they found scores of local firms ready and willing to assemble their garments. The local firms gradually moved from assembly into full-package production and may someday launch their own brands in foreign markets as well. Thus, Mexico's apparel firms, like their East Asian predecessors, are undergoing a process of upgrading.

I had this upgrading story in mind when I began to study the Dominican Republic's garment industry in the mid- to late 1990s. And I saw many seemingly familiar components of the process when I first ventured into Dominican garment plants in 1998. Local investors and entrepreneurs who had gained their initial access to world markets by assembling basic apparel for foreign buyers were moving into more complicated activities. They were cutting, dying, purchasing, and in a few cases making their own fabric. They were finishing and packaging their own garments. And they were beginning to discuss things like design and marketing. But they were neither boastful nor complacent. Nor were they upgrading—at least not in any meaningful sense of the word. On the contrary, they were worried because their profit margins were at best holding constant as more and more full-package producers came online, not only in the Dominican Republic and Mexico, but also in Guatemala, Honduras, China, and a number of other impoverished developing countries. These countries were not moving up the apparel commodity chain, I realized. The commodity chain was moving down to them.

Therefore, I complemented the established and not very controversial concept of upgrading with the equally necessary concept of downgrading, a process that occurs when the returns to a given economic activity are undermined by the very act of its diffusion.[3] As long as Korea, Taiwan, and Hong Kong were the only developing countries capable of producing full packages of clothing, I argued, they could capture relatively high returns from doing so and thereby upgrade their production profiles. But as more and more countries formally mimicked their Asian predecessors by moving from assembly to full-package production, they bid down the prices they could charge for such packages and thereby engendered an inferior substantive outcome. What fostered upgrading in Korea and Taiwan, I argued, would foster downgrading in the Caribbean Basin and Mexico—and quantitative data that I collected after carrying out the fieldwork for my case study would seem to support my interpretation (Schrank 2004).

This is not to say that the Caribbean and Central America would have been better off avoiding the apparel industry entirely. It employs hundreds of thousands of workers who would otherwise be unemployed. Nor is it to say that upgrading is artificial or impossible. It is neither, as the Asian experiences so aptly demonstrate.

It is, however, unlikely to occur more than a few times in the same industry using the same organization and technology, because the returns on a given activity or product tend to be an inverse function of the number of suppliers of the product. In other words, as more and more firms, regions, or countries try to upgrade their production profiles by imitating their respective first movers, they tend to turn the formal process of upgrading into the substantive reality of downgrading—with all that it entails for human and economic development. While I am now able to distinguish upgrading from downgrading with cross-national quantitative data (Schrank 2004), I did not have even the conceptual tools to understand the difference until I had undertaken fieldwork, listened to my respondents, and come to recognize that the same formal activity—purchasing new equipment, learning new skills, and so on—can have radically different consequences in different times and places.

Case Studies and Causal Mechanisms

Large-n researchers tend to focus on variables to the exclusion of agents or mechanisms (Abbott 1992; Hedström & Swedberg 1998), and they therefore tend to provide incomplete accounts of the outcomes they seek to explain. The standard regression model, for example, attributes variation in the score of a dependent variable to variation in a series of independent variables—not to the actions of different individuals with distinct preferences, opportunities, and constraints. While practitioners of large-n research frequently have a sense for the underlying causal story (i.e., Who are the individuals? What are their preferences? And what are the various opportunities and constraints?), they rarely explicate—let alone test—their instincts, and their explanations are therefore at best incomplete.

The problem is not simply the dearth of formal mathematical theory in sociology, political science, and especially anthropology, as some analysts have implied (see, e.g., Sørensen 1998), but the fact that the same quantitative evidence is frequently consistent with more than one underlying causal explanation. Take, for example, the literature on the relationship between governance and economic growth. A large body of evidence suggests that good governance—defined variously to include transparency, integrity, and administrative competence—is a necessary prerequisite of long-term growth. Economist Lloyd Reynolds, in his magisterial 1983 survey of the topic, identified "the administrative competence of government" as "the single most important" variable accounting for "the spread of economic growth to the Third World" (Reynolds 1983, p. 976). Others followed in his footsteps. And by the late 1990s, a number of investigators had deployed seemingly sophisticated survey-based indicators of state capacity to place the relationship between growth and governance on sounder empirical footing (Clague et al. 1997; Evans & Rauch 1999; Kaufmann & Kraay 2002).

But why does good governance foster growth? To mainstream economists, the answer is obvious: Competent government officials leave private actors to pursue their own interests. Private actors self-interestedly pursue economic activities that are in line with their countries' comparative advantages. And their economies grow accordingly—à la the East Asian newly industrializing economies (see, e.g., Riedel 1988).

But the answer is not necessarily so obvious. After all, critics of the mainstream approach hold that, rather than simply allowing the economy to find its own level, truly capable government officials build new and potentially more remunerative comparative advantages by pushing, prodding, and cajoling private actors into sectors with high barriers to entry. In other words, they do exactly the opposite of what they are supposed to do in mainstream economic theory. Robert Wade, for example, tells of Taiwanese customs officials who encouraged large chemical manufacturers to turn to local input suppliers by "arbitrarily" delaying their import permits (Wade 1993, p. 152; Rodrik 1997 offers a broadly similar account for Korea and Brazil). The strategy worked in the sense of localizing high value production. But it is not what mainstream economists think of when they hear the expression "good governance," let alone what they like to think of when they reflect on the Taiwanese "miracle."

No formal model would allow us to adjudicate between Wade's explanation of Taiwanese economic success and the explanations of his rivals. Nor would a better-designed survey-based indicator of administrative capacity. For the very same activity will have very different meanings and consequences in different contexts and yet yield the same score on a survey designed to measure the quality of governance. A respondent, asked whether import licenses are delayed "often," "sometimes," or "never," may answer "often" in both Taiwan and Kenya, and Taiwan and Kenya may thereby obtain similar scores on a measure of the quality of governance; the underlying reasons for the delays and revealed differences in living standards, however, are worlds apart—and unlikely to be adequately explained by large-n research alone.

Another example derives from the juxtaposition of the cross-national literature on good governance and my own fieldwork experience in Latin America. Evans and Rauch (1999) use survey data to measure the rationality (or "Weberianness") of the civil service in a broad sample of newly industrializing countries. They ask key informants from (or on) each country a series of questions about the nature of recruitment and retention in the country's civil service. One question asks how desirable government jobs are for graduates of the country's top universities. A high degree of desirability is treated as a sign of a high-quality civil service, that is, a sign that the civil service is able to attract the brightest graduates of the leading schools. Evans and Rauch clearly have a Japanese or Asian model in mind. After all, the brightest graduates of Tokyo University have traditionally opted for the civil service because of its high prestige, and the Japanese civil service has frequently been portrayed as highly capable (see, e.g., Johnson 1982). But in many developing countries—including a number of the Latin American countries in which I have carried out fieldwork—graduates of the leading universities want government posts, not because they are prestigious, but because they provide access to illicit wealth. Thus, a high degree of desirability signals not a rational civil service but its opposite: a porous one (Kurtz & Schrank 2004).

My point is neither to defend Wade's account of Taiwanese success nor to attack Evans and Rauch's scholarship. It is simply to defend Wade's method of intensive, case-based research as a necessary complement to cross-national scholarship—whatever its substantive merits. Large-n research is essential. But it is not without its limitations. Among other things, it tends to treat the causal mechanisms underlying the statistical equations as a black box. And small-n approaches will therefore retain their relevance for many years to come.

Case Study Research: Data Collection and Analysis

While large-n researchers treat classificatory ambiguity as a threat, small-n researchers view it as an opportunity. "What is my case a case of?" they ask.

"Ah, I know, it's a 'developmental state.'" Or an "agroindustrial bourgeoisie." Or a "democratic transition from below." By answering the question "What is my case a case of?" they invoke new concepts, develop fruitful hypotheses, and ultimately advance their social scientific research programs in countless ways. But in so doing, what type of data do they use? And how do they analyze it?

There is no uniform answer. While case studies have almost invariably been associated with qualitative data, their authors frequently invoke quantitative indicators and at times even deploy inferential statistical methods. For some examples of the way quantitative data are used in case studies, see Tilly's work *The Vendée* (1964), Bates's work on mine workers in Zambia (1971), and Laitin's analysis of Somalia (1971). The one commonality is that the authors of the best case studies are methodologically catholic; they let their questions drive their data collection and analytic procedures and not vice versa. Do you want to know how or why X did Y to Z? Use interview data, oral histories, or archival materials to gain insight into X's motivations and capacities. Do you want to know what type of people participated in Y? Use tabular data drawn from surveys, censuses, or other publicly available records to break down the demographic correlates of the process. Do you want to know whether Case 1 really looks like Case 2? Use secondary sources to gain a comprehensive understanding of the similarities and differences between the two cases. Practitioners of case-based research, in short, need to have a lot of different tools in their toolkits and a willingness to "purchase" even more.

Where should these purchases be made? A number of answers are obvious. Methodology classes are often a good place to start, and the fact that departments rarely offer classes on "case study methods" per se need not pose an overwhelming obstacle. Classes on ethnography, archival research, comparative historical methods, research design, and even statistics will prove invaluable, as will textbooks on related themes. But I think there are at least three less obvious places where practitioners of the case study can gain useful insights into the processes of data collection and analysis.

The first is dialogue with the large-n fundamentalists. Why turn to the case study's principal opponents for advice on how to write a case study? If my admittedly casual observations are at all accurate, the scholars who have authored the best case studies and comparative historical analyses have actively engaged—rather than isolated themselves from—their critics. In so doing, they have forced themselves to ask hard questions about just what they were trying to learn, where and how they planned to learn it, and whether they could in fact defend their conclusions with their data. They may not have found much common methodological ground in the end, but they almost invariably seem to have profited from the interchange.

It also took me a long time to discover a second important source of advice on data collection and analysis: the acknowledgements, prefaces, introductions, and appendixes to my favorite books. I had once been told that the easiest way to make it through graduate school was to read only the bare essentials: the summary chapter of a good book, perhaps the synopsized version of the book (published in a journal somewhere), or maybe even a book review or two. Nothing could be further from the truth. The books themselves not only feature essential substantive information but also contain an abundance of detail on themselves: on how they were written. Much of this detail can be found in the acknowledgments, preface, and introductory chapter. To whom did the author talk? When? Why? At whose prompting? With what results? The most useful of these works are reflexive and self-conscious but not solipsistic. They constitute, in a sense, roadmaps to effective fieldwork (Evans 1979).

And what do these roadmaps tell us? Well, one of the things they tell us, almost without exception, is that our friends, sources, and interlocutors in the field constitute a no less important source of insight into the process of data collection. You may know a lot about social or political theory. And you may know a lot about methodology. But unless you are a decidedly atypical young social scientist, your "native informants," for lack of a better term, know much, much more about their countries and contexts than you do. By listening to them, trusting them, and perhaps most importantly respecting them, you will almost certainly guarantee yourself a pleasant as well as productive fieldwork experience.

Notes

1. In theory, and sometimes in practice, one can apply quantitative methods to small samples and qualitative methods to large samples. For instance, Ronald Fisher's "exact test" for 2×2 contingency tables has at times been employed with sample sizes in the single digits. And large-n data collection efforts increasingly combine qualitative and quantitative analysis.

2. For a critique of this argument, see Hall (2003).

3. I have no idea whether the concept or word is original in the narrow sense. A number of other authors were floating similar notions at the same time. See, e.g., Kaplinsky 1998.

Supplemental References

Abbott, Andrew. (1992). "What Do Cases Do? Some Notes on Activity in Sociological Analysis." Pp. 53–82 in *What Is a Case? Exploring the Foundations of Social Inquiry,* edited by C. Ragin and H. Becker. Cambridge, UK: Cambridge University Press.

Bair, Jennifer and Gary Gereffi. (2001). "Local Clusters in Global Chains: The Causes and Consequences of Export Dynamism in Torreón's Blue Jeans Industry." *World Development* 29(11), 1885–1903.

Bates, Robert. (1971). *Unions, Parties, and Political Development: A Study of Mineworkers in Zambia.* New Haven, CT: Yale University Press.

Bennett, Andrew. (2001). "Case Study: Methods and Analysis." Pp. 1513–1519 in *International Encyclopedia of the Social and Behavioral Sciences,* edited by Neil J. Smelser and Paul Baltes. Amsterdam, The Netherlands: Elsevier.

Caporaso, James. (1995). "Research Design, Falsification, and the Qualitative-Quantitative Divide." *America Political Science Review* 89(2), 457–460.

Clague, Christopher, Philip Keefer, Stephen Knack, and Mancur Olson. (1997). "Institutions and Economic Performance: Property Rights and Contract Enforcement." Pp. 67–90 in *Institutions and Economic Development: Growth and Governance in Less-Developed and Post-Socialist Countries,* edited by Christopher Clauge. Baltimore, MD: Johns Hopkins University Press.

Dahrendorf, Ralf. (1968). "Market and Plan: Two Types of Rationality." In *Essays in the Theory of Society,* edited by Ralf Dahrendorf. London, UK: Routledge.

Evans, Peter and James Rauch. (1999). "Bureaucracy and Growth: A Cross-National Analysis of the Effects of 'Weberian' State Structures on Economic Growth." *American Sociological Review* 64(5), 748–765.

Gereffi, Gary. (1999). "International Trade and Industrial Upgrading in the Apparel Commodity Chain." *Journal of International Economics* 48, 37–70.

Hall, Peter. (2003). "Aligning Ontology and Methodology in Comparative Politics." In *Comparative Historical Analysis in the Social Sciences,* edited by James Mahoney and Dietrich Rueschemeyer. Cambridge, UK: Cambridge University Press.

Hedström, Peter and Richard Swedberg. (1998). "Social Mechanisms: An Introductory Essay." Pp. 1–31 in *Social Mechanisms: An Analytical Approach to Social Theory,* edited by Peter Hedström and Richard Swedberg. Cambridge, UK: Cambridge University Press.

Johnson, Chalmers. (1987). "Political Institutions and Economic Performance: The Government-Business Relationship in Japan, South Korea, and Taiwan." In *The Political Economy of the New Asian Industrialism,* edited by Frederic Deyo. Ithaca, NY: Cornell University Press.

———. (2000). *Blowback: The Costs and Consequences of American Empire.* New York: Henry Holt.

Kaplinsky, Raphael. (1998). "Globalisation, Industrialisation, and Sustainable Growth: The Pursuit of the Nth Rent." Discussion Paper No. 365, Institute for Development Studies, University of Sussex, UK.

Kaufmann, Daniel and Aart Kraay. (2002). "Growth Without Governance." *Economia* 3(1), 169–215.

Kurtz, Marcus. (1999). "Social Origins of Central American Democracy." *Journal of Interamerican Studies and World Affairs* 41(1), 87–96.

Kurtz, Marcus and Andrew Schrank. (2004). "Understanding and Misunderstanding Corruption and Growth in the International Economy." Presented at the annual meeting of the American Political Science Association, September 4, Chicago, IL.

Laitin, David. (1971). *Politics, Language, and Thought: The Somali Experience.* Chicago, IL: University of Chicago Press.

———. (1995). "Disciplining Political Science." *American Political Science Review* 89, 454–456.

Moore, Barrington, Jr. (1966). *Social Origins of Dictatorship and Democracy: Lord and Peasant in the Making of the Modern World.* Boston, MA: Beacon.

Orum, Anthony. (2001). "Case Study: Logic." Pp. 1509–1513 in *International Encyclopedia of the Social and Behavioral Sciences,* edited by Neil J. Smelser and Paul Baltes. Amsterdam, The Netherlands: Elsevier.

Paige, Jeffery. (1987) "Coffee and Politics in Central America." In *Crises in the Caribbean Basin: Meanings and Prospects,* edited by Richard Tardanico. Beverly Hills: Sage.

———. (1990). "The Social Origins of Dictatorship, Democracy, and Socialist Revolution in Central America." *Journal of Developing Societies* VI, 37–42.

Ragin, Charles C. (1987). *The Comparative Method: Moving Beyond Qualitative and Quantitative Strategies.* Berkeley: University of California Press.

Reynolds, Lloyd. (1983). "The Spread of Economic Growth to the Third World, 1850–1980." *Journal of Economic Literature* XXI, 941–980.

Riedel, James. (1988). "Economic Development in East Asia: Doing What Comes Naturally?" Pp. 1–38 in *Achieving Industrialization in East Asia,* edited by Helen Hughes. Cambridge, UK: Cambridge University Press.

Rodrik, Dani. (1997). "The 'Paradoxes' of the Successful State." *European Economic Review* 41, 411–442.

Schrank, Andrew. (2004). "Ready-to-Wear Development? Foreign Investment, Technology Transfer, and Learning-by-Watching in the Apparel Trade." *Social Forces* 83(1), 123–156.

———. (forthcoming). "Entrepreneurship, Export Diversification, and Economic Reform: The Birth of a 'Developmental Community' in the Dominican Republic." *Comparative Politics,* 38(1).

Sørensen, Aage. (1998). "Theoretical Mechanisms and the Empirical Study of Social Processes." Pp. 238–266 in *Social Mechanisms: An Analytical Approach to Social Theory,* edited by Peter Hedström and Richard Swedberg. Cambridge, UK: Cambridge University Press.

Topik, Steven. (2000). "Coffee Anyone? Recent Research on Latin American Coffee Societies." *Hispanic American Historical Review,* 80(2), 225–267.

Wade, Robert. (1993). "Managing Trade: Taiwan and South Korea as Challenges to Economics and Political Science." *Comparative Politics* 25(2), 147–167.

Woo-Cumings, Meredith. (1999). "Introduction: Chalmers Johnson and the Politics of Nationalism and Development." In *The Developmental State*, edited by Meredith Woo-Cumings. Ithaca, NY: Cornell University Press.

Wood, Elisabeth Jean. (2000). *Forging Democracy From Below: Insurgent Transitions in South Africa and El Salvador*. Cambridge, UK: Cambridge University Press.

Yashar, Deborah. (2002). "Democratic Pathways: Crossroads, Detours, and Dead Ends in Central America." In *The Making and Unmaking of Democracy: Lessons from History and World Politics*, edited by Theodore Rabb and Ezra Suleiman. New York: Routledge.

Bibliography on Case Studies

1. Overviews: Case Studies, Critics, and Rejoinders

Achen, Christopher and Duncan Snidal. (1989). "Rational Deterrence Theory and Comparative Case Studies." *World Politics* 41(2), 143–169.

Adams, Julia, Elisabeth Clemens, and Ann Shola Orloff. (2005). "Social Theory, Modernity, and the Three Waves of Historical Sociology." Pp. 1–74 in *Remaking Modernity: Politics, History and Sociology*, edited by Julia Adams, Elisabeth Clemens and Ann Shola Orloff . Durham, NC: Duke University Press.

Becker, Howard S. and Charles Ragin. (1992). *What Is a Case? Exploring the Foundations of Social Inquiry.* Cambridge, UK: Cambridge University Press.

Berk, Richard. (1991). "Toward a Methodology for Mere Mortals." *Sociological Methodology* 21, 315–324. See response to this by David Freedman (1991b), listed below.

Blalock, Hubert, Jr. (1991). "Are There Really Any Constructive Alternatives to Causal Modeling?" *Sociological Methodology* 21, 325–335. See response to this by David Freedman (1991b), listed below.

Campbell, Donald and Julian Stanley. (1966). *Experimental and Quasi-Experimental Designs for Research.* Chicago, IL: Rand McNally.

Chamberlin, Thomas C. (1965). "The Method of Multiple Working Hypotheses." *Science* 148(3671), 754–759. Reprint, *Science* 15 (1890).

Consortium on Qualitative Research Methods. Various resources. Retrieved August 30, 2005, from www.asu.edu/clas/polisci/cqrm/. The Consortium promotes case-based social scientific inquiry and maintains an essential website and a listserv that cover developments in the field.

Feagin, Joe R., Anthony M. Orum, and Gideon Sjoberg, eds. (1991). *A Case for the Case Study.* Chapel Hill: University of North Carolina Press.

Freedman, David. (1991a). "Statistical Models and Shoe Leather." *Sociological Methodology* 21, 291–313.

———. (1991b). "A Rejoinder to Berk, Blalock, and Mason." *Sociological Methodology* 21, 353–358.

Geis, Gilbert. (1991). "The Case Study Method in Sociological Criminology." Pp. 200–223 in *A Case for the Case Study*, edited by Joe Feagin, Anthony Orum, and Gideon Sjoberg. Chapel Hill: University of North Carolina Press.

Goldthorpe, John H. (1997). "Current Issues in Comparative Macrosociology: A Debate on Methodological Issues." *Comparative Sociological Research* 16(1), 1–26.

King, Gary, Robert O. Keohane, and Sidney Verba. (1994). *Designing Social Inquiry: Scientific Inference in Qualitative Research.* Princeton, NJ: Princeton University Press.

Lieberson, Stanley. (1985). *Making It Count: The Improvement of Social Research and Theory.* Berkeley: University of California Press.

———. (1991). "Small N's and Big Conclusions: An Examination of the Reasoning in Comparative Studies Based on a Small N of Cases." *Social Forces* 70(2), 307–320.

———. (1994). "More on the Uneasy Case for Using Mill-Type Methods in Small-N Comparative Studies." *Social Forces* 72(4), 1225–1237.

Mahoney, James. (1999). "Nominal, Ordinal, and Narrative Appraisal in Macrocausal Analysis." *American Journal of Sociology* 104(4), 1154–1196.

———. (2000). "Strategies of Social Research in Small-N Analysis." *Sociological Methods and Research* 28(4), 387–424.

Mason, William. (1991). "Freedman is Right as Far as He Goes, but There Is More, and It's Worse, Statisticians Could Help." *Sociological Methodology* 21, 337–351. See response to this by David Freedman (1991b), listed above.

Paige, Jeffery. (1999). "Conjuncture, Comparison, and Conditional Theory in Macrosocial Inquiry." *American Journal of Sociology* 105(3), 781–800.

Przeworksi, Adam and Henry Teune. (1970). *Logic of Comparative Social Inquiry.* New York: John Wiley and Sons.

Ragin, Charles C. (1994). *Constructing Social Research: The Unity and Diversity of Method.* Thousand Oaks, CA: Pine Forge Press.

———. (2000). *Fuzzy Set Social Science.* Chicago, IL: University of Chicago Press.

Ragin, Charles C. and Howard Becker, eds. (1992). *What Is a Case? Exploring the Foundations of Social Inquiry.* Cambridge, UK: Cambridge University Press.

Savolainen, Jukka. (1994). "The Rationality of Drawing Big Conclusions Based on Small Samples: In Defense of Mill's Methods." *Social Forces* 72(2), 1217–1224.

Stinchcombe, Arthur. (1968). *Constructing Social Theories.* New York: Harcourt, Brace, and World.

Tilly, Charles. (1997). "Means and Ends of Comparison in Macrosociology." *Comparative Sociological Research* 16, 43–54.

Yin, Robert K. (1989). *Case Study Research: Design and Methods.* Applied Social Research Methods Series. Newbury Park, CA: Sage.

2. The "One Shot" Case Study Revisited

Theory and Method

Campbell, Donald T. (1975). "Degrees of Freedom and the Case Study." *Comparative Political Studies* 8(2), 178–193. Ideally this should be read as an autocritique of Campbell and Stanley (1966), listed above.

Levi, Margaret. (2000). "Making a Case for Case Studies." *APSA-CP* 11, 19–21.
March, James, Lee Sproull, and Michal Tamuz. (1991). "Learning from Samples of One or Fewer." *Organization Science* 2(1), 1–13.

Good Examples

Collier, David. (1976). *Squatters and Oligarchs: Authoritarian Rule and Policy Change in Peru.* Baltimore, MD: Johns Hopkins University Press.
Evans, Peter. (1979). *Dependent Development: The Alliance of Multinational, State, and Local Capital in Brazil.* Princeton, NJ: Princeton University Press.
Johnson, Chalmers. (1982). *MITI and the Japanese Miracle: The Growth of Industrial Policy, 1925–1975.* Stanford, CA: Stanford University Press.
———. (1999). "The Developmental State: Odyssey of a Concept." In *The Developmental State*, edited by Meredith Woo-Cumings. Ithaca, NY: Cornell University Press.
Lipset, Seymour. (1950). *Agrarian Socialism: The Cooperative Commonwealth Federation in Saskatchewan: A Study in Political Sociology.* Berkeley: University of California Press.
Reno, William. (1995). *Corruption and State Politics in Sierra Leone.* Cambridge, UK: Cambridge University Press.
Sewell, William. (1996). "Political Events as Structural Transformations: Inventing Revolution at the Bastille." *Theory and Society* 25(6), 841–881.

Good Examples From U.S.-Based Research Sites

Allison, Graham. (1971). *The Essence of Decision.* Boston, MA: Little Brown.
Lipset, Seymour Martin, Martin Trow, and James S. Coleman. (1953). *Union Democracy.* Glencoe, IL: Free Press.
Vaughan, Diane. (1997). *The Challenger Launch Decision: Risky Technology, Culture, and Deviance at NASA.* Chicago, IL: University of Chicago Press.
Walton, John. (1992). *Western Times and Water Wars: State, Culture, and Rebellion in California.* Berkeley: University of California Press.

3. Comparative Case Approaches

Theory and Method

Collier, David and James Mahoney. (1996). "Insights and Pitfalls: Selection Bias in Qualitative Research." *World Politics* 49(1), 56–91.
Dion, Douglas. (1998). "Evidence and Inference in the Comparative Case Study." *Comparative Politics* 30(2), 127–146.
Geddes, Barbara. (1990). "How the Cases You Choose Affect the Answers You Get: Selection Bias in Comparative Politics." *Political Analysis* 2, 131–149.

Mill, John Stuart. (1970). "Two Methods of Comparison." In *Comparative Perspectives: Theories and Methods*, edited by Amitai Etzioni and Fredric Dubow. Boston, MA: Little Brown.

Ragin, Charles. (1981). "Comparative Sociology and the Comparative Method." *International Journal of Comparative Sociology* 22(1–2), 102–120.

Skocpol, Theda and Margaret Somers. (1980). "The Uses of Comparative History in Macrosocial Inquiry." *Comparative Studies in Society and History* 22(2), 174–197.

Good Examples

Aston, Trevor H. and Charles H. E. Philpin. (1987). *The Brenner Debate: Agrarian Class Structure and Economic Development in Pre-Industrial Europe.* Cambridge, UK: Cambridge University Press.

Bhagwati, Jagdish. (1986). "Rethinking Trade Strategy." In *Development Strategies Reconsidered*, edited by John Lewis and Valeriana Kallab. New Brunswick, NJ: Transaction Books.

Collier, Ruth Berins and David Collier. (1991). *Shaping the Political Arena: Critical Junctures, the Labor Movement, and Regime Dynamics in Latin America.* Princeton, NJ: Princeton University Press.

Evans, Peter. (1995). *Embedded Autonomy: States and Industrial Transformation.* Princeton, NJ: Princeton University Press.

Gourevitch, Peter. (1986). *Politics in Hard Times: Comparative Responses to International Economic Crises.* Ithaca, NY: Cornell University Press.

Kurtz, Marcus and Andrew Barnes. (2002). "The Political Foundations of Post-Communist Regimes: Marketization, Agrarian Legacies, or International Influences?" *Comparative Political Studies* 35(5), 524–553.

Luebbert, Gregory. (1991). *Liberalism, Fascism, or Social Democracy: Social Classes and the Political Origins of Regimes in Interwar Europe.* New York: Oxford University Press.

O'Donnell, Guillermo. (1973). *Modernization and Bureaucratic Authoritarianism: Studies in South American Politics.* Berkeley: Institute of International Studies, University of California.

Paige, Jeffery. (1975). *Agrarian Revolution: Social Movements and Export Agriculture in the Underdeveloped World.* New York: Free Press.

——. (1983). "Social Theory and Peasant Revolution in Vietnam and Guatemala." *Theory and Society* 12(6), 699–737.

——. (1997). *Coffee and Power: Revolution and the Rise of Democracy in Central America.* Cambridge, MA: Harvard University Press.

——. (1999). "Conjuncture, Comparison, and Conditional Theory in Macrosocial Inquiry." *American Journal of Sociology* 105(3), 781–800.

Skocpol, Theda. (1976). "A Structural Analysis of Social Revolutions." *Comparative Studies in Society and History* 18(2), 175–210.

——. (1979). *States and Social Revolutions: A Comparative Analysis of France, Russia, and China.* Cambridge, UK: Cambridge University Press.

4. Subnational Approaches

Theory and Method

Lijphart, Arend. (1971). "Comparative Politics and the Comparative Method." *American Political Science Review* 65(3), 682–693.

Snyder, Richard. (2001). "Scaling Down: The Subnational Comparative Method." *Studies in Comparative International Development* 36(1), 93–110.

Good Examples

Barnett, Michael. (1990). "High Politics Is Low Politics: The Domestic and Systemic Sources of Israeli Security Policy, 1967–1977." *World Politics* 42(4), 529–562.

Hamilton, Nora. (1982). *The Limits to State Autonomy: Post-Revolutionary Mexico.* Princeton, NJ: Princeton University Press.

Heller, Patrick. (2000). "Degrees of Democracy: Some Comparative Lessons from India." *World Politics* 52(4), 484–519.

Kohli, Atul. (1987). *The State and Poverty in India: The Politics of Reform.* Cambridge, UK: Cambridge University Press.

Locke, Richard. (1995). *Remaking the Italian Economy.* Ithaca, NY: Cornell University Press.

Putnam, Robert D., Robert Leonardi, and Raffaela Nanetti. (1995). *Making Democracy Work: Civic Traditions in Modern Italy.* Princeton, NJ: Princeton University Press.

Snyder, Richard. (2001). *Politics after Neoliberalism: Reregulation in Mexico.* Cambridge, UK: Cambridge University Press.

Tilly, Charles. (1964). *The Vendée: A Sociological Account of the Counter-Revolution of 1793.* Cambridge, MA: Harvard University Press.

5. "Doing" Case Studies

Theory and Method

Van Evera, Stephen. (1997). "What Are Case Studies? How Should They Be Performed?" In *Guide to Methods for Students of Political Science*, edited by Stephen Van Evera. Ithaca, NY: Cornell University Press.

Vaughan, Diane. (1992). "Theory Elaboration: The Heuristics of Case Analysis." In *What Is a Case? Exploring the Foundations of Social Inquiry*, edited by Howard S. Becker and Charles Ragin. Cambridge, UK: Cambridge University Press.

Walton, John. (1992). "Making the Theoretical Case." In *What Is a Case? Exploring the Foundations of Social Inquiry*, edited by Howard S. Becker and Charles Ragin. Cambridge, NY: Cambridge University Press.

6. Counterfactuals

Fearon, James. (1991). "Counterfactuals and Hypothesis Testing in Political Science." *World Politics* 43(2), 169–195.

Lebow, Richard Ned. (2000). "What's So Different About a Counterfactual?" *World Politics* 52(4), 550–585.

Good Examples

Desai, Manali. (2002). "The Relative Autonomy of Party Practices: A Counterfactual Analysis of Left Party Ascendancy in Kerala, India, 1934–1940." *American Journal of Sociology* 108(3), 616–657.

7. The "Negative Case" Approach

Theory and Method

Emigh, Rebecca Jean. (1997). "The Power of Negative Thinking: The Use of Negative Case Methodology in the Development of Sociological Theory." *Theory and Society* 26(5), 649–684.

Good Examples

Barrett, Richard and Martin King Whyte. (1982). "Dependency Theory and Taiwan: Analysis of a Deviant Case." *American Journal of Sociology* 87(5), 1064–1089.

Emigh, Rebecca Jean. (1998). "The Mystery of the Missing Middle Tenants: The 'Negative' Case of Fixed-Term Leasing and Agricultural Investment in Fifteenth Century Tuscany." *Theory and Society* 27(3), 351–375.

8. Concept Formation

Collier, David. (1995). "Trajectory of a Concept: 'Corporatism' in the Study of Latin American Politics." In *Latin America in Comparative Perspective*, edited by Peter Smith. Boulder, CO: Westview Press.

Collier, David and Steven Levitsky. (1997). "Democracy with Adjectives: Conceptual Innovation in Comparative Research." *World Politics* 49(3), 430–451.

Collier, David and James E. Mahon. (1993). "Conceptual Stretching Revisited: Adapting Categories in Comparative Analysis." *American Political Science Review* 87(4), 845–855.

Kurtz, Marcus. (2000). "Understanding Peasant Revolution: From Concept to Theory and Case." *Theory and Society* 29(1), 93–124.

Levitsky, Steven. (1998). "Institutionalization and Peronism: The Concept, the Case, and the Case for Unpacking the Concept." *Party Politics* 4(1), 77–92.

Romer, Paul. (1993). "Two Strategies for Economic Development: Using Ideas and Producing Ideas." *Proceedings of the World Bank Annual Conference on*

Development Economics 1992, supplement to the *World Bank Economic Review* (March), 63–91.

Sartori, Giovanni. (1970). "Concept Misformation in Comparative Politics." *American Political Science Review* 64(4), 1033–1053.

Srinivasan, T. N. and Jagdish Bhagwati. (2001). "Outward Orientation and Development: Are Revisionists Right?" In *Trade, Development and Political Economy: Essays in Honour of Anne Krueger*, edited by Deepak Lal and Richard Shape. London, UK: Palgrave.

3

Ethnographic Methods

Ethnography: Theory and Methods

Alma Gottlieb

What Is Ethnography?

Interviewing the minister of finance about current trends in the local economy. Riding in a taxi all day with an immigrant cab driver as he picks up and drops off his fares. Helping young mothers as they pound corn in adjoining courtyards and gossip about recent village events. Joining in a lesbian and gay rights march and observing relations between marchers and bystanders.

What do these disparate activities have in common? They are all examples of ethnography—a powerful, multistranded method first developed by cultural anthropologists and now adopted by researchers in many disciplines, from political scientists and economists to scholars of education and media studies. Why is ethnography so widely used? Put simply, ethnography offers an unparalleled set of methods for exploring and gaining insight

AUTHOR'S NOTE: I am grateful to Liora Bresler for insightful comments on this chapter; to Philip Graham, my partner in fieldwork and life; and, from the fieldwork methods courses and workshops I have taught over the years, to the many students who have always pushed me to articulate and hone my ideas and who keep reminding me by their own inspirational research that fieldwork is a process.

into people's values, beliefs, and behaviors. Qualitative methods, of which ethnography is the quintessential exemplar, seek to explain what quantitative observations actually mean to actual individuals. Moreover, qualitative methods have the potential to explore ruptures between individuals' stated opinions and beliefs (such as those they might express in survey questionnaires), on the one hand, and their actual behaviors, on the other hand, since the latter may not always reflect the former. Ideally, quantitative and qualitative methods can be harnessed to work together, as well-paired as couples on a dance floor.

What Is the Value of Doing Ethnography?

Among the methodologies available to social science researchers, ethnography is the only one based explicitly on the recognition of three fundamental and interrelated presuppositions: (a) that data are not just gathered like grapes on a vine but are also created by human effort; put more prosaically, the way in which information is collected affects the content of the data themselves; (b) that scholars who "produce data" are complex creatures whose perceptions and communications are shaped at every turn by the context in which they find themselves and the level of comfort—or discomfort—they experience in that context; and (c) that both the quality and the content of the "data" that a researcher "gathers" have as much to do with the researcher as they do with the informants or research participants.

These presuppositions are in turn premised on a philosophical orientation, developed by the branch of philosophy known as hermeneutics, that human life is about interpretation—that developing and working with systems of meaning constitute both the prime motive in, and the prime mode of, being human (Berger & Luckmann 1966; Cassirer 1944; Geertz 1973a; Langer 1942). It follows from this perspective that it is crucial to pay attention to intersubjectivity—the process of individuals encountering one another both empirically and psychologically—in the course of conducting research. Recent examples of works critically examining the theoretical foundations of longstanding anthropological practices (positivist and otherwise) include, among many others, Clifford and Marcus (1986); Harrison (1991); James, Hockey, and Dawson (1997); and Marcus and Fisher (1986). Indeed, qualitative researchers writing since the 1980s have increasingly worked through the productive implications of such a hermeneutic approach. While some qualitative methods emphasize externally imposed analytic models and downplay both subjectivity and intersubjectivity, the orientation of this chapter is informed by the hermeneutic perspective.

Let me illustrate the potential value of a hermeneutically informed qualitative approach—and the intellectual payoff it can offer—by way of a story from my own research. Before I began conducting my doctoral research in a group of small villages in Côte d'Ivoire, my graduate adviser counseled me to inaugurate my fieldwork by compiling basic census data in the village in which I would settle, noting names and ages of all residents, their clan membership, their relations to others in the household, and any other information that appeared relevant. The strategy seemed reasonable, and soon after settling into a village, I followed my adviser's instructions and began trying to collect primary census data. It was an unmitigated disaster. The residents would not even divulge what I assumed would be unproblematic facts, such as their own names or how many children they had, let alone clan affiliation or more private information (Gottlieb & Graham 1994, pp. 65–69). I immediately gave up on my census efforts and, for the next few months, settled for conducting innocuous conversations about the weather, the names of house parts, clothing styles, and anything else I hoped would be uncontroversial. Apparently, the residents of this village had reason to suspect my motives, and I would clearly need to make great efforts to win their trust before they would willingly share even basic aspects of their lives. Entrée into this community—one of my prime goals—would apparently be a protracted process, and delicately exploring the motives for their suspicion became a theme in my research that ultimately helped me understand their bitter experiences with French colonial domination earlier in the century.

Pursuing participant observation—better known among anthropologists as advanced hanging out—combined with systematically learning the local language, proved to be my primary research method during my first six months. Only after I could conduct a simple conversation in the local language (Beng) did people start talking with me about issues that mattered to them. In the end, I filled out my census cards on the run, jotting down demographic facts about lives and households as I came to know my neighbors. When I returned to the region five years later for another research project, one close friend confided that my initial attempt at a census had done even more damage than I had realized: Only then did I discover that on my previous visit, people had interpreted my questions as a sign that I was a spy for the government and intended to help the regime reinstate the French colonial system of forced labor (Gottlieb & Graham 1994, pp. 287–288). Had I *initially* attended to the hermeneutic dimensions of research and taken the time to build rapport before embarking on a census, I might have saved myself—and my Beng hosts and hostesses—much heartache.

My case is not unusual. Gaining rapport with a group of people can take far more time, attention, and imagination than one might anticipate.

Another real-life fieldwork story can illustrate the point well. A medical anthropologist, Denise Allen, planned a two-year doctoral research stint in a small town in Tanzania on the topic of childbirth and midwifery practices. Soon after moving into the town, she decided that during her entire first year, she would never carry a notebook with her as she walked around town. Out of concern that taking notes in front of people would raise too many suspicions, Allen deferred her note taking to evenings when she was alone in her room. Her first priority was earning people's trust, and she did this by eating meals with her neighbors, helping out with babysitting, and asking as few direct questions as possible. Only after a year of working to develop comfortable relations with her neighbors did Allen begin asking formal questions about her research topic, and only then did she begin writing in her notebook while observing births (Allen 2002).

Granted, Allen's is an extreme case, and most researchers lack the luxury of both time and money to carry out such a relaxed schedule. But the lesson is worth attending to. The more rushed you are, the more superficial will be the information you collect. Put simply, skimpy methods produce skimpy data. Conversely, the more time you take to get to know the people whose lives you are trying to understand, the more likely it is that they will take the time to share their honest reflections with you.

This principle is equally relevant in more familiar settings. A researcher in communications, Mary Anne Moffitt, envisaged a doctoral study of the reading habits of teenage American girls who read dozens or even hundreds of romance novels each year. From her formal interviews with a group of girls, she learned what they thought about the plots of the books, but she had a hunch that there was more to the girls' reading experiences than what they were telling her. To probe how the girls' responses to a survey on their experiences reading romance novels squared with their actual reading behaviors, she decided to add a qualitative component to her study. The girls agreed to allow Moffitt to follow them around on weekends as they spent hours at the local mall's bookstore. Here, Moffitt discovered the inner workings of an elaborate exchange network that had not come to light from her more formal surveys: One girl would buy a book and then share it with the others, with each book passed back and forth multiple times so as to reach the entire reading group. Although this project was initially conceived as a purely literary study, the charting of the girls' exchange networks through both a survey and a set of ethnographic observations provided it with a dynamic sociological perspective and helped put this initially more textually oriented study into broader perspective (Moffitt 1990; Moffitt & Wartella 1992).

Such cases point to the difference in scope between ethnography and survey research. While a national survey conducted over a period of a month may obtain data from 10,000 respondents and have statistical reliability and a low margin of error, ethnographers may spend a year living among and studying the lives of only three or four neighboring families. An ethnographic study may even focus extensively on one person's life in order to produce a full-scale biography of that individual, with nuanced discussions of all stages of the life cycle. Is there a payoff for this focus on depth rather than breadth?

Depth Versus Breadth

Think of the relationship between quantitative and qualitative methods as a seesaw. As if attached by a fulcrum, they form part of a single dynamic system, but at any given moment they produce two different, indeed sometimes incommensurable forms of knowledge: Quantitative methods produce breadth but sacrifice depth; qualitative methods produce depth, revealing a complexity that quantitative methods might miss, but they sacrifice breadth. Of course, this perfunctory description is something of a caricature; the best quantitative studies also build on at least some level of depth, and the best qualitative methods also offer at least some level of breadth. But at their most extreme, the two approaches have very different goals (on quantitative methods, see Chapter 7 in this volume).

Ethnography often produces spectacular results in terms of depth. A beautifully written ethnography based on long-term involvement in a community and fluency in the local language allows the reader to virtually taste the flavors of the local cuisine and smell the sea breezes. Most important, it allows the reader to gain a deep understanding of, and empathy for, lives lived and values held in a very different fashion from one's own (see, e.g., Bowen 1954; Briggs 1970; Cesara 1982; Dumont 1978; Fernea 1965, 1975; Lareau & Shultz 1996; Powdermaker 1967; Read 1965; Rabinow 1977; Stoller & Olkes 1987). Sometimes this understanding is of a group of people defined by their gender, as with Abu-Lughod's sensitive portrait of Bedouin women in Egypt (1993b); sometimes it is of a group of people who are related by affiliation to a political ideology, as with Crapanzano's disturbing portrait of racist whites living in late-apartheid South Africa (1985); sometimes it is even of a single individual whom the reader gets to know in exquisite detail, as in Shostak's renowned and intimate biography of a !Kung woman leading a somewhat traditional hunter-gatherer lifestyle in southern Africa (2000) or Crapanzano's provocative portrait of a male Moroccan tile maker (1980). All these results could be achieved only through fine-grained ethnographic research conducted extensively or even exclusively in the local language.

In the best of all possible worlds, every study would provide for both optimal depth and optimal breadth. In generously funded projects, this might be achieved through research teams consisting of both quantitatively and qualitatively oriented researchers who collaboratively design a study to take advantage of the skills and training of each team member. In more modest projects, a single scholar might seek training in both quantitative and qualitative research methods so as to craft a well-integrated research agenda aiming for a balance between the statistical breadth of quantitative methods and the cultural depth of qualitative methods (see Chapter 7 in this volume).

Ethnography as Social Science: Some Ethnographic Techniques

What techniques do ethnographers use in creating such evocative portraits of individuals and their social universe?

Many cultural anthropologists used to argue that ethnography is such a personal process that it cannot be taught. By contrast, nowadays few cultural anthropologists would espouse this quasi-mystical perspective. In fact, the current generation of anthropologists aims to demystify the process. Despite the uniqueness of each fieldwork experience, many scholars now suggest that much can be learned in advance from thinking and reading about others' experiences and mistakes in conducting research.

Graduate programs in anthropology often offer courses in fieldwork methods that are open to students in any discipline, and the National Science Foundation often offers such summer courses at one or more campuses around the United States. Most such courses provide an opportunity to conduct a modest fieldwork project locally, on the premise that it is preferable to make your worst mistakes during a trial run, when the success of your major research will not be affected.

A good field-methods course should offer intellectual and emotional tools to help you analyze and learn from your mistakes and deal with the frustrations that you will inevitably encounter in any fieldwork project. Let us explore briefly a few formal techniques that are often taught in such courses.

Language

The first and perhaps most important tool for conducting effective ethnography is language. If most residents of your research site speak a language other than one in which you are already fluent, you will reap great rewards if you work to become competent in that language *before* you embark on your study. If you are a U.S. citizen working on your doctorate at a U.S. university, you can apply for the federally funded Work-Study Program and for a FLAS (Foreign Language and Area Studies) fellowship, which funds a full year of language study on your campus. If your campus does not teach the language you need to learn, you can find a campus that does and then apply for a FLAS fellowship to study there for a summer or a semester. Even without a FLAS fellowship, you may be able to study a foreign language relevant to your research. Your institution may be part of a regional agreement that funds students to take courses at other universities. Ask your adviser or college dean about funding opportunities for language study both on and off campus. For suggestions on how to improve your knowledge of a new language through means other than formal coursework, and a general "pep talk" to give you courage if you are intimidated by language study, see Farber (1991).

Perhaps you will protest, "It takes too long to learn a language. I have to complete my doctorate in five years, and I can't possibly do this if I am taking extra courses outside my field." Well, perhaps it is the (folk) custom in your home department to complete a doctorate in five years. But folk customs are often far more pliable than they at first appear. Do not give up on studying the language before exploring the options!

If you will be conducting research in a developing nation, even if you already know the colonial language that is spoken in your planned field site (e.g., French, Spanish, or Portuguese), it is wise to spend some time learning the indigenous language that is native to most residents. The more people you can converse with comfortably in their first language, the richer your research will be. One graduate student I worked with devoted extraordinary energy in studying four languages before embarking on his doctoral research in a multilingual region of Senegal. His competence in the appropriate languages greatly strengthened his applications for dissertation research, which was ultimately funded by two national agencies. Equally important, his linguistic competence allowed him to hit the ground running once he began his research (Westgard 2006).[1]

Still you may object, "Why go through all this trouble when English is now a global language?" Contrary to increasingly common perceptions, only about 8% of the world's citizens are currently considered competent in English (Gordon 2000). Moreover, in many parts of the world where English is the official language, relying on English in effect means limiting yourself to speaking to elites and excluding the majority of the citizenry, who will inevitably have very different perspectives on whatever topic you are aiming to research.

Is it necessary to become fully fluent in the local language? Most people are genuinely touched when outsiders try to learn their language, and no matter how modest your level of competence, your attempts will probably be greatly appreciated. Winning people's trust and willingness to share their opinions can be accomplished far more easily and quickly once you have convinced them that you are on their side. And making at least some effort to speak their language is a prime way to demonstrate this.

A final objection you might have to language learning involves translation and interpretation. Surely ignorance of the local language will not prevent me from having access to non-English speakers, you may be thinking, since I can always engage the services of a reliable interpreter.

My response to this frequent objection is that interpreters can themselves create problems, however inadvertently (Gentzler 2001; Newmark 1991; Pochhacker & Shlesinger 2001; Schäffner & Kelly-Holmes 1995; Tymoczko & Gentzler 2002; and Wagner, Bech, & Martínez 2001, pp. 62–81). First, as in all skills, some interpreters are better trained and more competent than others, but you may not have much choice in whom to hire as an interpreter. You may discover the hard way that hiring an interpreter can be risky—for instance, when you find that your interpreter has mistranslated or incompletely translated essential conversations. Political agendas can also interfere in the delicate process of translation. Consider this example from my own research. In my first months of fieldwork in Côte d'Ivoire, I discovered that the young man I had engaged as an interpreter was delighted to translate pleasant conversations and information about traditional customs, but he refused to translate disputes and conversations about unpleasant or controversial topics. He hoped my work would bring renown to the Beng people via an imagined Voice of America radio broadcast, and he was adamant that I represent his people in a positive light. Our agendas were at loggerheads, and we eventually had to part company (Gottlieb & Graham 1994). As this example suggests, you will generally be much better off becoming as competent as you can in the local language(s) and using interpreters just to check your own understanding.

Once you have attained some level of competence in the locally spoken language(s), you can consider a range of ethnographic methods that will allow you to understand what people think about a particular issue or topic and how they experience some aspects of their lives.

A Potpourri of Ethnographic Methods

The classic formal ethnographic method remains the long interview with, ideally, several follow-up interviews. A short version of this is the one-shot, quick-and-dirty, prescheduled, short interview. This is certainly better than no interview, but it is far from optimal. The sorts of information and opinions that a person will give you in a short, structured conversation are quite different from—and often far more superficial than—the sorts of information and opinions that same person will give you in a more leisurely but less structured situation once he or she has come to know you and feels comfortable sharing more heterodox, complex, or even intimate thoughts with you. Fortunately, helpful guidelines on a variety of techniques for conducting different kinds of interviews are now readily available (see, e.g., Arksey & Knight 1999; Briggs 1986; Fontana & Frey 2000; Holstein & Gubrium 1995; Ives 1995; Kvale 1996; McCracken 1988; Rubin & Rubin 1995; Spradley 1979; also see Chapter 4 in this volume).

After your first interview, jot down further questions that occur to you as you read through your notes. Then try to schedule a follow-up interview. If your informant seems congenial, suggest a more informal venue for the second conversation. What your informant is willing to talk about in, say, a park or out-of-the-way café may be quite different from what he or she might say in an office or a living room crowded with noisy relatives. In Africa, I have had some of my most productive interviews in buses, where my informant and I spoke a language that the other passengers did not know, and my interlocutor felt free to share opinions about quite sensitive issues and even to divulge otherwise secret information (although for ethical reasons, I never published the latter). If you look creatively at your surroundings, you can propose a site where your respondents will feel relaxed enough to confide their thoughts. Ideally, you will be able to conduct a series of follow-up interviews in such sites, with greater levels of depth occurring each time.

Focus groups offer an intriguing variation on the individual interview. Citizens of democratically oriented nations may be aware of focus groups largely through reports that journalists provide, in which they summarize opinions offered by members of focus groups concerning political campaigns or issues. However, the relevance of this research technique goes far beyond the journalistic. Social scientists can make exciting use of focus groups in any number of research projects. The key lies in the selection of the focus group: The researcher should aim to assemble a set of individuals who will offer an informative spectrum of ideas about a particular subject but whose backgrounds are not so diverse that comparing their opinions becomes meaningless. Fortunately, excellent guides now exist to help you avoid the possible pitfalls, and make use of the great potential, of this valuable research method (see, e.g., Chapter 5 in this volume).

Attending to social connections among individuals leads us to consider a more active technique: the ethnographic charting of social networks. From work conducted in the mid-20th century in London (Bott 1971) and southern Africa (van Velsen 1964), social scientists have developed techniques to trace the networks that individuals maintain across a variety of identity factors and social groups (Freeman, White, & Kimball 1989; Schensul et al. 1999; Scott 1991; Wasserman & Faust 1994; Wasserman & Galaskiewicz 1994; Wellman & Berkowitz 1988). Researchers in several disciplines have expanded this method to study topics as diverse as AIDS (Frey 1989), conspiracy (Davis 1984), and organized crime (Klerks 2001)—and most recently, Al Qaeda networks (Krebs 2002a, 2002b).

Related to the charting of social networks is another classic technique long used by anthropologists and taught in many fieldwork courses and texts: the construction of genealogies. Even with the shrinking of families and their dispersal across the globe—or perhaps because of these epic changes—family relations remain key to many individuals. Uncovering what such relations mean to people in the face of new reproductive technologies, intercultural adoption, and other contemporary means for creating families is a central endeavor for many in the current generation of anthropologists (e.g. Franklin & McKinnon 2001; Franklin & Ragoné 1998; Graham 1996; Lomnitz & Lizaur 1987; McKinnon & Silverman 2005; Stone 2001; Strathern 1992; Weston 1991; Yanagisako & Delaney 1995). With helpful resources available for teaching the novice, you will not find it hard to learn how to develop an efficient shorthand to chart genealogies as a first step to exploring the meanings of kinship (whether biologically based or otherwise) in contemporary life (see, e.g., Barnard & Good 1984; Crane & Angrosino 1984, pp. 44–52).

Anthropologists have developed additional techniques to analyze other specific domains of social life. For example, scholars interested in rituals and other symbolically resonant events often make use of an analytic method created by the renowned anthropologist Victor Turner (1967). To understand the complex meanings embedded in any given site of cultural production, the analyst, Turner urged, should explore three levels of inquiry: exegetical (explicit exegesis or interpretations offered by informants), operational (how a symbol is actually deployed in a particular cultural practice), and positional (the range of culturally meaningful events in which a given symbol is deployed). Furthermore, to investigate the performative nature of legal proceedings, Turner developed the concept of "social drama" and associated methods for investigating such dramas (1957). Although Turner developed these two methods to understand initiation rituals and village-level legal battles, respectively, among the Ndembu of Zambia, he later adapted them for investigating sacred and secular rituals and performances of modern Western life as well (Turner 1975, 1988), and the methods remain impressively adaptable in any number of cultural settings.

So far, all the methods discussed in this chapter rely on verbal techniques, with the practice of asking people questions being central to these methods. Although ethnographers uncover impressive layers of meaning when they talk with people, conversation does not afford the only means of gaining insight into social life. If "a picture can tell a thousand words," ethnographers have begun to make good on this claim by incorporating visual images into their work. Even a casual museumgoer discovers the dramatic truths that the visual can uncover for the viewer. As research tools, still and video photography have the potential to harness such truths. We may not all be Walker Evans, but surely the way his photographs awakened an earlier generation of Americans to the appalling realities of poverty in rural America—or the central role of photojournalists' images from Hurricane Katrina in putting pressure on the Bush administration to attend to the ravages of race and class in America, the disturbing inefficiency of our federal emergency organization, and the risks of deferring prevention upgrades for large-scale infrastructural technologies such as levees—reminds us of the power of the visual (for engaging examples of the visual used to good effect in contemporary social science, see the journal *Visual Anthropology*). The development of digital technology in both still and video modes makes it increasingly appealing for ethnographers to explore these technologies as they become both more affordable and more user-friendly (see, e.g., Barbash & Taylor 1997; Bauer & Gaskell 2000; Biella 2001; Collier & Collier [1967] 1986; el Guindi 1998; Harper 1998).

Although visual methods such as still and video photography challenge the verbal domination of most scholarly research methods, all these methods nevertheless depend on the single sense of vision for making their point. Yet, as many thoughtful scholars have pointed out, privileging the visual sense dooms us to neglect the other senses, all of which play an active role in how we as humans experience the world (e.g., Howes 1991; Mauss [1938] 1973; Stoller 1989, 1997; Strathern 1997). Trying to put into operation this philosophical observation, some ethnographers have begun employing body-based techniques. For example, some researchers have developed a notational system called labanotation to chart bodily movements in dance and other body practices (see, e.g., Farnell 1995). Taking seriously the body and all the ways it communicates meaningfully to others can also allow us to pay attention to a group of people that most social scientists other than psychologists routinely neglect: infants (Gottlieb 2004). Developing means of analyzing body-based communications affords us new theoretical insights into important domains of human experience that Western scholarship often ignores.

Field Notes

Many issues present themselves with reference to the use of field notes. First, no matter which methods you employ, you will need to spend significant periods of time writing, reading over, and thinking about your notes while you conduct your research. Previous generations of scholars tended to regard the process of note taking as transparent and unproblematic, comprising an objective record of verifiable facts. By contrast, most contemporary ethnographers now view the practice as a site of cultural production that is deeply (if invisibly) informed by both cultural values and systems of unequal power relations.

Bresler (1997) explores the emotional consequences of the researcher's transition from quasi-member of a community to distant observer of the community during the process of taking and writing up research notes. Ottenberg (1990) goes so far as to question the hegemony of the *written* field note, pointing out that the process of thinking about, interpreting, and reinterpreting data—a process he intriguingly dubs headnotes—may be at least as important as the process of physically recording the data. As Ottenberg points out,

> the words in my written notes stay the same. . . . But my interpretations of them as my headnotes have altered. My headnotes and my written notes are in constant dialogue, and in this sense the field experience does not stop. (p. 146)

A small but growing body of social science literature discusses a variety of these and related provocative issues raised by the process of taking notes (Emerson, Fretz, & Shaw 1995; Sanjek 1990; Vermeulen & Roldán 1996). At the same time, computer software is now being developed that makes the task of writing up research notes appealingly systematic (e.g., Coward, Moore, & Wimbish 1998; Richards & Richards 1998).

In spite of the fact that ethnographers regularly make use of relatively formal, learnable techniques such as those discussed above, ethnography nevertheless remains as much art as science (Wolcott 1995). Thus, most ethnographers will tell you that intuition, the hallmark of artistic practice, can be as important as rational plans in making for successful research.

Ethnography as Art

First, there is the matter of serendipity. A beautifully planned research project may prove hopelessly unviable due to changed political circumstances that may necessitate dramatic revamping. For example, cultural anthropologist Michelle Johnson changed her doctoral research field site from West Africa to western Europe when the country in which she had already conducted a year of predissertation research, Guinea-Bissau, became embroiled in civil war. After moving her dissertation project to an expatriate, refugee community of Guineans living in the former colonial metropole of Lisbon, she began writing and publishing on previously unanticipated topics (Johnson 2002, 2006). Even when changes in research design are not necessitated by political upheavals, ethnographers may choose to alter their strategies and aims based on early findings. Another cultural anthropologist, Shanshan Du, originally intended to focus her doctoral research on the disturbing number of love-pact suicides among the Lahu, an ethnic minority group in Southwest China. But while conducting interviews, she discovered the extent to which a basic ideology of gender equality accounted for the suicide pacts and decided to focus instead on the broader issue of egalitarian gender relations among the Lahu (Du 2002).

Both these stories underscore how important it is to remain flexible in conducting research (Moore 1973). As you "collect data," your understanding of the local situation *should* keep changing. Attending to your own changing understanding may well suggest reorienting your original focus.

In addition to serendipity, there is also the human factor in conducting social science research. Attending to the humanity of research subjects suggests a consideration of our own humanity as researchers as well. If a previous generation of social scientists assumed the positivist premise commonly espoused in the natural sciences—that all researchers work as neutral observers in conditions that should approximate as much as possible the laboratory conditions of the physical sciences—many in the current generation of social scientists challenge this epistemological orientation. Rather than trying to neutralize our identities—a quest that many contemporary researchers think is doomed—many of us now ask, How do our own identities shape our research questions? And how do they shape the answers we receive from our informants?

One productive way to approach these questions is to assess the extent to which you are an insider or an outsider in your research community. This may appear to be a simple query, but globalization now produces such a complex interweaving of identities that the answer to this question is often murky. More and more of us are "halfies," straddling two—or more—identity borders (Abu-Lughod 1991). Let us take the case of two recently minted scholars.

Jonathan Zilberg, a middle-class student and sculptor of European/Jewish background born and raised in Harare but later educated in the United States, returned to Zimbabwe to conduct doctoral fieldwork. Most of his informants were black Christian Zimbabwean artists, some were white Christian or Jewish Zimbabwean art gallery owners, and later some were European gallery owners who dealt in Zimbabwean art. Was Zilberg a native in any of these communities? He embarked on this research in his homeland as if he were returning as a native, and he was treated as such by successful black sculptors among the artistic elite. Yet he was acutely aware that his skin color and class brought him privileged status compared with other sculptors who were quite poor and struggling (Zilberg 2000; also see Zilberg 1995a, 1995b).

Or consider another case that complicates the issue of "native." Cultural anthropologist JoAnn D'Alisera is an Italian American raised in a working-class neighborhood near New York City who conducted research with immigrants and refugees from Sierra Leone living in the metropolitan Washington, D.C., region. Initially she was teased by some peers and professors for doing "easy" fieldwork, not only in her home country, but in a familiar urban environment as well. The criticism ceased when she demonstrated that she had discovered an Africanized Washington that was as culturally different from her American experience as was the small village in northern Sierra Leone where she had conducted predissertation research (see D'Alisera 2004). Both these cases remind us that while one's national citizenship contributes to one's cultural identity, the two are not necessarily the same. For other recent stimulating discussions of this issue, see, for example, Altorki and El-Solh (1988), Amit (2000), Bresler (2002), D'Amico-Samuels (1991), Fahim (1982), Hong (1994), Jones (1982), Khare (1983), Kuwayama (2003), Messerschmidt (1982), Narayan (1993), and Ohnuki-Tierney (1984).

In any case, being fully native to a local community is not necessarily a guarantee that fieldwork will proceed smoothly. To the contrary, being a native can produce its own intellectual and emotional challenges. For example, Matti Bunzl, a gay, Viennese-born Jew who has conducted extensive research with gays and Jews in Vienna, found that the most serious challenge he faced during fieldwork was creating sufficient *distance* between himself and his research subjects to see them as subjects and not just friends (see Bunzl 2004).

In recent years, an outpouring of writing has explored such human factors in research (see the bibliography accompanying this chapter for some examples). Your own fieldwork will surely present its idiosyncratic challenges. Reading about others' experiences should at least help you mentally prepare for some of them and reduce the likelihood that unexpected challenges will overwhelm you.

What are the Pitfalls of Doing Ethnography?

For all its satisfactions, ethnography can also be deeply frustrating. Where there are people, there are inevitably misunderstandings, disputes, and imbroglios. As Nietzsche once wrote somewhat cynically, "Whether in conversation we generally agree or disagree with others is largely a matter of habit: the one tendency makes as much sense as the other" ([1878] 1999, aphorism 334).

Ethnographers have documented all manner of conflicts they have encountered with neighbors, rivals of their hosts, and even the police (see, e.g., Geertz 1973b; Straight 2002). In my own case, halfway through my doctoral fieldwork in Côte d'Ivoire, I found myself in a local village court holding a trial against the powerful chief of the village in which my husband and I were living (Gottlieb & Graham 1994, pp. 181–194). Although disputatious situations can become unpleasant and even dangerous, the hermeneutic perspective suggests that it is best to treat them as part of, rather than an obstacle to, your research, and as valuable lessons to be learned from your research experiences—as opposed to hindrances to your "real" study.

The topic of conflict raises a related issue: How do you know whether your informant is lying? And if you discover an informant is lying, what should you do about it? Even if your informant is not deliberately trying to deceive you, is the informant telling the whole story (Bernard et al. 1984; Nachman 1984; Salamone 1977)? Cross-checking information among several individuals is a classic technique whose nuances are explored in fieldwork methods literature and courses. At a more general level, the value of in-depth ethnography becomes apparent in this context: The longer you know your informants and the more fluently you can communicate with them in their own language, the better you will be at judging their reliability.

Still, the question itself raises certain epistemological issues. If you assume that there is a single, whole story to be told, you will probably never be satisfied. Indeed, with such an assumption, cross-checking all information across several informants may prove an exercise in frustration as each informant offers a variation of the previous informant's claims. Acknowledging the inevitability of this reality, many contemporary ethnographers operate on the more hermeneutic principle that every story is by definition incomplete, and that the richest ethnographic portrait comes from collecting and presenting several stories across divergent lines of class, ethnicity, religion, and gender rather than seeking just one as the single, authoritative version (Altheide & Johnson 1998).

Sampling decisions become critical with this set of assumptions. The hermeneutic approach insists that both the psychological and the demographic profile of any person you decide to ask about any given topic will determine the information you learn. It follows that you should give careful thought to how to select your informants. Consulting a reliable guide on this subject (e.g., Johnson 1990) will alert you to consider many factors that, at least ideally, should help guide your selection of informants. At the same time, it is important to acknowledge that you may not always have full control over who participates in your research. Some potential informants move away, fall sick, or refuse to join in the project for reasons of their own that you have no choice but to respect. Following the protocols of your campus institutional review board also legally obliges you to adhere to ethical guidelines in all your dealings with your research community.

Ethical Issues

Implicit in all the above is the more general question of ethical conduct. Most fieldwork courses and textbooks include a unit or chapter on ethical issues. But the truth is that ethical issues pervade every decision, great and small, that one makes during ethnographic research, and scholars now grapple with a far-ranging set of ethical questions that inhere in any qualitative research project.

In fact, submitting forms for approval by the institutional review board of your campus will alert you to a host of ethical issues that you will do well to think about while you are still in the early stages of designing your project. Perhaps most obvious among such issues looms the question of compensation. How can you avoid exploiting your research assistants (see, e.g., Sanjek 1993)? It is essential to consider how you will compensate informants for their participation. The time is long past for social scientists to expect people, especially impoverished people from developing world nations, to take time away from their own labor or other affairs to freely provide information for the sake of disinterestedly contributing to the goals of science. At the same time, notions of what constitutes acceptable forms of compensation are intimately bound with cultural values. A careful reading of Mauss's classic text (2000) on the nature of reciprocity will prepare you to think carefully about the general issues involved in gift-giving.

In some settings, cash payments will be most appropriate; in other settings, however, cash might be considered insulting or disruptive (Srivastava 1992). Bars of soap, bags of salt, bottles of peanut oil, baby clothes, and small cash payments were all gifts that young mothers especially appreciated in a study I conducted in West Africa concerning infancy and child rearing (Gottlieb 2004, pp. 3–37). Rather than such tangible goods, residents in other developing world and rural settings may prefer services that visiting researchers can provide, such as nursing care, translation into the colonial language, help with filling out complicated bureaucratic forms, help with reading for those with limited literacy skills, transportation to town, and information on specific topics of interest to those with little formal schooling. By contrast, a copy of your published works might be the most appropriate gift to offer highly educated elites in a different sort of project. Keep in mind that people in some places may feel perfectly comfortable specifying how they would like to be compensated for their time while others might consider it inappropriate, rude, or even taboo to discuss the question of compensation.

Beyond the immediate issue of how to appropriately compensate participants in your study loom many additional challenges that may be harder to anticipate. Field researchers often find themselves in difficult, even threatening positions that require immediate responses whose ethical implications are far from apparent in the heat of the moment. For example, is it better to expend a large proportion of your scarce research funds trying to save the life of a gravely sick infant with only a 50% chance of survival or to save the funds for other infants with a greater likelihood of recovery (Gottlieb 2004, pp. 249–260)? What are the particular challenges posed by conducting research on especially sensitive issues (Lee 1993; Renzetti & Lee 1992) or with specific populations, such as infants and children (Fine & Sandstrom 1988; Gottlieb 2004)? Is it ethical to use your professional expertise to help the U.S. and European military in their efforts to combat violence committed in the name of Islam (Gusterson 2003; Wax 2003)? By contrast, is it ethical to *avoid* conducting research in war-torn areas when so much of the contemporary world is, in one way or another, victimized by violence (Hoffman 2003)?

Broader issues concerning the shape of scholarly careers should also be the object of some reflection on your part as you think beyond the immediate research situation and contemplate writing plans. Should you use pseudonyms for specific individuals and places in your writings, and if so, how should you choose them (see, e.g., van der Geest 2003)? In what ways should "developed world" scholars collaborate with "developing world" scholars to avoid paternalism and racism, however inadvertent (see, e.g., Louis & Bartunek 1996; Smith 1999)? One of the most effective ways to anticipate how best to address dilemmas and issues posed by such questions is to read a broad selection of frank memoirs of field research written by anthropologists and other scholars who write honestly of the ethically complex situations they faced and how they responded (see the bibliography following this chapter) as well as to read more theoretical texts addressing the intellectual implications of ethical issues such as those broached above (see, e.g., Appell 1978; Bresler 1997; Brettell 1993; Caplan 2003; Cassell & Jacobs 1987; de Laine 2000; Fluehr-Lobban & Rhudy 2003; Katz, Ruby, & Gross 2003; Kimmel 1988; Kirsch 1999; Lee 1993; Mitchell 1993; Punch 1986; Salzano, Ferling, & Hurtado 2003; Scheper-Hughes 1995; and see Part II of this volume).

Personal Issues

Attending to the hermeneutic foundations of research means considering very personal issues. Increasingly, social scientists are acknowledging that what all researchers bring to their work is colored as much by emotional as by intellectual factors. It is important to think about how your own emotional biography may shape your research agenda—the basic question(s) and issue(s) you have chosen to address, the sorts of people you feel comfortable seeking out for answers, and the ways you intuitively tend to deal with whatever challenges you may encounter (Hunt 1989; Kleinman & Copp 1993; Wengle 1983).

Gender plays an enormously determinative role in shaping one's research experience, but until recently it has been a somewhat invisible factor (Bell, Caplan, & Karim 1993; Caplan 1988a, 1988b; Golde 1986; Gregory 1984; Keesing 1985; Kirsch 1999; Lewin & Leap 1996; Warren 1988; Whitehead & Conway 1986; Wolf 1996). Even now, it is mostly discussed in relation to female researchers but rarely male researchers. And issues specific to gay and lesbian anthropologists are only now beginning to be discussed (Lewin & Leap 1996). A related issue for fieldworkers concerns the intimate question of the impact of family members (spouse, children, or others) who may accompany you during your research. A few scholars have begun to write about the profound ways in which a spouse's presence may shape fieldwork (see, e.g., Ariëns & Strijp 1989; Firth 1972; Gottlieb & Graham 1994; Oboler 1986), but this remains an underresearched topic. More has been written about the impact of having your children accompany you to the field (Butler & Turner 1987; Cassell 1987; Sutton & Fernandez 1998), although this question raises many issues that need to be explored further; I am not aware of any published discussions of the role that other relatives may play in accompanying field researchers.

By contrast, loneliness can be a significant component of one's field experience, especially if one is not accompanied by family members. While some have questioned the possibility of friendship between a researcher and a member of the community being studied, given the inevitable power relations involved, others argue that meaningful friendship is indeed possible (Grindal & Salamone 1995). The interpersonally knotty as well as ethically problematic issues raised when such relationships become sexual have only recently begun to be broached in print (Kulick & Willson 1995; Tierney 2002; Watkins 2001).

At the same time that fieldwork can lead to personal entanglements—for better or for worse—with members of an adopted community, it can also lead to changes in intellectual orientation toward the world. A recent collection of essays documents some ways in which the rational world view that is a hallmark of Western thought has been challenged through ethnographers' profound encounters with non-Western cultural traditions (Young & Goulet 1994).

Writing

Over the past two decades, ethnographers have begun thinking both critically and creatively about their lives, not just as researchers, but also as authors (see, e.g., Geertz 1988). Rather than making the positivist assumption of previous generations of social scientists that ethnographic texts easily reflect a single objective and nonproblematic reality, many ethnographers now take a hermeneutic perspective and see texts as products created by the scholar-as-author on the basis of the author's *interpretation* of the data collected. Starting from this perspective, ethnographic writing can become a site for creative experimentation with voice and authorship. Some recent experimental ethnographies include Behar (1996), DeLoache and Gottlieb (2000), Narayan (1994), Stack (1996), Stoller (1999), Tedlock (1990), and Wolf (1992), among others. At the same time, two scholarly journals encourage experimental writing in the social sciences and related fields (*Anthropology and Humanism* and *Cultural Studies↔Critical Methodologies*), and the first of these journals now offers prizes in ethnographic poetry and fiction.

Complementing these somewhat literary works are a host of theoretical as well as pedagogical texts that critically examine the writing of ethnography (see, e.g., Becker 1986; Ben-Ari 1987; Davis 1992; Denzin 1997; Marcus & Cushman 1982; Richardson 1990, 1998; Thornton 1988; Van Maanen 1988; Wolcott 1990). A recent series of articles appearing in the widely circulated monthly newsletter of the American Anthropological Association reports on a "Writing Culture Planning Seminar" (held at the School of American Research, Santa Fe, New Mexico, October 2004), at which a small group of distinguished scholars and authors brainstormed about how to transform the discipline of anthropology into one that values good writing (*Anthropology News,* February 2005, March 2005, April 2005, May 2005, et al.). As you move from conducting fieldwork to writing about it, you may find yourself inspired to write not only clear, scholarly prose but also accessible texts that may make your expertise available to a broad educated readership. I tell the students in my Writing Ethnography classes: If a research project is worth funding, it is worth sharing your findings with the general public. Finding the voice to convey your passion for your subject to a broad readership may be an unexpected pleasure encountered as you write up your findings.

Conclusions

In this chapter, I have outlined both major satisfactions and major challenges posed by ethnographic research. For any given research project, how does one decide whether ethnography can contribute to answering the questions one hopes to address?

By way of example, let us consider an article recently published in a scholarly journal. In "War and Children's Mortality," Carlton-Ford, Hamill, and Houston (2000) use statistical tools to analyze the many ways in which children become casualties of contemporary wars, from direct combat to more indirect but nonetheless potent pathways of destruction. Noting that the data available to them are incomplete, the authors signal the gaps in data concerning access to safe water, and they question "the reliability of information about involvement in war" (p. 416). They conclude that "a more finely grained measurement of involvement in war should reveal more precisely *how* war has its impact on children's mortality" (p. 417; my emphasis).

A qualitative ethnographic investigation of these issues would have filled in these frustrating gaps in the extant data sets. Such an approach would have added a human dimension to this statistical report on children and war, providing a portrait of suffering that would lend a human face to the numbers. Elsewhere, scholars have taken up the daunting challenge of conducting ethnographic field research in war zones, and recent texts resulting from qualitative research carried out in zones of violence are moving indeed (see, e.g., Hoffman 2003; Kelleher 2003; Nordstrom 1997; Nordstrom & Robben 1995; Quesada 1998; Sluka 2000).

In the end, as this case suggests, the complementarity of quantitative and qualitative methods can only enrich the findings of the research. Whether you are a researcher already trained in quantitative methods or a student just beginning your training in the social sciences, making qualitative techniques central to a research project should prove exciting because of their potential to make the human stories behind large "data sets" and theoretical models come alive.

Note

1. If the language that is spoken locally in your research site is still undocumented and not yet taught anywhere, do not despair. Generations of travelers and scholars have managed to learn unwritten languages while living in a community. Try to prepare yourself ahead of time for the general grammatical and other linguistic structures you are likely to encounter by taking a field linguistics course. If this proves impossible, read a guide such as Burling's *Learning a Field Language* (1984).

Supplemental References

Allen, Denise Roth. (2002). *Managing Motherhood, Managing Risk: Fertility and Danger in West Central Tanzania*. Ann Arbor: University of Michigan Press.

Carlton-Ford, Steve, Ann Hamill, and Paula Houston. (2000). "War and Children's Mortality." *Childhood* 7(4), 401–419.

Cassirer, Ernst. (1944). *An Essay on Man*. New Haven, CT: Yale University Press.

Crapanzano, Vincent. (1985). *Waiting: The Whites of South Africa*. New York: Random House.

Davis, Roger H. (1984). *Social Network Analysis: An Aid in Conspiracy Investigations*. Washington, DC: Federal Bureau of Investigation, U.S. Dept. of Justice.

Du, Shanshan. (2002). *"Chopsticks Only Work in Pairs:" Gender Unity and Gender Equality*. New York: Columbia University Press.

Franklin, Sarah & Helena Ragoné, eds. (1998). *Reproducing Reproduction: Kinship, Power, and Technological Innovation*. Philadelphia, PA: University of Philadelphia Press.

Gentzler, Edwin. (2001). *Contemporary Translation Theories*, 2d ed. Clevedon, UK: Channel View Publications for Multilingual Matters.

Gordon, Raymond G., Jr., ed. (2000). "ENGLISH: a language of United Kingdom." *Ethnologue 14*. Retrieved November 1, 2005, from www.ethnologue.com/show_language.asp?code=ENG_

Howes, David. (1991). *The Varieties of Sensory Experience*. Toronto, Canada: University of Toronto Press.

Johnson, Michelle. (2002). "Being Mandinga, Being Muslim: Transnational Debates on Personhood and Religious Identity in Guinea-Bissau and Portugal." Ph.D. dissertation, Department of Anthropology, University of Illinois at Urbana-Champaign.

———. (2006). "Making Mandinga or Making Muslims? Debating Female Circumcision, Ethnicity, and Islam in Guinea-Bissau and Portugal." In *Trancultural Bodies: Female Genital Cutting in Global Context*, edited by Ylva Hernlund and Bettina Shell-Duncan. Piscataway, NJ: Rutgers University Press.

Klerks, Peter. (2001). "The Network Paradigm Applied to Criminal Organizations: Theoretical Nitpicking or a Relevant Doctrine for Investigators? Recent Developments in the Netherlands." *Connections* 24(3), 53–65.

Langer, Susanne. (1942). *Philosophy in a New Key*. Cambridge, MA: Harvard University Press.

Mauss, Marcel. ([1938] 1973). "Techniques of the Body." Translated by Ben Brewster. *Economy and Society* 2(1), 70–87.

———. ([1950] 2000). *The Gift: The Form and Reason for Exchange in Archaic Societies*. Translated by W. D. Halls. New York: W. W. Norton.

Moffitt, Mary Anne Smeltzer. (1990). "Understanding Middle-Class Adolescent Leisure: A Cultural Studies Approach to Romance Novel Reading." Ph.D.

dissertation, Institute of Communications Research, University of Illinois at Urbana-Champaign.

Moffitt, Mary Anne Smeltzer and Ellen S. Wartella. (1992). "Youth and Reading: A Survey of Leisure Reading Pursuits of Female and Male Adolescents." *Reading Research and Instruction* 31(2), 1–17.

Newmark, Peter. (1991). *About Translation*. Clevedon, UK: Channel View Publications for Multilingual Matters.

Nietzsche, Friedrich. ([1878] 1999). "Human, All-Too-Human; Man in Society; Aphorism 334; and In Conversation." In *Sämtliche Werke: Kritische Studienausgabe*, vol. 2, edited by Giorgio Colli and Mazzino Montinari. Munich, Germany: Deutscher Taschenbuch Verlag.

Peacock, James. (2001). *The Anthropological Lens: Harsh Light, Soft Focus*, 2d ed. Cambridge, UK: Cambridge University Press.

Schäffner, Christina. (1999). *Translation and Norms*. Clevedon, UK: Channel View Publications for Multilingual Matters.

———, ed. (2000). *Translation in the Global Village*. Clevedon, UK: Channel View Publications for Multilingual Matters.

Schäffner, Christina and Helen Kelly-Holmes, eds. (1995). *Cultural Functions of Translation*. Clevedon, UK: Channel View Publications for Multilingual Matters.

Strathern, Andrew J. (1997). *Body Thoughts*. Ann Arbor: University of Michigan Press.

Strathern, Marilyn. (1992). *Reproducing the Future: Essays on Anthropology, Kinship and the New Reproductive Technologies*. New York: Routledge.

Tymoczko, Maria and Edwin Gentzler, eds. (2002). *Translation and Power*. Amherst: University of Massachusetts Press.

Wagner, Emma, Svend Bech, and Jesús M. Martínez. (2001). *Translating for the European Union Institutions*. Manchester, UK: St. Jerome Publications.

Yanagisako, Sylvia and Carolyn Delaney, eds. (1995). *Naturalizing Power: Essays in Feminist Cultural Analysis*. New York: Routledge.

Zilberg, Jonathan. (1995a). "Shona Sculpture's Struggle for Authenticity and Value." *Museum Anthropology* 19(1), 3–24.

———. (1995b). "Yes, It's True: Zimbabweans Love Dolly Parton." *Journal of Popular Culture* [special issue: *Anthropology and Popular Culture*] 29(1), 111–125.

Bibliography on Ethnography

1. Theory and Methods

Theoretical Issues in Conducting Ethnographic Research

Amit, Vered, ed. (2000). *Constructing the Field: Ethnographic Fieldwork in the Contemporary World*. New York: Routledge.

Asad, Talal. (1973). *Anthropology and the Colonial Encounter*. New York: Humanities Press.

Berger, Peter L. and Thomas Luckmann. (1966). *The Social Construction of Reality: A Treatise in the Sociology of Knowledge*. Garden City, NY: Doubleday.

Bernard, Harvey Russel, Peter Killworth, David Kronenfeld, and Lee Sailer. (1984). "The Problem of Informant Accuracy." *Annual Review of Anthropology* 13, 495–517.

Bohannan, Paul and Dirk van der Elst. (1998). *Asking and Listening: Ethnography as Personal Adaptation*. Prospect Heights, IL: Waveland Press.

Bresler, Liora. (2002). "The Interpretive Zone in International Qualitative Research." In *International Research in Education: Experience, Theory and Practice*, edited by Liora Bresler and Alexandre Ardichvili. New York: Peter Lang.

Burawoy, Michael, et al., eds. (1991). *Ethnography Unbound: Power and Resistance in the Modern Metropolis*. Berkeley: University of California Press. See especially the Introduction and Conclusion.

Clifford, James and George Marcus, eds. (1986). *Writing Culture*. Berkeley: University of California Press.

Denzin, Norman K. (1997). *Interpretive Ethnography: Ethnographic Practices for the 21st Century*. Thousand Oaks, CA: Sage.

Denzin, Norman K. and Yvonne S. Lincoln, eds. (1998). *The Landscape of Qualitative Research: Theories and Issues*. London, UK: Sage.

Fabian, Johannes. ([1983] 2002). *Time and the Other: How Anthropology Makes Its Object*, 2d ed. New York: Columbia University Press.

Fahim, Hussein, ed. (1982). *Indigenous Anthropology in Non-Western Countries*. Durham, NC: Carolina Academic Press.

Freeman, Derek. (1996). *Margaret Mead and Samoa*. Ringwood, Victoria, Australia: Penguin Books.

Geertz, Clifford. (1973b). "Thick Description: Towards an Interpretive Theory of Culture." In *The Interpretation of Cultures*, edited by Clifford Geertz. New York: Basic Books.

Glaser, Barney G. and Anselm L. Strauss. (1967). *The Discovery of Grounded Theory: Strategies for Qualitative Reasoning.* Chicago, IL: Aldine Publishing Company.

Gupta, Akhil and James Ferguson, eds. (1997). *Anthropological Locations: Boundaries and Grounds of a Field Science.* Berkeley: University of California Press.

Harrison, Faye V., ed. (1991). *Decolonizing Anthropology: Moving Further Toward an Anthropology for Liberation.* Washington, DC: American Anthropological Association.

Hoddinot, John and Stephen Devereux, eds. (1992). *Fieldwork in Developing Countries.* London, UK: Harvester Wheatsheaf.

Hong, Keelung. (1994). "Experiences of Being a 'Native' While Observing Anthropology." *Anthropology Today* 10(3), 6–9.

Jackson, Bruce. (1987). *Fieldwork.* Urbana: University of Illinois Press.

James, Alison, Jenny Hockey, and Andrew Dawson, eds. (1997). *After Writing Culture: Epistemology and Praxis in Contemporary Anthropology.* New York: Routledge.

Jones, Delmos J. (1982). "Towards a Native Anthropology." In *Anthropology for the Eighties,* edited by Johnetta B. Cole. New York: Free Press.

Kuwayama, Takami. (2003). "'Natives' as Dialogic Partners: Some Thoughts on Native Anthropology." *Anthropology Today* 19(1), 8–13.

Marcus, George E. (1998). *Ethnography Through Thick and Thin.* Princeton, NJ: Princeton University Press.

Marcus, George E. and Michael Fischer. (1986). *Anthropology as Cultural Critique: An Experimental Moment in the Human Sciences.* Chicago, IL: University of Chicago Press.

Messerschmidt, Donald A., ed. (1982). *Anthropologists at Home in North America: Methods and Issues in the Study of One's Own Society.* Translated by W. D. Halls. Cambridge, UK: Cambridge University Press.

Narayan, Kirin. (1993). "How Native Is the 'Native' Anthropologist?" *American Anthropologist* 95(3), 671–686.

Ohnuki-Tierney, Emiko. (1984). "'Native' Anthropologists." *American Ethnologist* 11(3), 584–586.

Olwig, Karen Fog and Kirsten Hastrup, eds. (1997). *Siting Culture: The Shifting Anthropological Object.* New York: Routledge.

Pochhacker, Franz and Miriam Shlesinger, eds. (2001). *The Interpreting Studies Reader.* New York: Routledge.

Rosaldo, Michelle and Louise Lamphere. (1974). *Woman, Culture, and Society.* Stanford, CA: Stanford University Press.

Sanjek, Roger. (1993). "Anthropology's Hidden Colonialism: Assistants and Their Ethnographers." *Anthropology Today* 9(2), 13–18.

Smith, Linda Tuhiwai. (1999). *Decolonizing Methodologies: Research and Indigenous Peoples.* London, UK: Zed Books.

Stewart, Alex. (1998). *The Ethnographer's Method.* Thousand Oaks, CA: Sage.

Weiss, Robert. (1994). *Learning From Strangers.* New York: Free Press.

Wolcott, Harry F. (1995). *The Art of Fieldwork.* Walnut Creek, CA: AltaMira Press.

Wulff, Robert and Shirley Fiske. (1988). *Anthropological Praxis: Translating Knowledge Into Action*. Boulder, CO: Westview Press.

Theoretical Issues in Writing Ethnography

Abu-Lughod, Lila. (1991). "Writing Against Culture." In *Recapturing Anthropology: Working in the Present*, edited by Richard Fox. Santa Fe, NM: School of American Research Press.

Agar, Michael. (1996). *The Professional Stranger: An Informal Introduction to Ethnography*. San Diego, CA: Academic Press.

Altheide, David and John M. Johnson. (1998). "Criteria for Assessing Interpretive Validity in Qualitative Research." In *Collecting and Interpreting Qualitative Materials*, edited by Norman K. Denzin and Yvonna S. Lincoln. Thousand Oaks, CA: Sage.

Becker, Howard S. (1986). *Writing for Social Scientists*. Chicago, IL: University of Chicago Press.

Ben-Ari, Eyal. (1987). "On Acknowledgment in Ethnographies." *Journal of Anthropological Research* 43(1), 63–84.

Brettell, Caroline B., ed. (1993). *When They Read What We Write*. Westport, CT: Bergin and Garvey.

Bruner, Edward. (1982). "Ethnography as Narrative." Pp. 139–158 in *The Anthropology of Experience*, edited by Victor Turner and Edward Bruner. Urbana: University of Illinois Press.

Clifford, James. (1988). "On Ethnographic Authority." In *The Predicament of Culture: Twentieth-Century Ethnography, Literature, and Art*, edited by James Clifford. Cambridge, MA: Harvard University Press.

Davis, John. (1992). "Tense in Ethnography: Some Practical Considerations." Pp. 205–220 in *Anthropology and Autobiography*, edited by Judith Okely and Helen Callaway. London, UK: Routledge.

Geertz, Clifford. (1988). *Works and Lives: The Anthropologist as Author*. Stanford, CA: Stanford University Press.

Gordon, Deborah. (1988). "Writing Culture, Writing Feminism: The Poetics and Politics of Experimental Ethnography." *Inscriptions* 3/4, 7–24.

Marcus, George E. and Dick Cushman. (1982). "Ethnographies as Texts." *Annual Review of Anthropology* 11, 25–69.

Richardson, Laurel. (1990). *Writing Strategies: Reaching Diverse Audiences*. Newbury Park, CA: Sage.

———. (1998). "Writing: A Method of Inquiry." In *Collecting and Interpreting Qualitative Materials*, edited by Norman K. Denzin and Yvonna S. Lincoln. Thousand Oaks, CA: Sage.

Sanjek, Roger. (1991). "The Ethnographic Present." *Man* 26, 609–628.

Stack, Carol. (1993). "Writing Ethnography: Feminist Critical Practice." *Frontiers: A Journal of Women's Studies* 8(3).

Strathern, Marilyn. (1987). "Out of Context: The Persuasive Fictions of Anthropology." *Current Anthropology* 28, 251–281.

Thornton, Robert J. (1988). "The Rhetoric of Ethnographic Holism." *Cultural Anthropology* 3(3), 285–303.

van der Geest, Sjaak. (2003). "Confidentiality and Pseudonyms: A Fieldwork Dilemma from Ghana." *Anthropology Today* 19(1), 4–18.

van Maanen, John. (1988). *Tales of the Field: On Writing Ethnography*. Chicago, IL: University of Chicago Press.

Wolcott, Harry F. (1990). *Writing Up Qualitative Research*. Newbury Park, CA: Sage.

Specific Methods in Ethnographic Research

Arksey, Hilary and Peter T. Knight. (1999). *Interviewing for Social Scientists: An Introductory Resource With Examples*. Thousand Oaks, CA: Sage.

Baker, R., C. Brick, and A. Todd. (1996). "Methods Used in Research With Street Children in Nepal." *Childhood* 3, 171–193.

Barbash, Ilisa and Lucien Taylor. (1997). *Cross-Cultural Filmmaking: A Handbook for Making Documentary and Ethnographic Films and Videos*. Berkeley: University of California Press.

Barnard, Alan and Anthony Good. (1984). *Research Practices in the Study of Kinship*. Orlando, FL: Academic Press.

Bauer, Martin W. and George Gaskell, eds. (2000). *Qualitative Research With Text, Image and Sound*. Thousand Oaks, CA: Sage.

Bernard, H. Russell. (1998). *Handbook of Methods in Cultural Anthropology*. Walnut Creek, CA: AltaMira Press.

———. (2002). *Research Methods in Anthropology: Qualitative and Quantitative Approaches*, 3d ed. Walnut Creek, CA: AltaMira Press.

Biella, Peter. (2001). "Ur-List: Web List for Visual Anthropology Resources." Retrieved September 1, 2005, from www.usc.edu/dept/elab/urlist/index.html

Briggs, Charles. (1986). *Learning How to Ask: A Sociolinguistic Appraisal of the Role of the Interview in Social Science Research*. Cambridge, UK: Cambridge University Press.

Burgess, Robert G., ed. (1982). *Field Research: A Sourcebook and Field Manual*. London, UK: G. Allen and Unwin.

Burling, Robbins. (1984). *Learning a Field Language*. Ann Arbor: University of Michigan Press.

Collier, John, Jr., and Malcolm Collier. ([1967] 1986). *Visual Anthropology: Photography as a Research Method,* rev. ed. Albuquerque: University of New Mexico Press.

Coward, David, Barbara Moore, and John Wimbish. (1998). *Application Guide to Shoebox Anthropology*. Waxhaw, NC: JAARS, Inc./International Computing and Telecommunications Services, for the Summer Institute for Linguistics.

Crane, Julia and Michael V. Angrosino. (1984). *Field Projects in Anthropology: A Student Handbook,* 2d ed. Prospect Heights, IL: Waveland Press.

Crapanzano, Vincent. (1984). "Life-Histories" [review article]. *American Anthropologist* 86, 953–960.

De Munck, Victor and Elisa J. Sobo. (1998). *Using Methods in the Field: A Practical Introduction and Casebook.* Walnut Creek, CA: AltaMira Press.

Denzin, Norma K. and Yvonna S. Lincoln, eds. (1994). *Handbook of Qualitative Research.* Thousand Oaks, CA: Sage.

———. (1998). *Collecting and Interpreting Qualitative Materials.* Thousand Oaks, CA: Sage.

De Vos, A., ed. (2000). *Narrative Analysis Cross Culturally: The Self as Revealed in the Thematic Apperception Text.* Lanham, MD: Rowman and Littlefield Publishers.

el Guindi, Fadwa. (1998). "From Pictorializing to Visual Anthropology." In *Handbook of Methods in Cultural Anthropology,* edited by Harvey Russell Bernard. Walnut Creek, CA: AltaMira Press.

Ellen, Roy F. (1984). *Ethnographic Research: A Guide to General Conduct.* London, UK: Academic Press.

Emerson, Robert, Rachel Fretz, and Linda Shaw. (1995). *Writing Ethnographic Fieldnotes.* Chicago, IL: University of Chicago Press.

Farber, Barry J. (1991). *How to Learn Any Language: Quickly, Easily, Inexpensively, Enjoyably and On Your Own.* Sacramento, CA: Citadel Press.

Fine, Gary Alan and Kent L. Sandstrom. (1988). *Knowing Children: Participant Observation With Minors.* Newbury Park, CA: Sage.

Fontana, Andrea and James H. Frey. (2000). "The Interview: From Structured Questions to Negotiated Text." In *Handbook of Qualitative Research,* 2d ed., edited by Norman K. Denzin and Yvonne S. Lincoln. Thousand Oaks, CA: Sage.

Freeman, Linton C., Douglas R. White, and A. Romney Kimball, eds. (1989). *Research Methods in Social Network Analysis.* Fairfax, VA: George Mason University Press.

Harper, Douglas. (1998). "On the Authority of the Image: Visual Methods at the Crossroads." In *Collecting and Interpreting Quality Materials,* edited by Norman K. Denzin and Yvonna S. Lincoln. Thousand Oaks, CA: Sage.

Holstein, James A. and Jaber F. Gubrium. (1995). *The Active Interview.* Thousand Oaks, CA: Sage.

Honingman, John J. (1982). "Sampling in Ethnographic Fieldwork." In *Field Research,* edited by Robert Burgess. London, UK: Allen and Unwin.

Ives, Edward. (1995). *The Tape-Recorded Interview: A Manual for Field Workers in Folklore and Oral History,* 2d ed. Knoxville: University of Tennessee Press.

Johnson, Allen. (1978). *Quantification in Cultural Anthropology: An Introduction to Research Design.* Stanford, CA: Stanford University Press.

Johnson, Jeffrey C. (1990). *Selecting Ethnographic Informants.* Newbury Park, CA: Sage.

Krebs, Valdis. (2002a). "Mapping Networks of Terrorist Cells." *Connections* 24(3), 43–52.

———. (2002b). "Connecting the Dots—Tracking Two Identified Terrorists." *Orgnet.com.* Retrieved September 2, 2005, from www.orgnet.com/tnet.html

Kvale, Steinar. (1996). *Interviews: An Introduction to Qualitative Research Interviewing.* Thousand Oaks, CA: Sage.

Langness, Lewis L. and Gelya Frank. (1981). *Lives: An Anthropological Approach to Biography*. Novato, CA: Chandler and Sharp Publications.

LeCompte, Margaret Diane and Jean J. Schensul. (1999a). *Analyzing and Interpreting Ethnographic Data*. Vol. 5 of *Ethnographer's Toolkit*. Walnut Creek, CA: AltaMira Press.

———. (1999b). *Designing and Conducting Ethnographic Research*. Vol. 1 of *Ethnographer's Toolkit*. Walnut Creek, CA: AltaMira Press.

Lee, Raymond M. (1993). *Doing Research on Sensitive Topics*. London, UK: Sage.

Louis, Meryl Reis and Jean M. Bartunek. (1996). *Insider/Outsider Team Research*. Thousand Oaks, CA: Sage.

Marshall, Catherine and Gretchen B. Rossman. (1995). *Designing Qualitative Research*, 2d ed. Thousand Oaks, CA: Sage.

McCracken, Grant. (1988). *The Long Interview*. Newbury Park, CA: Sage.

Mitchell, Richard G., Jr. (1993). *Secrecy and Fieldwork*. Newbury Park, CA: Sage.

Moore, Janet R. (1973). "The Best-Laid Plans—Research Pre-Design and Field Revision." *Anthropological Quarterly* 46, 7–14.

Pelto, Pertti and Greta Pelto. (1978). *Anthropological Research: The Structure of Inquiry*, 2d ed. Cambridge, UK: Cambridge University Press.

Piore, Michael J. (1979). "Qualitative Research Techniques in Economics." *Administrative Science Quarterly* 24, 560–569.

Renzetti, Claire M. and Raymond M. Lee, eds. (1992). *Researching Sensitive Topics*. Newbury Park, CA: Sage.

Richards, Thomas J. and Lyn Richards. (1998). "Using Computers in Qualitative Research." In *Collecting and Interpreting Qualitative Materials*, edited by Norman K. Denzin and Yvonna S. Lincoln. Thousand Oaks, CA: Sage.

Rubin, Irene and Herbert J. Rubin. (1995). *Qualitative Interviewing: The Art of Hearing Data*. Thousand Oaks, CA: Sage.

Salamone, Frank. (1977). "The Methodological Significance of the Lying Informant." *Anthropological Quarterly* 50(3), 117–124.

Sanjek, Roger, ed. (1990). *Fieldnotes: The Makings of Anthropology*. Ithaca, NY: Cornell University Press.

Schensul, Jean J., Margaret Diane LeCompte, Bonnie K. Nastasi, and Stephen P. Borgotti. (1999). *Enhanced Ethnographic Methods: Audiovisual Techniques, Focused Group Interviews, and Elicitation*. Vol. 3 of *Ethnographer's Toolkit*. Walnut Creek, CA: AltaMira Press.

Schensul, Jean J., Margaret Diane LeCompte, Robert T. Trotter, Ellen K. Cromley, and Merrill Singer. (1999). *Mapping Social Networks, Spatial Data, and Hidden Populations*. Vol. 4 of *Ethnographer's Toolkit*. Walnut Creek, CA: AltaMira Press.

Schensul, Stephen L., Jean J. Schensul, and Margaret Diane LeCompte. (1999). *Essential Ethnographic Methods: Observation, Interviews, and Questionnaires*. Vol. 2 of *Ethnographer's Toolkit*. Walnut Creek, CA: AltaMira Press.

Schoepfle, Werner. (1987). *Systematic Fieldwork: Ethnographic Analysis and Data Management*. Newbury Park, CA: Sage.

Scott, John. (1991). *Social Network Analysis: A Handbook*. Newbury Park, CA: Sage.

Spradley, James. (1979). *The Ethnographic Interview*. New York: Holt, Rinehart, Winston.

———. (1980). *Participant Observation*. New York: Holt, Rinehart, Winston.

Srivastava, Vinay Kumar. (1992). "Should Anthropologists Pay Their Respondents?" *Anthropology Today* 8(6), 16–20.

Vermeulen, Han F. and Arturo Alvarez Roldán, eds. (1996). *Fieldwork and Fieldnotes*. London, UK: Routledge.

Wasserman, Stanley and Katherine Faust. (1994). *Social Network Analysis: Methods and Applications*. Cambridge, UK: Cambridge University Press.

Wasserman, Stanley and Joseph Galaskiewicz, eds. (1994). *Advances in Social Network Analysis: Research in the Social and Behavioral Sciences*. Thousand Oaks, CA: Sage.

Wellman, Barry and Stephen D. Berkowitz, eds. (1988). *Social Structures: A Network Approach*. Cambridge, UK: Cambridge University Press.

Ethical Issues in Conducting Ethnographic Research

American Anthropological Association. (2002). *Final Report of the Eldorado Task Force*, 2 vols. Retrieved September 2, 2005, from www.aaanet.org/edtf. An assessment of the debate over the work among the Yanomamö of Napoleon Chagnon and James Neel, accused of being unethical by Patrick Tierney (2002) in *Darkness in El Dorado*; see also Caplan 2003, Cantor 2000, Hagen et al. 2001, Salzano et al. 2003, Tierney 2002.

Appell, George N. (1978). *Ethical Dilemmas in Anthropological Inquiry: A Case Book*. Waltham, MA: African Studies Association/Crossroads Press.

Bresler, Liora. (1997). "Towards the Creation of a New Code of Ethics in Qualitative Research." *Council of Research in Music Education* 130, 17–29.

Cantor, Nancy. (2000). [Statement by the provost of the University of Michigan about *Darkness in El Dorado*, by Patrick Tierney.] University of Michigan. Retrieved September 2, 2005, from www.umich.edu/~urel/darkness.html. An assessment of the debate over the work among the Yanomamö of Napoleon Chagnon and James Neel, accused of being unethical by Patrick Tierney (2002) in *Darkness in El Dorado;* see also American Anthropological Association 2002, Caplan 2003, Hagen et al. 2001, Salzano et al. 2003, Tierney 2002.

Caplan, Pat, ed. (2003). *The Ethics of Anthropology: Debates and Dilemmas*. New York: Routledge. An assessment of the debate over the work among the Yanomamö of Napoleon Chagnon and James Neel, accused of being unethical by Patrick Tierney (2002) in *Darkness in El Dorado;* see also American Anthropological Association 2002, Cantor 2000, Hagen et al. 2001, Salzano et al. 2003, Tierney 2002.

Cassell, Joan and Sue-Ellen Jacobs, eds. (1987). *Handbook on Ethical Issues in Anthropology*. Special Publication no. 23. Washington, DC: American Anthropological Association.

de Laine, Marlene. (2000). *Fieldwork, Participation and Practice: Ethics and Dilemmas in Qualitative Research*. Thousand Oaks, CA: Sage.

Fluehr-Lobban, Caroline and Robyn Rhudy, eds. ([1991] 2003). *Ethics and the Profession of Anthropology: A Dialogue for Ethically Conscious Practice*, 2d ed. Philadelphia: University of Pennsylvania Press.

Gusterson, Hugh. (2003). "Comment: Defending the Nation? Ethics and Anthropology after 9/11. Anthropology and the Military—1968, 2003, and Beyond?" *Anthropology Today* 19(3), 25–26.

Hagen, Edward H., Michael E. Price, and John Tooby. (2001). "Preliminary Report" [on allegations against Napoleon Chagnon and James Neel]. University of California at Santa Barbara. Retrieved September 2, 2005, from www.anth.ucsb.edu/ucsbpreliminaryreport.pdf. An assessment of the debate over the work among the Yanomamö of Napoleon Chagnon and James Neel, accused of being unethical by Patrick Tierney (2002) in *Darkness in El Dorado;* see also American Anthropological Association 2002, Caplan 2003, Cantor 2000, Salzano et al. 2003, Tierney 2002.

Hoffman, Danny. (2003). "Frontline Anthropology: Research in a Time of War." *Anthropology Today* 19(3), 9–12.

Katz, John Stuart, Jay Ruby, and Larry Gross, eds. (2003). *Image Ethics in the Digital Age*. Minneapolis: University of Minnesota Press.

Kimmel, Allan J. (1988). *Ethics and Values in Applied Social Research*. Newbury Park, CA: Sage.

Kirsch, Gesa E. (1999). *Ethical Dilemmas in Feminist Research: The Politics of Location, Interpretation, and Publication*. Albany: State University Press of New York.

Punch, Maurice. (1986). *The Politics and Ethics of Fieldwork*. Beverly Hills, CA: Sage.

Salzano, Francisco M., John E. Ferling, and A. Magdalena Hurtado, eds. (2003). *Lost Paradises and the Ethics of Research and Publication*. New York: Oxford University Press. An assessment of the debate over the work among the Yanomamö of Napoleon Chagnon and James Neel, accused of being unethical by Patrick Tierney (2002) in *Darkness in El Dorado;* see also American Anthropological Association 2002, Caplan 2003, Cantor 2000, Hagen et al. 2001.

Schensul, Jean J., Margaret Diane LeCompte, et al. (1999). *Using Ethnographic Data: Interventions, Public Programming, and Public Policy*. Vol. 7 of *Ethnographer's Toolkit*. Walnut Creek, CA: AltaMira Press.

Scheper-Hughes, Nancy. (1995). "The Primacy of the Ethical: Propositions for a Militant Anthropology." *Current Anthropology* 36(3), 409–440.

Stoll, David. (2001). [Review of *Darkness in El Dorado*, by Patrick Tierney] *New Republic*, March 19, pp. 34–38.

Straight, Bilinda, ed. (2002). *Anthropology and Humanism* [special issue: *Conflict at the Center of Ethnography*] 27(1).

Tierney, Patrick. (2002). *Darkness in El Dorado: How Scientists and Journalists Devastated the Amazon*. New York: Norton. Critique of Napoleon Chagnon, *Yanomamö* [The Fierce People], 3d ed. New York: Holt, Rinehart and

Winston, [1968] 1983; see also American Anthropological Association 2002, Caplan 2003, Cantor 2000, Hagen et al. 2001, and Salzano et al. 2003 for further debate.

Watkins, Joe. (2001). "Briefing Paper for Consideration of the Ethical Implications of Sexual Relationships between Anthropologists and Members of a Study Population." *American Anthropological Association*. Retrieved September 2, 2005, from www.aaanet.org/committees/ethics/bp6.htm

Wax, Murray. (2003). "Comment: Defending the Nation? Ethics and Anthropology after 9/11. Wartime Dilemmas of an Ethical Anthropology." *Anthropology Today* 19(3), 23–24.

Wilson, K. (1992). "Thinking About the Ethics of Fieldwork." In *Fieldwork in Developing Countries*, edited by S. Devereux and J. Hoddinott. London, UK: Harvester Wheatsheaf.

Family, Gender, and Other Personal Issues in Conducting Ethnographic Research

Ariëns, Ilva and Ruud Strijp, eds. (1989). *Focaal* [special issue: *Anthropological Couples*] 10.

Bell, Diane, Pat Caplan, and Wazir Jahan Karim, eds. (1993). *Gendered Fields: Women, Men and Ethnography*. New York: Routledge.

Butler, Barbara and Diane Michalski Turner, eds. (1987). *Children and Anthropological Research*. New York: Plenum Press.

Caplan, Pat. (1988a). "Engendering Knowledge: The Politics of Ethnography (Part 1)." *Anthropology Today* 14(5), 8–12.

———. (1988b). "Engendering Knowledge: The Politics of Ethnography (Part 2)." *Anthropology Today* 14(6), 14–17.

Cassell, Joan, ed. (1987). *Children in the Field: Anthropological Perspectives*. Philadelphia, PA: Temple University Press.

Cesara, Manda. (1982). *Reflections of a Woman Anthropologist: No Hiding Place*. New York: Academic Press. Frank account of fieldwork in Zambia written pseudonymously by a respected anthropologist.

D'Amico-Samuels, Deborah. (1991). "Undoing Fieldwork: Personal, Political, Theoretical and Methodological Implications." In *Decolonizing Anthropology: Moving Further Toward an Anthropology for Liberation*, edited by Faye V. Harrison. Washington, DC: American Anthropological Association.

Fernea, Elizabeth Warnock. (1975). *A Street in Marrakech: A Personal Encounter With the Lives of Moroccan Women*. New York: Doubleday.

Firth, Rosemary. (1972). "From Wife to Anthropologist." In *Cross Cultural Boundaries: The Anthropological Experience*, edited by Solon Kimball and James B. Watson. San Francisco, CA: Chandler.

Golde, Peggy, ed. (1986). *Women in the Field: Anthropological Experiences*, 2d ed. Urbana: University of Illinois Press.

Gregory, James. (1984). "The Myth of the Male Ethnographer and the Woman's World." *American Anthropologist* 86(2), 316–327.

Howell, Nancy. (1990). *Surviving Fieldwork: A Report of the Advisory Panel on Health and Safety in Fieldwork*. Special Publication no. 26. Washington, DC: American Anthropological Association.

Hunt, Jennifer C. (1989). *Psychoanalytic Aspects of Fieldwork*. Newbury Park, CA: Sage.

Keesing, Roger. (1985). "Kwaio Women Speak: The Micropolitics of Autobiography in a Solomon Island Society." *American Anthropologist* 87(1), 27–39.

Kleinman, Sherryl and Martha A. Copp. (1993). *Emotions and Fieldwork*. Newbury Park, CA: Sage.

Kulick, Don and Margaret Willson, eds. (1995). *Taboo: Sex, Identity, and Erotic Subjectivity in Anthropological Fieldwork*. New York: Routledge.

LeCompte, Margaret Diane, Jean J. Schensul, R. Margaret Weeks, and Merrill Singer. (1999). *Researcher Roles and Research Partnerships*. Vol. 6 of *Ethnographer's Toolkit*. Walnut Creek, CA: AltaMira Press.

Lee, Raymond M. (1994). *Dangerous Fieldwork*. Thousand Oaks, CA: Sage.

Lewin, Ellen and William L. Leap, eds. (1996). *Out in the Field: Reflections of Lesbian and Gay Anthropologists*. Urbana: University of Illinois Press.

Oboler, Regina S. (1986). "For Better or Worse: Anthropologists and Husbands in the Field." In *Self, Sex and Gender in Cross-Cultural Fieldwork*, edited by Tony Larry Whitehead and Mary Ellen Conaway. Urbana: University of Illinois Press.

Sutton, David and Renate Lellap Fernandez, eds. (1998). *Anthropology and Humanism* [special issue: *In the Field and at Home: Families and Anthropology*] 23(2).

Warren, Carol A. B. (1988). *Gender Issues in Field Research*. Newbury Park, CA: Sage.

Wengle, John. (1983). *Ethnographers in the Field: The Psychology of Research*. Birmingham: University of Alabama Press.

Whitehead, Tony Larry and Mary Ellen Conway, eds. (1986). *Self, Sex, and Gender in Cross-Cultural Fieldwork*. Urbana: University of Illinois Press.

Wolf, Diane L., ed. (1996). *Feminist Dilemmas in Fieldwork*. Boulder, CO: Westview Press.

2. Case Studies

Memoirs of Ethnographic Research

Alverson, Marianne. (1987). *Under African Sun*. Chicago, IL: University of Chicago Press.

Bowen, Elenore Smith [Laura Bohannan]. (1954). *Return to Laughter*. New York: Harper and Brothers/Doubleday. Written pseudonymously by anthropologist Laura Bohannan; written as a novel but grounded in actual fieldwork among the Tiv of Nigeria.

Briggs, Jean. (1970). *Never in Anger: Portrait of an Eskimo Family*. Cambridge, MA: Harvard University Press.

Campbell, Howard. (2001). *Mexican Memoir: A Personal Account of Anthropology and Radical Politics in Oaxaca.* Westport, CT: Bergin and Garvey.

Chagnon, Napoleon. (1974). *Studying the Yanomamö.* New York: Holt, Rinehart and Winston.

Crapanzano, Vincent. (1972). *The Fifth World of Foster Bennett: Portrait of a Navaho.* New York: Viking Press. A rare account of a failed fieldwork project from an undergraduate summer study.

DaVita, Philip, ed. (1990). *The Humbled Anthropologist: Tales From the Pacific.* Belmont, CA: Wadsworth Press.

DeSoto, Hermine G. and Nora Dudwick, eds. (2000). *Fieldwork Dilemmas: Anthropologists in Postsocialist States.* Madison: University of Wisconsin Press.

Dumont, Jean-Paul. (1978). *The Headman and I: Ambiguity and Ambivalence in the Fieldworking Experience.* Austin: University of Texas Press.

Fernea, Elizabeth Warnock. (1965). *Guest of the Sheik: An Ethnography of an Iraqi Village.* New York: Doubleday.

Geertz, Clifford. (1973a). "Deep Play: Notes on the Balinese Cockfight." In *The Interpretation of Cultures*, edited by Clifford Geertz. New York: Basic Books.

Gottlieb, Alma and Philip Graham. ([1993] 1994). *Parallel Worlds: An Anthropologist and a Writer Encounter Africa.* Chicago, IL: University of Chicago Press.

Grindal, Bruce T. and Frank Salamone, eds. (1995). *Bridges to Humanity: Narratives on Anthropology and Friendship.* Prospect Heights, IL: Waveland Press.

Khare, Ravindra S. (1983). "Between Being Near and Distant: Reflections on Initial Approaches and Experiences of an Indian Anthropologist." In *Fieldwork: The Human Experience*, edited by Robert Lawless, Vinson H. Sutlive, Jr., and Mario D. Zamora. New York: Gordon and Breach.

Kim, Choong Soon. (1977). *An Asian Anthropologist in the South: Field Experiences with Blacks, Indians, and Whites.* Knoxville: University of Tennessee Press.

Lareau, Annette and Jeffrey Shultz, eds. (1996). *Journeys Through Ethnography: Realistic Accounts of Fieldwork.* Boulder, CO: Westview Press.

Malinowski, Bronislaw. ([1967] 1989). *A Diary in the Strict Sense of the Term*, 2d ed. London, UK: Athlone. A frank diary of fieldwork in the Trobriand Islands that was not intended for publication and caused a scandal when it was published posthumously.

Mead, Margaret. (1977). *Blackberry Winter: My Earlier Years.* New York: HarperCollins.

———. ([1977] 1979). *Letters From the Field, 1925–1975.* New York: Harper.

Mitchell, William E. (1988). "A Goy in the Ghetto: Gentile-Jewish Communication in Fieldwork Research." In *Anthropology for the Nineties: Introductory Readings*, edited by Johnetta Cole. New York: Free Press/Macmillan.

Nachman, Steven. (1984). "Lies My Informants Told Me." *Journal of Anthropological Research* 40, 536–555.

Nordstrom, Carolyn and Antonius Robben, eds. (1995). *Fieldwork Under Fire: Contemporary Studies of Violence and Survival.* Berkeley: University of California Press.

Powdermaker, Hortense. (1967). *Stranger and Friend: The Ways of the Anthropologist*. New York: W. W. Norton.

Rabinow, Paul. (1977). *Reflections on Fieldwork in Morocco*. Berkeley: University of California Press.

Read, Kenneth. (1965). *The High Valley: An Autobiographical Account of Two Years Spent in the Central Highlands of New Guinea*. New York: Scribner's.

Stoller, Paul and Cheryl Olkes. (1987). *In Sorcery's Shadow: A Memoir of Apprenticeship Among the Songhay of Niger*. Chicago, IL: University of Chicago Press.

Young, David E. and Jean-Guy Goulet, eds. (1994). *Being Changed by Cross-Cultural Encounters*. Peterborough, Ontario, Canada: Broadview Press.

Examples of Excellent or Experimental Ethnographic Writing

Abu-Lughod, Lila. (1986). *Veiled Sentiments*. Berkeley: University of California Press.

———. (1993a). "A Tale of Two Pregnancies." In *Women Writing Culture*, edited by Ruth Behar and Deborah Gordon. Berkeley: University of California Press.

———. (1993b). *Writing Women's Worlds: Bedouin Stories*. Berkeley: University of California Press. Winner of the 1994 Victor Turner Prize in Ethnographic Writing.

Basso, Keith. (1996). *Wisdom Sits in High Places: Landscape and Language Among the Western Apache*. Albuquerque: University of New Mexico Press. Winner of the 1997 Victor Turner Prize in Ethnographic Writing, winner of the 2001 J. I. Staley Prize from the School of American Research, and winner of the 1996 Western States Book Award for Creative Nonfiction.

Behar, Ruth. (1996). *The Vulnerable Observer: Anthropology That Breaks Your Heart*. Boston, MA: Beacon.

Bodley, John. (1990). *Victims of Progress,* 4th ed. Mountain View, CA: Mayfield.

Briggs, Jean L. (1999). *Inuit Morality Play: The Emotional Education of a Three-Year-Old*. New Haven, CT: Yale University Press. Winner of the 1999 Victor Turner Prize in Ethnographic Writing and winner of the 1999 Boyer Prize.

Brown, Karen McCarthy. (1991). *Mama Lola: A Voodoo Priestess in Brooklyn*. Berkeley: University of California Press. Winner of the 1992 Victor Turner Prize in Ethnographic Writing and winner of the 1991 American Academy of Religion Award for Best First Book in the History of Religion.

Cohen, Lawrence. (1998). *No Aging in India: Alzheimer's, the Bad Family, and Other Modern Things*. Berkeley: University of California Press. Winner of the 1998 Victor Turner Prize in Ethnographic Writing.

Crapanzano, Vincent. (1980). *Tuhami: Portrait of a Moroccan*. Chicago, IL: University of Chicago Press.

Daniel, E. Valentine. (1984). *Fluid Signs: Being a Person the Tamil Way*. Berkeley: University of California Press.

DeLoache, Judy S. and Alma Gottlieb, eds. (2000). *A World of Babies: Imagined Child-care Guides for Seven Societies*. Cambridge, UK: Cambridge University Press.

Desjarlais, Robert. (1997). *Shelter Blues: Sanity and Selfhood Among the Homeless.* Philadelphia: University of Pennsylvania Press. Winner of the 2003 Victor Turner Prize in Ethnographic Writing.

Duneier, Mitchell. (1999). *Sidewalk.* New York: Farrar, Straus and Giroux. An urban ethnography of street vendors in Greenwich Village; see methods sections and epilogue.

Gottlieb, Alma. (2004). *The Afterlife Is Where We Come From: The Culture of Infancy in West Africa.* Chicago, IL: University of Chicago Press.

Gottlieb, Alma and Philip Graham. ([1993] 1994). *Parallel Worlds: An Anthropologist and a Writer Encounter Africa.* New York: Crown. Winner of the 1993 Victor Turner Prize in Ethnographic Writing.

Klima, Alan. (2002). *The Funeral Casino: Meditation, Massacre, and Exchange With the Dead in Thailand.* Princeton, NJ: Princeton University Press. Winner of the 2003 Victor Turner Prize in Ethnographic Writing.

Lavie, Smadar. (1990). *The Poetics of Military Occupation.* Berkeley: University of California Press.

Luhrman, Tanya M. (2000). *Of Two Minds: The Growing Disorder in American Psychiatry.* New York: Knopf. Winner of the 2001 Victor Turner Prize in Ethnographic Writing.

Mattingly, Cheryl. (1998). *Healing Dramas and Clinical Plots: The Narrative Structure of Experience.* New York: Cambridge University Press. Winner of the 2001 Victor Turner Prize in Ethnographic Writing.

McLeod, Jay. (1995). *Ain't No Makin' It: Aspirations and Attainments in a Low Income Neighborhood.* Boulder, CO: Westview Press. Urban ethnography of two groups of poor male youth—one black, one white—failing at upward mobility.

Narayan, Kirin. (1989). *Storytellers, Saints and Scoundrels: Folk Narrative and Hindu Religious Teaching.* Philadelphia: University of Pennsylvania Press. Winner of the 1990 Victor Turner Prize in Ethnographic Writing.

———. (1994). *Love, Stars, and All That.* New York: Washington Square Press. An ethnographic novel.

Plath, David. (1980). *Long Engagements: Maturity in Modern Japan.* Palo Alto, CA: Stanford University Press.

Raffles, Hugh. (2002). *In Amazonia: A Natural History.* Princeton, NJ: Princeton University Press. Winner of the 2003 Victor Turner Prize in Ethnographic Writing.

Sharp, Henry S. (2001). *Loon: Memory, Meaning, and Reality in a Northern Dene Community.* Lincoln: University of Nebraska Press. Winner of the 2002 Victor Turner Prize in Ethnographic Writing.

Shostak, Marjorie. ([1981] 2000). *Nisa: The Life and Words of a !Kung Woman.* Cambridge, MA: Harvard University Press.

Stack, Carol. (1996). *Call to Home: African Americans Reclaim the Rural South.* New York: Basic Books. Winner of the 1997 Victor Turner Prize in Ethnographic Writing.

Steedly, Mary Margaret. (1993). *Hanging Without a Rope: Narrative Experience in Colonial and Postcolonial Karoland*. Princeton, NJ: Princeton University Press. Winner of the 1994 Victor Turner Prize in Ethnographic Writing.

Stoller, Paul. (1999). *Jaguar*. Chicago, IL: University of Chicago Press. An ethnographic novel about West African immigrants in NYC.

Tedlock, Dennis. (1990). *Days From a Dream Almanac*. Urbana: University of Illinois Press. Winner of the 1991 Victor Turner Prize in Ethnographic Writing.

Trawick, Margaret. (1990). *Notes on Love in a Tamil Family*. Berkeley: University of California Press.

Tsing, Anna. (1993). *In the Realm of the Diamond Queen: Marginality in an Out-of-the-Way Place*. Princeton, NJ: Princeton University Press. Winner of the 1994 Harry J. Benda Prize in Southeast Asian Studies, Southeast Asia Council, Association for Asian Studies.

Wafer, Jim. (1991). *The Taste of Blood: Spirit Possession in Brazilian Candomble*. Philadelphia: University of Pennsylvania Press. Winner of the 1992 Victor Turner Prize in Ethnographic Writing.

Wiener, Margaret. (1994). *Visible and Invisible Realms: Power, Magic, and Colonial Conquest in Bali*. Chicago, IL: University of Chicago Press. Winner of the 1995 Victor Turner Prize in Ethnographic Writing.

Wolf, Margery. (1992). *A Thrice-Told Tale: Feminism, Postmodernism, and Ethnographic Responsibility*. Stanford, CA: Stanford University Press.

A Selection of Ethnographies That Exemplify Specific Research Techniques

Altorki, Soraya and Camillia Fawzi El-Solh. (1988). *Arab Women in the Field: Studying Your Own Society*. Syracuse, NY: Syracuse University Press. Two Arab anthropologists explore issues of gender, society, and politics.

Bott, Elizabeth. (1971). *Family and Social Networks: Roles, Norms, and External Relationships in Ordinary Urban Families*, 2d ed. New York: Free Press.

Bunzl, Matti. (2004). *Symptoms of Modernity: Jews and Queers in Late-Twentieth-Century Vienna*. Berkeley: University of California Press.

Carsten, Janet. (2000). "Knowing Where You've Come From: Ruptures and Continuities of Time and Kinship in Narratives of Adoption Reunions." *Journal of the Royal Anthropological Institute*, n.s. 6, 687–704.

D'Alisera, JoAnn. (2004). *An Imagined Geography: Sierra Leonean Muslims in America*. Philadelphia: University of Pennsylvania Press.

Farnell, Brenda. (1995). *Do You See What I Mean? Plains Indian Sign Talk and the Embodiment of Action*. Austin: University of Texas Press.

Franklin, Sarah and Susan McKinnon, eds. (2001). *Relative Values: Reconfiguring Kinship Studies*. Durham, NC: Duke University Press.

Frey, Sharon L. (1989). "Network Analysis as Applied to a Group of AIDS Patients Linked by Sexual Contact." B.S. thesis, Department of Psychology, University of Illinois at Urbana-Champaign.

Graham, Allan. (1996). *Kinship and Friendship in Modern Britain*. Oxford, UK: Oxford University Press.

Kelleher, William F., Jr. (2003). *The Troubles in Ballybogoin: Memory and Identity in Northern Ireland*. Ann Arbor: University of Michigan Press.

Lomnitz, Larissa Adler and Marisol Perez Lizaur. (1987). *A Mexican Elite Family, 1820–1980: Kinship, Class, Culture*. Princeton, NJ: Princeton University Press.

McKinnon, Susan and Sydel Silverman, eds. (2005). *Complexities: Beyond Nature and Nurture*. Chicago, IL: University of Chicago Press.

Nordstrom, Carolyn. (1997). *A Different Kind of War Story*. Philadelphia: University of Pennsylvania Press.

Ottenberg, Simon. (1990). "Thirty Years of Fieldnotes: Changing Relationships to the Text." In *Fieldnotes: The Makings of Anthropology*, edited by Roger Sanjek. Ithaca, NY: Cornell University Press.

Quesada, James. (1998). "Suffering Child: An Embodiment of War and Its Aftermath in Post-Sandinista Nicaragua." *Medical Anthropological Quarterly* 12(1), 51–73.

Sluka, Jeffrey, ed. (2000). *Death Squad: The Anthropology of State Terror*. Philadelphia: University of Pennsylvania Press.

Stoller, Paul. (1989). *The Taste of Ethnographic Things: The Senses in Anthropology*. Philadelphia: University of Pennsylvania Press.

———. (1997). *Sensuous Scholarship*. Philadelphia: University of Pennsylvania Press.

Stone, Linda, ed. (2001). *New Directions in Anthropological Kinship*. Lanham, MD: Rowman & Littlefield.

Terrorist Networks (special issue). (2001). *Connections: Official Journal of the International Network for Social Network Analysis* 24(3).

Turner, Victor. (1957). *Schism and Continuity in an African Society*. Manchester, UK: Manchester University Press.

———. (1967). *The Forest of Symbols*. Ithaca, NY: Cornell University Press.

———. (1975). *Dramas, Fields, and Metaphors: Symbolic Action in Human Society*. Ithaca, NY: Cornell University Press.

———. (1988). *The Anthropology of Performance*. New York: Performing Arts Journal Publ.

van Velsen, Jaan. (1964). *The Politics of Kinship: A Study in Social Manipulation Among the Lakeside Tonga of Nyasaland*. Manchester, UK: Manchester University Press for the Rhodes-Livingstone Institute.

Westgard, Bjørn. (Forthcoming). "'Wisdom That Grows and Knowledge That Flies': Negotiating Translocal Knowledge and Health Development in Senegal." In *Health Knowledge and Belief Systems in Africa*, edited by Toyin Falola. Durham, NC: Carolina Academic Press.

Weston, Kath. (1991). *Families We Choose: Lesbians, Gays, Kinship*. New York: Columbia University Press.

Zilberg, Jonathan. (2000). "White Rhodesian Jewry and Contemporary African Art, 1947–1992." Talk presented at conference titled *Metropolitan Non-Dominant Groups as (Parts of) Local Elites in Colonial and Post-Colonial Societies*, May 17, Department of Social Anthropology, University of Manchester, UK.

A Few Classic Ethnographies

Evans-Pritchard, Edward E. (1940). *The Nuer*. Oxford, UK: Clarendon Press.

Firth, Raymond. (1936). *We, the Tikopia*. London, UK: Allen and Unwin.

Malinowski, Bronislaw. ([1922] 1984). *Argonauts of the Western Pacific*. Prospect Heights, IL: Waveland Press.

Mead, Margaret. (1928). *Coming of Age in Samoa*. New York: William Morrow.

Bibliography: Ethnography

4

Oral Histories

Oral Histories as Methods and Sources

Tamara Giles-Vernick

O ral history methods can illuminate dimensions of the past that other methodologies investigating the past, such as archival or statistical tools and sources, cannot. In places where documentary evidence is slim (such as in parts of Africa for certain historical periods), oral histories can provide insights into the past that might otherwise remain inaccessible to social scientists. Such methods have usefully revealed the ways in which particular people recall past livelihoods, conflicts, political authority, self-conceptions, and social practices.

Oral history as a source and a method has been central to the development of African history. White, Miescher, and Cohen have recently observed that "no element has served as a clearer signature of and for African historiography than the development of a central position for the *oral source* and *oral history* within the programs of recovering the African past" (2001, p. 2). The late-19th-century African American activist and intellectual George Washington Williams was among the first to employ oral history methods, interviewing Africans who suffered the abuses of the Congo Independent State (Dworkin 2003). And in the 20th century, anthropologists' and folklorists' studies of oral epics profoundly influenced Africanist historians, who contended that oral traditions could illuminate African societies' pasts (Finnegan 1970, 1977; de Heusch 1982; Ong 1982; Scheub 1975, 1977).

Even where copious documentary sources exist, researchers can fruitfully employ oral history as a research tool. Studies of a workers' strike, a riot, the establishment of a new church, a particular educational process, an economic depression, and the development or demise of a political movement, for instance, might be substantially richer if social scientists could understand how participants in these past events and processes understood themselves, how these events and processes unfolded, and why certain people chose (or refused) to participate in them (Passerini 1987, 1992; Portelli 1991, 1997). This rationale was partly the basis of the development of oral history methods and evidence in the mid-20th century. Historians sought to investigate new subjects of historical inquiry and to recover the "voices" of eyewitnesses to and participants in major historical changes. Among the earliest transcripts at the Columbia University Oral History Research Office (begun under historian Allan Nevins in 1948) is an oral history of draft riots during the American Civil War. The development of social and later feminist histories, which sought to excavate "history from below," facilitated the use of oral accounts to shed light on the experiences of former slaves, workers, and women.

This impulse to elucidate the perspectives of ordinary people has persisted for decades. Allen Isaacman's (1996) study of peasant labor processes and their interaction with the colonial state in Mozambique focuses, not on the well-documented colonial administrators and markets, but rather on cotton-producing farmers, especially women. Basing his analysis on extensive interviews with these farmers, Isaacman traces the diverse material effects of forced cotton cultivation and also farmers' "cultural understanding of how work should be defined and valued" (1996, p. 5). Whether these methods can shed light on what "actually" happened is up for debate, but they *can* allow researchers to gain insight into what Stephan Miescher has described as "moments of subjective reflection about the past" (2001, p. 163), a focus that can be of critical use in exploring not only changing notions of the self but also political, cultural, and economic processes and practices in the past. Oral history methodologies can also tell us something about the ways in which people produce, evaluate, and transmit knowledge about the past, and thus these methodologies can be useful in studies of popular or elite intellectual change (Basso 1984; Behar 1986; Brown 2001; Casey 1987; Connerton 1989; Fentress & Wickham 1992; Halbwachs 1992; Klein 2000; Malkki 1995; Matsuda 1996; Monson 2000; Nora [1984] 1997; Roberts & Roberts 1996; Samuel 1994; Shaw 2002; Tonkin 1992).

Hence, the major advantages of oral history methods lie in the fact that they, unlike other investigative methods into the past, can help to illustrate in specific, rich, and deeply engaging ways that people understand their changing selves in relation to broad historical processes. Without oral history methods, we cannot hope to gain any insight into ordinary people who did not write about their conceptions of themselves or of the historical moments in which they lived (Barber 1991; Behar 1993; Brown 2001; Comaroff & Comaroff 1992; Fabian & Matulu 1997; Giles-Vernick 1996; Hunt 1999; Roberts & Roberts 1996; Tonkin 1992; Vaughan 2001). Some historians have argued that oral histories can shed light on "historical consciousness," but they have not interrogated what historical consciousness is or its relationship to history as a discipline (Vaughan 2001). If remembrances have the capacity to illuminate how people understand themselves and interpret their own pasts, then oral historians must heed Alon Confino's caution concerning "memory and *mentalités*." Historians, he argues, need to distinguish "memory as a heuristic device and memory as part of the mental equipment of a society, of an age" (1997, p. 1403).

Oral history methods provide a glimpse into how people of the past constructed their worlds—what they believed, imagined, and valued. These methods can translate for readers what large, seemingly impersonal processes might have meant to those who participated in, contributed to, ignored, opposed, or even imagined them. That our informants filter such interpretations through their perceptions of contemporary personal, social, political, and economic relations makes them all the more exciting and revealing as sources.

In addition, while some scholars once criticized oral historians' predominant focus on "oral traditions," many now recognize that the collection and analysis of such sources can provide valuable glimpses into the making of elite power. Pioneering oral historian Jan Vansina, working on the precolonial past in equatorial Africa, initially based his methodology on "oral traditions," accounts passed down for more than one generation, and not on "oral histories," which he defined as eyewitness accounts of past events. He and others argued that oral traditions could illuminate African societies' pasts through careful extraction of historical truths from spoken texts (Vansina 1965, 1985; Irwin 1981; Henige 1974, 1982). But after African independence, historical scholars, some of whom were Vansina's former students, criticized the elite perspectives embedded in oral traditions and sought instead to focus on broader, more variegated perspectives on political, social, and economic change in the past and to recover how ordinary people lived, acted, and exercised "agency" in past historical events and processes (Cohen 1977, 1989; Miller 1980; Tonkin 1992). Africanist and South Asian scholars, focusing on the more recent colonial and postindependence eras, produced numerous analyses based largely on such oral accounts.

Oral historical methods can illuminate the contemporary processes by which tellers of oral traditions help to constitute elite power through their recitations of the past (Austen 1999). Similarly, in examining other genres of oral historical expression, social scientists have highlighted how tellers, singers, and celebrants perform such genres to affirm political power and relations or to articulate political autonomy or dissent (Guss 2000; Yankah 2001).

Finally, oral history methods enable researchers to gain insight into how people use their pasts (Cohen & Odhiambo 1989, 1992; Jewsiewicki & Newbury 1986; Ogot 2001; Shaw 2002; Thompson 2000; Vansina 1994; Vaughan 2001). While oral historians once assumed that the process of collecting oral accounts and integrating them into a master narrative produced histories that informants found useful, more recent debates over the nature of oral historical methods and evidence have propelled these researchers to distance themselves from the notion that they write histories *for* their informants. Rather, a researcher drawing from oral histories can produce studies that may achieve "an understanding of a people, through a study of their treasure chest, the profounder aspects of their culture, knowledge of their history, literature, and world-view . . . not for curiosity, or out of antiquarian interest, but as fit explanation for contemporary situations" (Ogot 2001, p. 32). And these productions provide narratives for informants to express their own conceptions and interpretations of their pasts and to deploy those interpretations in their own contemporary struggles (Cohen & Odhiambo 1989, 1992; Cinnamon 2002; Maddox forthcoming; Ranger 1999).

The very nature of oral histories and their relationship to other research methods and sources, including ethnography, have not only been debated by researchers themselves but have also recently come under scrutiny by governmental and academic institutions. Until 2003, oral historians were subject to institutional review board (IRB) oversight. This oversight required that oral historians submit extensive documentation to these review boards about their research projects. In their effort to ensure protection of human research subjects, IRBs would thus evaluate the aims and methods of oral history studies, the selection of informants, the acquisition of informed consent, and the specific advantages and risks associated with the research. But in 2003, the U.S. Office of Human Research Protection (part of the U.S. Department of Health and Human Services) concluded an agreement with the Oral History Association and the American Historical Association affirming that oral history projects differed fundamentally from other kinds of research involving human subjects and thus no longer needed clearance and supervision by IRBs. These organizations concluded that there were several justifications for this exclusion, the most important of which was that oral histories do not rely on standardized questionnaires and do not produce "generalizable" or "predictive" knowledge. Rather, oral historians generate highly specific knowledge about the past. Some critics[1] have deplored this exclusion of oral histories from institutional and Health and Human Services oversight, arguing that oral historians "ced[ed] their scientific research credentials." Many oral historians, however, would embrace the highly specific nature of the knowledge that their methods generate. Moreover, some academic institutions, including the University of Minnesota, continue to require that oral historians submit to IRB oversight.

The challenges of oral historical methods are several, from their collection to their interpretation and writing. In the first place, it may be easy to identify potential informants when writing a proposal, but locating actual people and encouraging them to talk about their pasts may prove more difficult. Sometimes potential informants move away permanently or temporarily from the researcher's region of research. They can fall ill or die. Indeed, some oral history projects documenting historical events in the first decades of the 20th century are now impossible to conduct because of the difficulty of finding living informants. I recently had to revise significantly a research project that relied heavily on oral histories, because so few people were still living who could talk about the events I had hoped to investigate. The demands of informants' work or social relations may make it difficult for them to find time to talk about the past. In agricultural societies, for instance, leisure time is scarce during the growing season, and researchers may have problems finding people who are willing to recount or discuss their pasts. Sometimes, potential informants fear interacting with researchers and talking about their pasts because this act could have dangerous political consequences. Political disputes may provoke some people to dissuade a researcher from interacting with potentially valuable informants, or even worse, researchers may find themselves unwittingly embroiled in disputes simply because of the people with whom they interact (Adenaike & Vansina 1996; Geiger 1997).

Even once researchers have identified and located real informants, they also need to recognize that the transmission of historical knowledge is a specific social process in which they are participants. Researchers cannot simply "open up" an informant as they do a book or an archival dossier to retrieve historical evidence. And they cannot appear before a complete stranger and demand that he or she describe in intimate detail an event that happened 50 years ago. The historical "evidence" that one seeks through oral historical methods is often part of a body of knowledge about the past that certain people possess. In some societies, such as Mande societies in West Africa, *jeliw* (griots or bards) are specialists trained to learn, elaborate on, and perform historical knowledge. Elsewhere, tellers of oral histories do not undertake special training, but they do possess knowledge of the past for particular social, political, or cultural reasons. Hence, a researcher may have to develop appropriate social relations with potential informants before learning about the past, just as young people within that particular society must. Such efforts may require a substantial investment in learning the language(s) of informants. But most important, they demand a commitment to developing a sense of mutual comfort, respect, and trust between the researcher and informant. (Indeed, the very term "informant" seems an impoverished one for the rich, dynamic interactions between researchers and the people who teach them about the past). The process of creating such a relationship can take a significant amount of time (Brown 2001).

Although researchers and their informants may have cultivated such relationships, the process of using oral history methods (as well as the resulting accounts) has the potential to confuse and disappoint both parties. Sometimes, informants simply do not understand what a researcher wants to know; perhaps the researcher does not know their language well enough, or perhaps there exist specific ways of asking about the past that the researcher has not yet mastered (Briggs 1986). Nor are all informants equally knowledgeable or eloquent about their pasts. They may forget, too, although this process of forgetting is never "natural" but needs in itself to be explored (Passerini 1987; Vaughan 2001; White 2000; more generally, see Trouillot 1995). And finally, informants can decide to recount their pasts for many reasons and in many different ways. Relations with audiences (real or imagined), with the researcher, and with the broader political and economic processes can all profoundly influence the interactions between the researcher and the informant, the conduct of oral historical methods, and the accounts that tellers recount (Ibrahim 2001; Malkki 1995; Mbilinyi 1989; Peel 1984; Tonkin 1992; Vaughan 2001; Willis 1996). Tellers can omit, elide, or prevaricate for any number of reasons, all of which investigators need to explore (White 2000). And in some contexts, tellers may decide to use an investigator's oral historical methods as a means of expressing their own political and economic agendas. Researchers thus need ample time and research support, not to mention an inclination to develop these social relations, to learn appropriate ways of asking questions and to weather the disappointment of encounters with preoccupied, inarticulate, or forgetful informants.

Mundane as it may seem, the actual technological process of "capturing" and storing an oral account can pose real challenges. There are many ways of recording an account, from taking notes to recording on digital video recorders. And they all have their risks. Taking notes of words, gestures, and interactions while at the same time concentrating on the significance of all these expressions and pondering future questions can befuddle even the most experienced field researcher. And nobody rests tranquil knowing that it is easy to lose notes or to see them destroyed by hostile political authorities or even by fire, water, or termites (Sanjek 1990). Recording equipment may do a better job of documenting the social interactions and performance of historical knowledge, but it is never foolproof. Not only might some informants feel ill at ease when recorded, but equipment can break down, get stolen or lost, or muffle or even erase previous recordings. To my chagrin, I have lost more than my share of recordings because my equipment faltered in humid conditions. To avoid these problems, researchers should choose a technology with which they are comfortable and be sure to make additional copies of notes and recordings, storing them in multiple (and safe) locations.

Researchers also need to grapple with how to interpret the complex and multilayered meanings of oral histories. In the 1970s, as oral historians began to reject the elite perspectives of purveyors of oral traditions in favor of recovering what they imagined to be the "voices" of ordinary people, they adopted a broad range of methods that they anticipated would capture the perspectives of the previously "silenced." Profoundly influenced by social and feminist histories, they sought to excavate an alternative narrative of the past, assuming that ruling elites had ignored and suppressed a nonelite "voice" that could provide a different and perhaps more authentic rendering of past events. They conducted formal and informal interviews, amassed life histories from dialogues with informants, engaged in informal conversations with individuals and groups, listened to tales and praise poems, and learned songs—all methods that remain widely used today (Bozzoli 1991; Briggs 1986; Davison 1989; Mbilinyi 1989; Menchu 1984; Miller 1980; Mintz [1960] 1974; Smith 1964; Vail & White 1991). But scholars interpreting oral histories need to remain aware that these methods and the narratives that they generate do not provide unmediated access to truths about the past any more than any other form of historical evidence can. Informants can speak in many, and sometimes contradictory, "voices" for diverse purposes and audiences; the very process of interpretation extracts informants' words from a complex social and political context and integrates these words into scholars' master narratives. As Megan Vaughan has emphasized,

> Voices are voices, not choruses; they cry in the wilderness of history and speak, apparently directly, to experience. They represent another kind of fantasy of authenticity, our access to the "real thing." . . . Inserted into our texts at appropriate moments, "African voices" could also help the historian, especially the non-African historian, to negotiate the politics of the production of knowledge, for through these "voices" we could feign "to make the world

speak itself and speak itself as a story." Completely inadequate as this was as a response to certain postcolonial criticisms, it has shown a capacity to fend off a few of the tamer wolves, for if you gave space to "voices" of the Africans oppressed in your text, then you were also "giving voice," or so it seemed to some. (Vaughan 2001, pp. 65–66)

And just as scholars need to remain skeptical of assumptions about the univocality and authenticity of the "voice," so too do they need to examine carefully the genres that those "voices" generated. Of life history methods, Corinne Kratz has usefully queried, "How does a conversation become 'a life'? And how do conversational lives become 'life histories'?" (Kratz 2001, p. 127). She astutely concludes that "A life told at different times and settings may present different selves and emphasize different themes. . . . My own attempts to 'do life histories' . . . demonstrated the variable forms that these conversations can take" (Kratz 2001, p. 150).

What scholars now subsume under the rubric of "historical accounts" can include embodied expressions, objects, and sites that are linked to, but are not themselves narrative accounts of, the past. A researcher needs to remain attuned to the specific and multiple ways in which people express their pasts, as well as what such expressions illuminate about those pasts. Peter Nabokov's *A Forest of Time* (2002) explores the myriad through which American Indians have interpreted, expressed, and deployed their histories. And although there are numerous critiques of interpreting the products of oral history methods as "authentic" and "true," it remains very difficult, particularly for historians, to resist interpreting oral historical narratives as depicting the past "as it really happened" and thus to privilege such accounts as "truth" (Hacking 1995; Confino 1997). But when we confront fantasies and falsehoods in such narratives, these interpretive strategies seem altogether inadequate. Several historians and social scientists have urged researchers to resist this temptation and instead to examine the subjective "worlds" that informants create through such fantasies and falsehoods. White, for instance, has compellingly argued that a false testimony (as well as misunderstandings and confusion) can provide "a rich and vivid account when read for what it describes; but it is an account historians cannot use if they seek to label it true or false." Indeed, she contends,

A false section of an interview is . . . not a problem; the words of a reliable informant might be reliable but have no particular authority. False sections of testimony do not make the informant unreliable but may make her reveal more. . . . (2001, pp. 298–299)

Researchers frequently use their oral historical accounts along with other kinds of historical evidence. In interpreting the diverse genres that oral history methods produce, they must also consider what relations they want to draw between those diverse kinds of evidence. White has criticized the use of "documentary material to flesh out, contextualize, and even explain the words of . . . informants" (1995, p. 1381). This interpretive strategy effectively boils down such accounts to a series of claims that can be verified or proved false, and it fails to account for the ways in which people situate these claims within bodies of historical knowledge and the epistemologies that they use to evaluate and to interpret the past (Fabian & Matulu 1997; Giles-Vernick 2002; Nabokov 2002; Skaria 1999).

Finally, one has to decide what to write about, an ethical problem that ethnographers share. As in ethnographic work, part of the very process of oral historical method involves creating a social relationship between researchers and their interlocutors, who might divulge information that they do not want imparted to others. Moreover, oral historical researchers do their work in contexts that may be politically volatile, and their writings may have profound implications for how contemporary disputes play out. In such contexts of shared confidences, researchers have an ethical responsibility not to divulge secrets that betray confidences, endanger the lives or livelihoods of their informants, inflict shame on informants or their families, or provoke violent political struggles. Steering clear of these ethical breaches and potential political conflagrations in the processes of writing and publication is not always so straightforward, and some social scientists have found that they have had to distinguish carefully in their publications between writing *about* sensitive or confidential concerns and divulging these concerns (McCurdy 1996). Moreover, in some contexts, informants have seen researchers as a conduit for disseminating their own interpretations of the past and present.

Obviously, oral history methods are not appropriate for every social science investigation. Their usefulness depends partly on the questions a researcher wants to pose, and also on the very nature of the researcher. Oral history methods cannot, of course, contribute much to studies unconcerned with historical inquiry, nor will they yield unassailable evidence for reconstructing the past "as it actually happened." And researchers have to decide for themselves whether they feel comfortable scouting out informants, gaining their confidence, and asking difficult questions about pasts that may be uncomfortable, awkward, or even painful to recall. Not every researcher possesses an overwhelming desire to pry into other people's most personal recollections or to badger potential tellers of the past to "teach history." Not everyone wants to engage in the painstaking task of transcribing and translating the words of informants. And not every historical moment may be appropriate for recounting of the past; much still depends on how potential tellers understand their own places within contemporary political, economic, and social contexts. Hence, not every researcher should feel compelled to integrate oral history tools into his or her methodologies. Nonetheless, in historical studies that focus on subjective understandings of social, political, economic, intellectual, or cultural change, and in contexts in which potential informants are alive and willing to speak, researchers may find that oral history can be a most powerful tool of inquiry.

Note

1. Among the critics is a reviewer of this volume.

Supplemental References

Cinnamon, John. (2002). "Genealogies of Knowledge Production and the Ethnographic Imagination in Gabonese Fieldwork." Presented at WARA Symposium, *Fieldwork in Africa*, June 12–15, Dakar, Senegal.

Comaroff, John and Jean Comaroff. (1992). *Ethnography and the Historical Imagination*. Chicago, IL: University of Chicago Press.

Dworkin, Ira. (2003). "American Hearts: African American Writings on the Congo, 1890–1915." Ph.D. dissertation, City University of New York.

Giles-Vernick, Tamara. (1996). "Na lege ti guiriri (On the road of History): Mapping Out the Past and Present in M'Bres Region, Central African Republic." *Ethnohistory* 43(2), 245–275.

Kratz, Corinne. (2001). "Conversations and Lives." In *African Words, African Voices: Critical Practices in Oral History*, edited by Luise White, Stephan Miescher, and David William Cohen. Bloomington: Indiana University Press.

Maddox, Gregory. (Forthcoming). *Writing the Gogo: An Intellectual History*. Portsmouth, NH: Heinemann.

Malkki, Liisa. (1995). *Purity and Exile*. Chicago, IL: University of Chicago Press.

Mbilinyi, Marjorie. (1989). "'I'd Have Been a Man': Politics and the Labor Process in Producing Personal Narratives." In *Interpreting Women's Lives: Feminist Theory and Personal Narratives*, edited by Personal Narratives Group. Bloomington: Indiana University Press.

McCurdy, Sheryl. (1996). "Learning the Dance, Initiating Relationships." In *Pursuit of History: Fieldwork in Africa*, edited by Carolyn Keyes Adenaike and Jan Vansina. Portsmouth, NH: Heinemann.

Miescher, Stephan F. (2001). "The Life Histories of Boakye Yiadom (Akasease Kofi of Abetifi, Kwaku): Exploring the Subjectivity and 'Voices' of a Teacher-Catechist in Colonial Ghana." In *African Words, African Voices: Critical Practices in Oral History*, edited by Luise White, Stephan Miescher, and David William Cohen. Bloomington: Indiana University Press.

Ogot, Bethwell A. (2001). "The Construction of Luo Identity and History." In *African Words, African Voices: Critical Practices in Oral History*, edited by Luise White, Stephan Miescher, and David William Cohen. Bloomington: Indiana University Press.

Ranger, Terence. (1999). *Voices From the Rocks: Nature, Culture, and History in the Matopos*. Bloomington: Indiana University Press.

Vansina, Jan. (1965). *Oral Tradition: A Study in Historical Methodology*. Translated by H. M. Wright. Chicago, IL: Aldine.

Vaughan, Megan. (2001). "Reported Speech and Other Kinds of Testimony." In *African Words, African Voices: Critical Practices in Oral History*, edited by Luise White, Stephan Miescher, and David William Cohen. Bloomington: Indiana University Press.

White, Luise. (1995). "They Could Make Their Victims Dull: Gender and Genres, Fantasies and Cures in Colonial Southern Uganda." *American Historical Review* 100(5), 1379–1402.

———. (2001). "True Stories: Narrative, Event, History, and Blood in the Lake Victoria Basin." In *African Words, African Voices: Critical Practices in Oral History*, edited by Luise White, Stephan Miescher, and David William Cohen. Bloomington: Indiana University Press.

Yankah, Kwesi. (2001). "Nana Ampadu, the Sung-Tale Metaphor, and Protest Discourse in Contemporary Ghana." In *African Words, African Voices: Critical Practices in Oral History*, edited by Luise White, Stephan Miescher, and David William Cohen. Bloomington: Indiana University Press.

Bibliography on Oral History

1. Oral Traditions

Theory and Method

Akyeampong, Emmanuel and Pashington Obeng. (1995). "Spirituality, Gender and Power and Asante History." *International Journal of African Historical Studies* 28(3), 481–508.

American Anthropological Association. (2002). *Final Report of the El Dorado Task Force*, 2 vols. Retrieved September 2, 2005, from www.aaanet.org/edtf.

Barber, Karen. (1991). *I Could Speak Until Tomorrow*. Washington, DC: Smithsonian.

Barber, Karen and Paulo F. De Moreas Farias, eds. (1989). *Discourse and Its Disguises: The Interpretation of African Oral Texts*. Birmingham, UK: Centre of West African Studies, University of Birmingham.

Beidelman, Thomas. (1970). "Myth, Legend, and Oral History." *Anthropos* 65, 74–97.

Cohen, David William. (1989). "The Undefining of Oral Tradition." *Ethnohistory* 36(1), 9–18.

Connerton, Paul. (1989). *How Societies Remember*. Cambridge, UK: Cambridge University Press.

De Heusch, Luc. (1982). *The Drunken King*. Bloomington: Indiana University Press.

Feierman, Steven. (1974). *The Shambaa Kingdom*. Madison: University of Wisconsin Press.

———. (1990). *Peasant Intellectuals*. Madison: University of Wisconsin Press.

Finnegan, Ruth H. (1970). *Oral Literature in Africa*. London, UK: Clarendon.

———. (1977). *Oral Poetry: Its Nature, Significance, and Social Context*. New York: Cambridge University Press.

———. (1992). *Oral Traditions and the Verbal Arts: A Guide to Research Practice*. London, UK: Routledge.

Hamilton, Carolyn. (1998). *Terrific Majesty*. Cambridge, MA: Harvard University Press.

Henige, David. (1974). *The Chronology of Oral Tradition*. Oxford, UK: Clarendon Press.

———, ed. *History in Africa*. Annual journal published by the African Studies Association.

Krech, Shepard, III. (1991). "The State of Ethnohistory." *Annual Review of Anthropology* 20, 345–375.

Larson, Pier. (1995). "Multiple Narratives, Gendered Voices: Remembering the Past in Highland Central Madagascar." *International Journal of African Historical Studies* 28(2), 295–325.

Miller, Joseph, ed. (1980). *The African Past Speaks*. Folkstone, UK: Archon.

Ong, Walter. (1982). *Orality and Literacy: The Technologizing of the World*. London, UK: Methuen.

Peel, John David Yeadon. (1984). "Making History: The Past in the Ijesha Present." *Man* 19(1), 111–132.

Scheub, Harold. (1975). *The Xhosa Ntsomi*. Oxford, UK: Clarendon Press.

———. (1977). *African Oral Narratives, Proverbs, Riddles, Poetry, and Song*. Boston, MA: G. K. Hall.

Schoffeleers, J. Matthew. (1992). *River of Blood*. Madison: University of Wisconsin Press.

Shoemaker, Nancy, ed. (2002). *Clearing a Path: Theorizing the Past in Native American Studies*. New York: Routledge.

Skaria, Ajay. (1999). *Hybrid Histories: Forests, Frontiers, and Wildness in Western India*. Delhi, India: Oxford University Press.

Spear, Thomas. (1981). "Oral Traditions: Whose History?" *Journal of Pacific History* 16, 133–148.

———. (2003). "Neo-Traditionalism and the Limits of Invention in British Colonial Africa." *Journal of African History* 44(1), 3–27.

Tedlock, Dennis. (1983). *The Spoken Word and the Work of Interpretation*. Philadelphia: University of Pennsylvania Press.

Thompson, Paul. (2000). *The Voice of the Past: Oral History*, 3d ed. Oxford, UK: Oxford University Press.

Vail, Leory and Landeg White. (1991). *Power and the Praise Poem*. Charlottesville: University Press of Virginia.

Vansina, Jan. (1985). *Oral Traditions as History*. Madison: University of Wisconsin Press. This is a revision of Vansina's 1965 work listed in the Supplemental References, above.

———. (1994). *Living With Africa*. Madison: University of Wisconsin Press.

White, Luise, Stephan Miescher, and David William Cohen, eds. (2001). *African Words, African Voices: Critical Practices in Oral History*. Bloomington: Indiana University Press.

Good Examples

Apter, Andrew. (1992). *Black Critics and Kings*. Chicago, IL: University of Chicago Press.

Austen, Ralph, ed. (1999). *In Search of Sunjata: The Mande Oral Epic as History, Literature, and Performance*. Bloomington: Indiana University Press.

Feinberg, Richard. (1998). *Oral Traditions of Anuta: A Polynesian Outlier in the Solomon Islands*. Oxford, UK: Oxford University Press.

Harms, Robert. (1981). *River of Wealth, River of Sorrow*. New Haven, CT: Yale University Press.

Bibliography: Oral History

Irwin, Paul. (1981). *Liptako Speaks*. Princeton, NJ: Princeton University Press.

Krech, Shepard, III. (1999). *The Ecological Indian: Myth and History*. New York: W.W. Norton.

Larson, Pier. (2000). *History and Memory in the Age of Enslavement*. Portsmouth, NH: Heinemann.

Law, Robin. (1977). *The Oyo Empire*. Oxford, UK: Clarendon Press.

Lomnitz, Larissa Adler and Marisol Perez Lizaur. (1987). *A Mexican Elite Family, 1820–1980*. Princeton, NJ: Princeton University Press.

Morphy, Howard and Frances Morphy. (1984). "Myths of Ngalakan History: Ideology and Images of the Past in Northern Australia." *Man* 19, 459–475.

Newbury, David. (1991). *Kings and Clans*. Madison: University of Wisconsin Press.

Price, Richard. (1990). *Alabi's World*. Baltimore, MD: Johns Hopkins University Press.

Rumsey, Alan and James Weiner, eds. (2001). *Emplaced Myth: Space, Narrative, and Knowledge in Aboriginal Australia and Papua New Guinea*. Honolulu: University of Hawaii Press.

Vansina, Jan. (1978). *The Children of Woot*. Madison: University of Wisconsin Press.

2. Oral History

Theory and Method

Adenaike, Carolyn Keyes and Jan Vansina, eds. (1996). *In Pursuit of History: Fieldwork in Africa*. Portsmouth, NH: Heinemann.

Basso, Ellen B. (1995). *The Last Cannibals: A South American Oral History*. Austin: University of Texas Press.

Basso, Keith. (1984). "Stalking With Stories: Names, Places, and Moral Narratives Among the Western Apache." Pp. 19–55 in *Text, Play, and Story: The Construction and Reconstruction of Self and Society*, edited by Stuart Plattner. Washington, DC: American Ethnological Society.

———. (1996). *Wisdom Sits in Places: Landscape and Language Among the Western Apache*. Albuquerque: University of New Mexico Press.

Bauman, Richard. (1986). *Story, Performance, and Event: Contextual Studies of Oral Narrative*. Cambridge, UK: Cambridge University Press.

Briggs, Charles. (1986). *Learning How to Ask: A Sociolinguistic Appraisal of the Interview in Social Science Research*. Cambridge, UK: Cambridge University Press.

Casey, Edward. (1987). *Remembering: A Phenomenological Study*. Bloomington: Indiana University Press.

Confino, Alon. (1997). "Collective Memory and Cultural History: Problems of Method." *American Historical Review* 102(5), 1386–1403.

Darien-Smith, Kate and Paula Hamilton, eds. (1994). *Memory and History in Twentieth Century Australia*. Oxford, UK: Oxford University Press.

Fabian, Johannes and Tshbumba Kanda Matulu. (1997). *Remembering the Present: Painting and Popular History in Zaire*. Berkeley: University of California Press.

Fentress, James, and Chris Wickham. (1992). *Social Memory*. Oxford, UK: Blackwell.

Geiger, Susan. (1996). "Tanganyikan Nationalism as Woman's Work: Life Histories, Collective Biography and Changing Historiography." *Journal of African History* 37(3), 465–478.

Gengenbach, Heidi. (1993). "Truth-Telling and the Politics of Women's Life History Research in Africa: A Reply to Kirk Hoppe." *International Journal of African Historical Studies* 27(3), 619–627. See Hoppe (1993), listed below.

Guss, David M. (2000). *The Festive State: Race, Ethnicity, and Nationalism as Cultural Performance*. Berkeley: University of California Press.

Hacking, Ian. (1995). *Rewriting the Soul: Multiple Personality and the Sciences of Memory*. Princeton, NJ: Princeton University Press.

Halbwachs, Maurice. (1992). *On Collective Memory*. Edited and translated by Lewis A. Coser. Chicago, IL: University of Chicago Press.

Henige, David. (1982). *Oral Historiography*. London, UK: Longman.

Hofmeyr, Isabel. (1993). *We Spend Our Years as a Tale That Is Told: Oral Historical Narrative in a South African Chiefdom*. Portsmouth, NH: Heinemann.

Hoppe, Kirk. (1993). "Whose Life Is It Anyway?" *International Journal of African Historical Studies* 26(3), 623–636. See Gengenbach (1993), listed above, for reply to Hoppe (1993).

Hunt, Nancy Rose. (1999). *A Colonial Lexicon of Birth Ritual, Medicalization, and Mobility in the Congo*. Durham, NC: Duke University Press.

Ibrahim, Abdullahi. (2001). "The Birth of the Interview: The Thin and the Fat of It." In *African Words, African Voices: Critical Practices in Oral History*, edited by Luise White, Stephan Miescher, and David William Cohen. Bloomington: Indiana University Press.

International Journal of Oral History.

Jewsiewicki, Bogumil, and David Newbury, eds. (1986). *African Historiographies: What History for Which Africa?* Beverly Hills, CA: Sage.

Klein, Kerwin Lee. (2000). "On the Emergence of Memory in Historical Discourse." *Representations* 69 (winter), 127–150.

Klein, Martin. (1989). "Studying the History of Those Who Would Rather Forget: Oral History and the Experience of Slavery." *History in Africa* 16, 209–217.

Loftus, Elizabeth. (1979). *Eyewitness Testimony*. Cambridge, MA: Harvard University Press.

Matsuda, Matt. (1996). *The Memory of the Modern*. New York: Oxford University Press.

Nora, Pierre. ([1984] 1997). *Les Lieux de Memoire*. Paris, France: Gallimard.

Ochs, Elinor and Lisa Capps. (2001). *Living Narrative: Creating Lives in Everyday Storytelling*. Cambridge, MA: Harvard University Press.

Oral History Review

Personal Narratives Group. (1989). *Interpreting Women's Lives*. Bloomington: Indiana University Press.

Portelli, Alessandro. (1997). *The Battle of Valle Giulia: Oral History and the Art of Dialogue*. Madison: University of Wisconsin Press.

Roberts, Mary Nooter and Allen F. Roberts. (1996). *Memory: Luba Art and the Making of History*. New York: Museum for African Art.

Rosaldo, Renato. (1980). "Doing Oral History." *Social Analysis* 4, 89–99.

Samuel, Raphael. (1994). *Theatres of Memory*. London, UK: Verso.

Sanjek, Roger, ed. (1990). *Fieldnotes: The Makings of Anthropology*. Ithaca, NY: Cornell University Press.

Thompson, Paul. (1988). *The Voice of the Past*. Oxford, UK: Oxford University Press.

Tonkin, Elizabeth. (1992). *Narrating Our Pasts: The Social Construction of Oral History*. Cambridge, UK: Cambridge University Press.

Trouillot, Rolph. (1995). *Silencing the Past: Power and the Production of History*. Boston, MA: Beacon.

White, Luise. (2000). *Speaking With Vampires: Rumor and History in Colonial Africa*. Berkeley: University of California Press.

Yates, Frances A. (1966). *The Art of Memory*. London, UK: Pimlico.

Good Examples

Akyeamong, Emmanuel. (2001). *Between the Sea and the Lagoon: An Eco-Social History of the Anlo of Southeastern Ghana c. 1850 to Recent Times*. Athens: Ohio University Press.

Behar, Ruth. (1986). *Santa Maria del Monte: The Presence of the Past in a Spanish Village*. Princeton, NJ: Princeton University Press.

———. (1993). *Translated Woman: Crossing the Border With Esperanza's Story*. Boston, MA: Beacon Press.

Berry, Sara. (1985). *Fathers Work for Their Sons*. Berkeley: University of California Press.

Bozzoli, Belinda (with Mmantho Nkotsoe). (1991). *Women of Phokeng*. Portsmouth, NH: Heinemann.

Brown, Karen McCarthy. (2001). *Mama Lola: A Voodoo Priestess in Brooklyn*. Berkeley: University of California Press.

Carruthers, Mary. (1990). *The Book of Memory: A Study of Memory in Medieval Culture*. Cambridge, UK: Cambridge University Press.

Chafe, William H., Raymond Gavins, and Robert Korstad. (2001). *Remembering Jim Crow: African Americans Tell About Life in the Segregated South*. New York: New Press in association with Lyndhurst Books of the Center for Documentary Studies of Duke University.

Cohen, David William. (1977). *Womunafu's Bonuafu: A Study of Authority in a Nineteenth-Century African Community*. Princeton, NJ: Princeton University Press.

Cohen, David William and E. S. Atieno Odhiambo. (1989). *Siaya: The Historical Anthropology of an African Landscape*. London, UK: J. Currey.

Cohen, David William and E. S. Atieno Odhiambo. (1992). *Burying SM: The Politics of Knowledge and the Sociology of Power in Africa*. Portsmouth, NH: Heinemann.

Cole, Jennifer. (2001). *Forget Colonialism: Sacrifice and the Art of Memory in Madagascar*. Berkeley: University of California Press.

Davison, Jean. (1989). *Voices From Mutira*. Boulder, CO: Lynne Rienner Publishers.

Draaisma, Douwe. (2000). *Metaphors of Memory: A History of Ideas About the Mind*. Cambridge, UK: Cambridge University Press.

Feldman, Allen. (1991). *Foundations of Violence: The Narrative of the Body and Political Terror in Northern Ireland*. Chicago, IL: University of Chicago Press.

Geiger, Susan. (1997). *TANU Women: Gender and Culture in the Making of Tanganyikan Nationalism: 1955–1965*. Portsmouth, NH: Heinemann.

Giles-Vernick, Tamara. (2002). *Cutting the Vines of the Past: Environmental Histories of the Central African Rain Forest*. Charlottesville: University of Virginia Press.

Gill, Tom. (2001). *Men of Uncertainty: The Social Organization of Day Laborers in Contemporary Japan*. Albany, NY: State University of Albany Press.

Gilsenan, Michael. (1996). *Lords of the Lebanese Marches: Violence and Narrative in an Arab Society*. Berkeley: University of California Press.

Guss, David M. (2000). *The Festive State: Race, Ethnicity, and Nationalism as Cultural Performance*. Berkeley: University of California Press.

Isaacman, Allen. (1996). *Cotton Is the Mother of Poverty: Peasants, Work, and Rural Struggle in Colonial Mozambique, 1938–1961*. Portsmouth, NH: Heinemann.

Kapucinski, Ryszard. (1983). *The Emperor*. New York: Harcourt Brace Jovanovich.

Keegan, Timothy. (1988). *Facing the Storm*. London, UK: Zed.

LeVine, Sarah. (1979). *Mothers and Wives*. Chicago, IL: University of Chicago Press.

Marks, Shula. (1987). *Not Either an Experimental Doll*. Pietermaritzburg, South Africa: University of Natal Press.

Monson Jamie. (2000). "Memory, Migration, and the Authority of History in Southern Tanzania, 1860–1950." *Journal of African History* 41(3), 347–372.

Menchu, Rigoberta. (1984). *I, Rigoberta Menchu*. London, UK: Verso.

Mintz, Sidney. ([1960] 1974). *Worker in the Cane: A Puerto Rican Life*. New York: Norton.

Mirza, Sarah and Margaret Strobel. (1989). *Three Swahili Women*. Bloomington: Indiana University Press.

Munson, Henry. (1984). *The House of Si Abd Allah*. New Haven, CT: Yale University Press.

Nabokov, Peter. (2002). *A Forest of Time: American Indian Ways of History*. Cambridge, UK: Cambridge University Press.

Passerini, Luisa. (1987). *Fascism in Popular Memory: The Cultural Experience of the Turin Working Class*. Cambridge, UK: Cambridge University Press.

———. (1992). "Memory and Totalitarianism." *In International Yearbook of Oral History and Life Stories*, vol. 1. London, UK: Oxford University Press.

Portelli, Alessandro. (1991). *The Death of Luigi Trastulli and Other Stories: Form and Meaning in Oral History*. Albany: State University of New York Press.

Preston, Richard J. (2002). *Cree Narrative: Expressing the Personal Meanings of Events*, 2d ed. Montreal, Canada: McGill-Queen's University Press.

Bibliography: Oral History

Ranger, Terrence. (1995). *Are We Not Also Men?* Harare, Zimbabwe: Heinemann.

Rathbone, Richard. (1993). *Murder and Politics in Colonial Ghana*. New Haven, CT: Yale University Press.

Robertson, Claire. (1997). *Trouble Showed the Way*. Bloomington: Indiana University Press.

Roy, Beth. (1994). *Some Trouble With Cows: Making Sense of Social Conflict*. Berkeley: University of California Press. See section in bibliography on "Oral Life History: Case Studies."

Rozenzweig, Roy and David Thelen. (2000). *The Presence of the Past: Popular Uses of History in American Life*. New York: Columbia University Press.

Schmidt, Elizabeth. (1992). *Peasants, Traders and Wives*. Portsmouth, NH: Heinemann.

Shaw, Rosalind (2002). *Memories of the Slave Trade: Ritual and the Historical Imagination in Sierra Leone*. Chicago, IL: University of Chicago Press.

Shostak, Marjorie. ([1981] 2000). *Nisa*. New York: Vintage Books.

Shumaker, Lyn. (2001). *Africanizing Anthropology: Fieldwork, Networks, and the Making of Cultural Knowledge in Central Africa*. Durham, NC: Duke University Press.

Smith, Mary. (1964). *Baba of Karo: A Woman of the Muslim Hausa*. London, UK: Faber and Faber.

Spence, Jonathan D. (1984). *The Memory Palace of Mateo Ricci*. New York: Viking Press.

Van Onselen, Charles. (1996). *The Seed Is Mine*. New York: Hill and Wang.

Werbner, Richard. (1991). *Tears of the Dead*. Edinburgh, Scotland: Edinburgh University Press.

White, Geoffrey M. (1991). *Identity Through History: Living Stories in a Solomon Islands Society*. Cambridge, UK: Cambridge University Press.

White, Landeg. (1987). *Magomero*. Cambridge, UK: Cambridge University Press.

Whitehead, Neil L. (2003). *Histories and Historicities in Amazonia*. Lincoln: University of Nebraska Press.

Willis, Justin. (1996). "Two Lives of Mpamizo: Useful Dissonance in Oral History." *History in Africa* 23, 319–332.

Wright, Marcia. (1993). *Strategies of Slaves and Women*. New York: L. Barber Press.

5

Focus Groups

Focus Group Interviews

Susan E. Short

Imagine eight 30 something single women sitting around a table over coffee discussing the advantages and disadvantages of the pill, the diaphragm, the condom, and other forms of contraception. A moderator facilitates their discussion, and a note taker and tape recorder capture their interaction for a researcher to review and analyze at a later date. This description is an example of a focus group interview.

The moderator could be the lead researcher on the project but often is not. The women could be acquaintances or intimates but are probably strangers who have something in common. A similar geographic or social space may facilitate their participation. They will agree and disagree, interrupting one another from time to time. Some will talk more than others. Some will talk about themselves. Others will talk about other people they know. The discussion heads in unanticipated directions on several occasions.

AUTHOR'S NOTE: I am grateful to Abigail Harrison, Brooke Harrington, Ellen Perecman, and Sara Curran for their helpful comments on this chapter.

Focus groups, or small group interviews characterized by group interactions, have a long history in the social sciences (Bogardus 1926; Merton, Fiske, & Kendall 1990; Morgan 1997). They are also common in health education research (Kitzinger 1994). In applied settings, they are widely used in market research (Manoff 1985).

Researchers have debated and rarely agreed on the advantages and disadvantages of focus group discussions. As a method, focus groups occupy an intermediate space that is not the usual terrain for either quantitative or qualitative researchers of the more purist ilk. Focus group interviews can share characteristics of survey research in that individuals are asked to participate in what is usually a structured interview on a predesignated topic, often with a moderator or researcher who "drops in" for the interview and then leaves with data to be analyzed back in the office. At the same time, focus group interviews can share characteristics of ethnographic research in that the emphasis is on open-ended questions that produce text-based data that need to be transcribed and analyzed with a qualitative tool kit. The individuals who participate are often strategically selected for attributes deemed relevant to the research question, and researchers may develop relationships with informants over time through repeated local interviews. Focus groups can differ along numerous axes, including formality, degree of structure, familiarity of participants with one another, and the involvement of lead researchers. Focus groups are sometimes used in combination with established quantitative methods and in survey research (Knodel 1997). Open-ended discussion on themes related to a planned survey can aid in the development of survey questions or help to refine an instrument before pretesting. Focus groups have also been used to assess construct validity or to aid in the interpretation of quantitative results (see, e.g., Entwisle et al. 1996; Knodel, Havanon, & Sittitrai 1990; Short et al. 2002). While a regression model might suggest an association between two variables, it does not explain why such an association exists. Focus groups designed to include individuals who might provide insight into a particular relationship can be used to develop interpretations for observed relationships.

Focus groups have also been used in combination with established qualitative methods. Focus group interviews on violence can yield different data from individual interviews on violence (Hollander 2004). Group interviews can be used to gain insight into normative understandings of issues. They can provide insight into the way individuals discuss (or do not discuss) selected topics. Body language, uncomfortable pauses, and patterns of eye contact, in addition to verbal cues, can indicate topics of greater or lesser comfort (Wellings, Branigan, & Mitchell 2000).

In research I conducted on family relationships in the context of high HIV/AIDS prevalence in southern Africa, I found that informal group interviews provided valuable insights beyond those generated by structured, in-depth interviews. The group discussions were especially useful for elaborating the normative prescriptions against HIV testing and condom use among couples in serious romantic and sexual relationships. Discussions in the group context focused more on what can and cannot be done in relationships today, while parallel discussions in individual interviews focused more on individual-level explanations for behavior. The group laughter at the idea of a couple seeking (free) HIV tests before initiating a sexual relationship, and the conversations that ensued, yielded rich data about relationships in this context. As a result, the individual-level and group-level data complement one another in ways that enhance ongoing analyses.

Whether focus groups are appropriate as a stand-alone method of data collection is a subject of ongoing discussion. Michell (1999) argues against using them to the exclusion of other methods, citing the potential for the silencing of voices, especially when group members have ongoing social relations. Because of small-group dynamics, minority opinions can be silenced, or group members with less power may be less willing to present their views (Hollander 2004; Morgan 1997). For this reason, some researchers conduct individual interviews as well. Others recognize the influence of group context on product but do not pair focus groups with individual interviews; indeed, numerous researchers have published useful studies based solely or primarily on focus group data (e.g., Henderson et al. 2000; Krause et al. 2000; Peracca, Knodel, & Saengtienchai 1998), although sometimes the larger research projects from which their analyses were drawn included other forms of data.

Overall, I suggest that focus group techniques are most valuable when researchers (a) adopt this method when they seek data best provided by group interaction; (b) design and carry out the interviews so that they elicit the desired group interaction; and (c) analyze the data in a way that reflects the method by which they were collected. The key is to use focus groups deliberately to achieve a specific research goal. Because focus group interviews feature small group interaction, they are not a substitute for individual interviews.

Focus Group, Focused Group, and Group Interviews

What are the characteristics that make a group conversation on a research-relevant topic a focus group interview? Do focus group interviews require a particular interview technique? Can group discussions that occur in the field as part of a village ethnography be called focus group discussions? The semantic debate that surrounds focus group interviews can be bewildering. At issue is the slippery meaning of the term "focus group interview" or "focus group discussion."

Morgan defines focus groups as "a research technique that collects data through group interaction on a topic determined by the researcher" (1997, p. 6). This definition is inclusive of interviews with groups that gather naturally in a particular space, as long as the conversation of the group is organized around a research-relevant topic. Others prefer to reserve the term "focus group interview" for a more narrowly defined set of group interviews in which participants are invited because they meet a set of inclusion criteria.

The term "focus" (or "focused") refers to the fact that a moderator intervenes to shape the discussion using researcher-determined strategy. Often, the discussion will be orchestrated around a topic or common experience, but it is possible to design a research strategy that elicits conversation within a strategically selected group on participant-initiated topics that emerge.

Part of the semantic confusion surrounding "focus group interviews" stems from the conflation of the term "focused interview" with "focus *group* interview." The former was described by Merton, Fiske, and Kendall (1990) in *The Focused Interview: A Manual of Problems and Procedure*s, a book on research methods originally published in 1956. Paraphrasing the authors (1990, p. 3), the "focused interview" is a research method in which (a) interviewees experience a particular situation; (b) the particulars of the situation are analyzed by a social scientist, who generates hypotheses based on this analysis; (c) interview guides based on the hypotheses are developed; and (d) interviews are conducted that focus on the subjective experiences of the interviewees and ascertain their "definitions of the situation." Example situations include listening to a particular radio program or participating in a social situation such as a political rally. Significantly, the authors include a chapter on the "group interview," but most of the volume focuses on the research technique as it relates to individual interviews.

In the introduction to the second edition, Merton suggests that there is intellectual continuity between what he and colleagues called "focused interviews" and what others call "focus groups" (Merton et al. 1990, p. xxix). Indeed, parallels exist. My reading suggests the difference is emphasis. Merton, Fiske, and Kendall (1990) described a specific, four-part interview strategy that emphasizes the "focus" in an interview. They describe how to create and capitalize on focus, such as by providing a common stimulus and exploring a priori hypotheses, when interviewing individuals or groups. By contrast, more recent usage of the term "focus group" highlights the group aspect of the interview. Interview formats, including the degree of focus and structure, can vary considerably, but the group aspect is universal.

One final term deserves introduction: "focus group discussion." Some researchers substitute "discussion" for "interview" to highlight the interaction among participants in focus group interviews. More recently, some researchers have used the term "peer group discussion" to refer to a specific type of focus group discussion that involves adolescents. With peer group discussions, familiarity among participants is acknowledged or encouraged. Peer group discussions can take place among school children who attend the same school and as a consequence have a relationship with one another before and after the interview, or they can be carried out by designing longitudinal focus groups that bring together the same children repeatedly (Barbour & Kitzinger 1999; Bohmer & Kirumira 2000; Harrison, Xaba, & Kunene 2001). The focus group definition used here, namely, a research technique that generates data based on group interaction, does not require that the topic of a focus group interview be predetermined by the researcher, though most often it will be. This definition also highlights the group aspect of the interview rather than the interview strategy.

Emphasizing the Group in Focus Group

Social science research, and sociological research in particular, is predicated on the assertion that groups or collectivities are more than simple sums of the individuals who comprise them (see, e.g., Wolff 1950 on Simmel). It follows that it would be a-sociological to use the group interview as a convenient way to interview many individuals at once.

How do focus group interviews and individual interviews differ? A key difference is the unit of analysis. With focus groups, the unit of analysis is the group, not the individual. Participants respond directly to a moderator's questions and also to comments made by other members of the group. The discussion (and any individual response) is affected by the social contexts represented by the group. For example, adolescent boys discuss their attitudes toward girls differently in individual interviews than in focus group discussions with other adolescent boys. We might surmise that their responses would be even more different had they been expressed in groups that included adolescent girls. This issue is not unique to focus group interviews but is perhaps exaggerated by the group format. It is a feature that researchers might seek to use to strategic advantage. By contrast, in individual interviews, in which the individual is the unit of analysis, some researchers might attempt to minimize the effect of interaction, or "interviewer effects."

Good focus groups capitalize on process. They can be especially generative when group members interact to develop an explanation or accomplish a task. Participants ask questions of one another that differ from those of the researcher or moderator, and their responses to one another introduce alternate interpretations of the ongoing dialogue. The same individual might offer one view early in the interview and later revise it as others in the group react, comment, and express their own ideas.

There can be a discomfort with focus groups among those who take the epistemological position that positivistic research paradigms are the most legitimate research paradigms. Focus groups, arguably more than other interview techniques, require comfort with interactionist perspectives. Their very design is often built around variations in context. For example, a researcher interested in the organization of child care might interview young parents. However, recognizing the importance of context to the discussion, the researcher might design focus groups that include three sets of interviews: one set with mothers only; another with fathers only; and a third with mothers and fathers together. The sensitivity of responses to the context of a focus group can raise concern about response validity, or the "truthfulness" of participants. However, answers that shift with shifting contexts need not point to poor validity. They more likely point to an opportunity for insight.

How are participant-observation methods different from focus group interviews? For one thing, participant-observation methods are usually much less "contrived" or formal than focus group interviews and allow for observation of group interaction in a more naturalistic environment. As such, participant observation may be better suited than focus groups to research related to reasons for attending Alcoholics Anonymous meetings, for example. On the other hand, focus groups might be particularly useful for exploring normative ideas about what it means to be a "good mother" among women with different employment experiences, a conversation likely difficult to observe in a naturalistic setting.

Because group discussion can seem natural and easy in daily life, it is reasonable to think that group interviews would be easy to orchestrate. But without explicit goals and careful planning, one is likely to end up with a scenario in which the moderator asks questions and the individuals sitting in a circle respond in turn, as in the following sample transcript:

Moderator asks first question.

Participant A answers.

Participant B answers.

Participant C answers.

Participant D answers.

Participant E answers.

Then the pattern repeats itself:

Moderator asks second question.

Participant A answers

Participant B answers.

Participant C responds "I don't know."

Participant D responds "don't know."

Participant E answers.

And so on.

This sample transcript mirrors an actual interview shared with me by another researcher puzzling over the lack of group interaction. The "don't know" responses indicate that each group member thought he or she was expected to give "an answer" as opposed to entering into a discussion. Focus groups in which there is limited verbal interaction fail to take advantage of the strength of the focus group design.

Fortunately, there are now numerous books that provide guidance on how to conduct focus groups (see the 6-volume *Focus Group Kit* published by Sage, for example; also Edmunds 1999; Greenbaum 2000; Krueger 1994; Morgan 1997; Stewart & Shamdasani 1990). They provide terrific detail on the mechanics of carrying out interviews, particularly structured group interviews in the United States, but tend to be less useful in helping social science researchers decide when focus groups are appropriate or how best to construct appropriate content. Those decisions require that researchers consider carefully their research question and how data collected in group interviews can best contribute to specific research goals.

Sorting Through Relationships

The relationship between the researcher and the research participants varies considerably among those who use focus groups. At one end of the continuum are those who hire professionals to conduct focus groups for them. While these researchers may set the inclusion criteria for the focus group interviews, it is unlikely they will ever meet the participants or see or listen to the interviews. If they have contact with participants at all, their contact will probably be limited to analyzing the transcripts of the sessions. Some researchers may choose to hire professional moderators because the researchers do not have the requisite language skills to conduct or observe the interviews. Or given that personal characteristics of the moderator, such as age, gender, and class, are known to influence the focus group discussion, a researcher may judge it inappropriate for him or her to moderate, or even observe, a particular group. Indeed, power and identity are critical to "access" in the collection of research materials (Harrington 2003).

At the other end of the continuum are researchers who view focus group interviews as an appropriate vehicle for participatory research. In successful focus groups, the ideas that emerge in the course of the discussion are developed, shaped, and interpreted by the participants. In this way, focus group participants might be seen as collaborators in the research endeavor. Krueger and King (1998) adopt this view and suggest a nuts-and-bolts approach to involving community members in focus groups. They emphasize the training of volunteers to conduct focus groups and highlight the advantages of process over product for the purposes of evaluation research. Baker and Hinton (1999) also approach the arena of participatory research with an emphasis on collaboration. They explore how focus groups can be used to create valid results as well as a partnership between researchers and the informant community and define focus group exceedingly broadly, as follows:

> any group-based research activity that is grounded in regular interaction among the participants such that it becomes a social and political forum in its own right . . . [including] focused discussions in natural groupings, structured group exercises with targeted participants, and debate or activities facilitated by community members. (Baker & Hinton 1999, p. 79)

As participatory research methods gain acceptance in mainstream social science, it seems plausible that focus groups will increasingly be used as a tool to help formalize the incorporation of community members in research. At the same time, scholars caution that careful attention must be paid to power differentials in the design, execution, and analysis of these interviews (see, e.g., Baker & Hinton 1999). Participation does not necessarily produce co-representation.

It is not just relationships between researchers and participants that matter. The relationships among participants are an equally important design detail when planning focus group interviews. Researchers must decide whether homogeneous or heterogeneous groups best serve the research goals. This is a critical design issue for at least two reasons. First, group composition can affect elicitation, although perhaps not in as formulaic a way as once thought. Groups of like members can produce comfortable venues for expression. At the same time, groups of unlike members can generate disagreement and greater cause to explain individual points of view (Hollander 2004). Second, if group variation is used strategically, it has the potential to facilitate investigation of the ways in which social context shapes discussion of the issues under study.

Last, if groups are not observed in naturalistic settings, researchers also need to weigh the advantages and disadvantages of recruiting individuals who know one another. While researchers used to favor strangers over acquaintances or intimates, more recently there is growing recognition that degree of familiarity is yet another aspect of interview context that can be manipulated systematically to achieve research goals. One research strategy may be to facilitate familiarity and shared history among participants who may not have known each other at the start of an interview. For example, Bohmer and Kirumira (2000) and Harrison, Xaba, and Kunene (2001) used repeated focus groups with adolescents over time to develop a context more conducive to discussion of sexual behavior.

Ethical Issues

Ethical issues arise in the course of any research project. Several that pertain to group interviews deserve specific mention. The first is confidentiality. In individual interviews, researchers have a high degree of control over the information that is shared during the course of an interview. As part of any informed consent procedure, they can elaborate what will and will not be done with this information. In group interviews, participants are usually asked to agree to keep information confidential. However, it is difficult, if not impossible, for any researcher to enforce confidentiality.

Dynamics during the interviews, as they relate to confidentiality, can also be especially complicated when participants know each other. For example, it can be difficult to prevent participants from making disclosures about others in the group. When they do so, they may reveal information that other group members would have chosen to keep private.

At the same time, Kitzinger and Farquhar (1999) argue that, whenever possible, "sensitive moments" should not be suppressed. They note that such situations can be analytically useful in the research process because they serve to map out the boundaries of acceptable discourse (p. 156). A unique challenge for focus group researchers is the need to protect the welfare of participants while at the same time creating a safe space for sensitive moments in discussion.

Next Steps

The available manuals and books can be very helpful for planning and executing focus group research. Morgan (1997), in particular, is a straightforward treatment and a good introduction. It reflects more of a social science orientation than some of the other "how-to" books. Barbour and Kitzinger (1999) will appeal to those with no or little experience using focus group techniques, as well as those who already use them. It is an edited volume that features examples of research with focus groups. Interactionist in orientation, many of the chapters address methodological questions concerning focus group interviews. Morgan and Krueger's (1998) the *Focus Group Kit* is oriented to research in the United States. It may be useful as a reference for researchers thinking through specific organizational issues, such as how to craft invitation letters and whether to serve food.

Analysis of Focus Group Data

The analysis of focus group data is an underdeveloped area in sociological research methods. Handbooks for the analysis of qualitative data more generally might be useful. Volume 6 in the *Focus Group Kit* (Krueger 1998) addresses the topic of analysis. However, while it is written for focus groups specifically, much of the volume highlights in bullet format general principles related to analysis rather than specific strategies for the analysis of focus group interviews. Basic coding of content is addressed in Frankland and Bloor (1999); analysis of sensitive moments in Kitzinger and Farquhar (1999); and conversation analysis in Myers and Macnaghten (1999).

Nuanced analysis of focus group data ideally takes into account the group aspect of the interview (Wellings, Branigan, & Mitchell 2000). As the field increasingly moves toward software for textual analysis, how best to incorporate the group in analysis will require careful consideration; narrative thread can be especially complex in group interviews. Interruptions, the absence of material, and sequencing of comments can complicate analysis, as can the insertion of observational data. Yet these challenges deserve systematic consideration.

Let me close with one observation and one practical suggestion. First, the location of focus group research on the quantitative-qualitative research continuum is a factor that leads to criticism of the method. There are those who dismiss focus group techniques because they are often conducted with a nonrandom sample of individuals, and so inferences to a population cannot be drawn easily; or, generalizability, a characteristic of research highly valued by quantitative researchers, is not met. At the same time, others criticize focus group techniques because they fall short by ethnographic standards. There is often very little individual-specific context. Research participants are essentially abstracted from the social landscape, coming together in an unnatural environment to contemplate issues not typically discussed by strangers. I hope this chapter has served to clarify why one might use focus group interviews. Focus group techniques are not inherently good or bad; their value and appropriateness depend on how they are integrated into a research project.

Finally, I offer a practical suggestion. To determine whether focus group interviews are an appropriate data collection technique for your qualitative, quantitative, or mixed-method project, it might be helpful to think about the broadest range of group techniques possible. In order to gather relevant information when reviewing the literature on focus groups, consider search terms that include "group interviews," "group discussions," "focused interviews," and "focused group interviews." Even if you plan highly structured focus group interviews, the materials from this broader set of research techniques may be helpful in developing your project.

Supplemental References

Aubel, Judi. (1994). "Guidelines for Studies Using the Group Interview Technique" (Paper no. 2). Training Papers in Population and Family Welfare Education in the Worksetting. Geneva, Switzerland: United Nations Population Fund.

Baker, Rachel and Rachel Hinton. (1999). "Do Focus Groups Facilitate Meaningful Participation in Social Research?" In *Developing Focus Group Research: Politics, Theory and Practice*, edited by Rosaline S. Barbour and Jenny Kitzinger. London: Sage.

Balmer, Don H., E. Gikundi, M. C. Billingsley, F. G. Kihuho, M. Kimani, J. Wang'ondu, and H. Njoroge. (1997). "Adolescent Knowledge, Values, and Coping Strategies: Implications for Health in Sub-Saharan Africa." *Journal of Adolescent Health* 21, 33–38.

Barbour, Rosaline S. and Jenny Kitzinger, eds. (1999). *Developing Focus Group Research: Politics, Theory and Practice*. London: Sage.

Bogardus, Emory S. (1926). "The Group Interview." *Journal of Applied Sociology* 10, 372–382.

Bohmer, Lisa and Edward K. Kirumira. (2000). "Socio-Economic Context and the Sexual Behavior of Ugandan Out of School Youth." *Culture, Health, and Sexuality* 2(3), 269–285.

Edmunds, Holly. (1999). *The Focus Group Research Handbook*. Chicago: NTC Business Books.

Frankland, Jane and Michael Bloor. (1999). "Some Issues Arising in the Systematic Analysis of Focus Group Interviews." In *Developing Focus Group Research: Politics, Theory and Practice*, edited by Rosaline S. Barbour and Jenny Kitzinger. London: Sage.

Greenbaum, Thomas L. (2000). *Moderating Focus Groups: A Practical Guide for Group Facilitation*. Thousand Oaks, CA: Sage Publications.

Harrington, Brooke. (2003). "The Social Psychology of Access in Ethnographic Research." *Journal of Contemporary Ethnography* 32(5), 592–625.

Harrison, Abigail, Nonhlanha Xaba, and Pinky Kunene. (2001). "Understanding Safe Sex: Gender Narratives of HIV and Pregnancy Prevention by Rural South African School-Going Youth." *Reproductive Health Matters* 9(17), 63–71.

Henderson, Gail, Barbara Entwisle, Li Ying, Yang Mingliang, Xu Siyuan, and Zhai Fengying. (2000). "Re-Drawing the Boundaries of Work: Views on the Meaning of Work (*Gongzuo*)." In *Redrawing Boundaries: Work, Households, and Gender in China*, edited by Barbara Entwisle and Gail E. Henderson. Berkeley: University of California Press.

Hollander, Jocelyn A. (2004). "The Social Context of Focus Groups." *Journal of Contemporary Ethnography* 33(5), 602–637.

Kitzinger, Jenny. (1994). "The Methodology of Focus Groups: the Importance of Interaction Between Research Participants." *Sociology of Health and Illness* 16(1), 103–121.

Kitzinger, Jenny and Clare Farquhar. (1999). "The Analytical Potential of 'Sensitive Moments' in Focus Group Discussions." In *Developing Focus Group Research: Politics, Theory and Practice*, edited by Rosaline S. Barbour and Jenny Kitzinger. London: Sage.

Knodel, John. (1997). "A Case for Nonanthropological Qualitative Methods for Demographers." *Population and Development Review* 23(4), 847–853.

Knodel, J., N. Havanon, and W. Sittitrai. (1990). "Family-size and the Education of Children in the Context of Rapid Fertility Decline." *Population and Development Review* 16(1), 31–62.

Krause, N., L. M. Chatters, T. Meltzer, and D. L. Morgan. (2000). "Using Focus Groups to Explore the Nature of Prayer in Later Life." *Journal of Aging Studies* 14(2), 191–212.

Krueger, Richard A. (1994). *Focus Groups 2nd ed: A Practical Guide for Applied Research*. Thousand Oaks, CA: Sage.

———. (1998). *Analyzing and Reporting Focus Group Results*. Focus Group Kit 6. Thousand Oaks, CA: Sage.

Krueger, Richard A. and Jean A. King. (1998). *Involving Community Members in Focus Groups*. Focus Group Kit 5. Thousand Oaks, CA: Sage.

Manoff, Richard. (1985). *Social Marketing: New Imperative for Public Health*. New York: Praeger.

Merton, Robert K., Marjorie Fiske, and Patricia L. Kendall. (1990). *The Focused Interview: A Manual of Problems and Procedures,* 2d ed. New York: Free Press.

Michell, Lynn. (1999). "Combining Focus Groups and Interviews: Telling How It Is; Telling How It Feels." In *Developing Focus Group Research: Politics, Theory and Practice*, edited by Rosaline S. Barbour and Jenny Kitzinger. London: Sage.

Morgan, David L. (1996). "Focus Groups." *Annual Review of Sociology* 22, 129–152.

———. (1997). *Focus Groups as Qualitative Research*. Thousand Oaks, CA: Sage.

———. (1998a). *Planning Focus Groups*. Focus Group Kit 2. Thousand Oaks, CA: Sage.

———. (1998b). *The Focus Group Guidebook*. Focus Group Kit 1. Thousand Oaks, CA: Sage.

———. (1998c). "Practical Strategies for Combining Qualitative and Quantitative Methods: Applications to Health Research." *Qualitative Health Research* 8(3), 362–376.

Morgan, David L. and Richard A. Krueger. (1998). *The Focus Group Kit*. Volumes 1–6. Thousand Oaks, CA: Sage.

Myers, Greg and Phil Macnaghten. (1999). "Can Focus Groups be Analysed as Talk?" In *Developing Focus Group Research: Politics, Theory and Practice*, edited by Rosaline S. Barbour and Jenny Kitzinger. London: Sage.

Schensul, Jean J., M. D. LeCompte, B. K. Nastasi, and S. P. Borgatti. (1999). *Enhanced Ethnographic Methods: Audiovisual Techniques, Focused Group Interviews, and Elicitation Techniques*. Walnut Creek, CA: AltaMira Press.

Short, Susan E., Feinian Chen, Barbara Entwisle, and Zhai Fengying. (2002). "Maternal Work and Time Spent in Child Care in China: A Multimethod Approach." *Population and Development Review* 28(1), 31–57.

Singleton, Royce A., Jr., and Bruce C. Straits. (2005). *Approaches to Social Research*, 4th ed. New York: Oxford University Press.

Wellings, Kaye, Patrick Branigan, and Kristi Mitchell. (2000). "Discomfort, Discord, and Discontinuity as Data: Using Focus Groups to Research Sensitive Topics." *Culture, Health, and Sexuality* 2(3), 255–267.

Wolff, Kurt H., ed. and trans. (1950). *The Sociology of Georg Simmel*. New York: Free Press.

Bibliography on Focus Groups

Beck, Leif C., W. L. Trombetta, and Scott Share. (1986). "Using Focus Group Sessions Before Decisions Are Made." *North Carolina Medical Journal* 47(2), 73–74.

Entwisle, Barbara, Ronald Rindfuss, David Guilkey, Aphichat Chamratrithirong, Sara Curran, and Yothin Sawangdee. (1996). "Community and Contraceptive Choice in Rural Thailand: A Case Study of Nang Rong." *Demography* 33(1), 1–11.

Frey, James E. and Andrea Fontan. (1991). "The Group Interview in Social Research." *Social Science Journal* 28(2), 175–187.

Greenbaum, Thomas L. (1988). *The Practical Handbook and Guide to Focus Group Research*. Lexington, MA: D. C. Heath.

Knodel, John. (1995). "Focus Groups as a Qualitative Method for Cross-Cultural Research in Social Gerontology." *Journal of Cross-Cultural Gerontology* 10(1), 7–20.

——. (1997). "The Closing of the Gender Gap in Schooling: The Case of Thailand." *Comparative Education* 33(1), 61–86.

Knodel, John, Napaporn Havanon, and Anthony Pramualratana. (1984). "Fertility Transition in Thailand: A Qualitative Analysis." *Population and Development Review* 10(2), 297–328.

Knodel, John, Chanpen Saengtienchai, and Werasit Sittitrai. (1995). "The Living Arrangements of Elderly in Thailand: Views of the Populace." *Journal of Cross-Cultural Gerontology* 10(1), 79–111.

Miles, Matthew and Michael A. Huberman. (1994). *Qualitative Data Analysis*. Thousand Oaks, CA: Sage.

Morgan, David L. (1993). *Successful Focus Groups: Advancing the State of the Art*. Newbury Park, CA: Sage. See especially chapters 2, 3, and 8.

——. (1997). *Focus Groups as Qualitative Research*, 2d ed. Thousand Oaks, CA: Sage.

Morgan, David L. and Richard A. Krueger. (1988). *The Focus Group Kit*. Volumes 1–6. Thousand Oaks, CA: Sage.

Peracca, Sara, John Knodel, and Chanpen Saengtienchai. (1998). "Can Prostitutes Marry? Thai Attitudes Toward Female Sex Workers." *Social Science & Medicine* 41(2), 255–267.

Stewart, David W. and Prem N. Shamdasani. (1990). *Focus Groups: Theory and Practice*. Newbury Park, CA: Sage.

6

Surveys and Secondary Data Sources

Using Survey Data in Social Science Research in Developing Countries

Albert Park

The goal of this chapter is to introduce some of the major issues related to the use of survey data in social science research in developing countries. I will not address all aspects of survey research; nor will my treatment of the issues selected be comprehensive. Rather, my intention is to provide a broad roadmap of important issues to be addressed so that scholars embarking on field research in developing countries can think more systematically about (a) the potential value of quantitative data in research design, (b) how to find and use survey data collected by others, (c) when and how to conduct one's own survey, and (d) how to best utilize survey data in one's analysis. My insights are drawn from my own field research experiences as an economist, primarily in China, and come disproportionately from studies of economic development. Nonetheless, the main points are relevant to social scientists in other fields as well. One of my goals is to provide advice I wish I had been given at an earlier stage in my career, even though I am quite sure that many lessons can be learned only through firsthand experience.

Quantitative Data in Research Design

Ever since Charles Booth (1889) first attempted to measure poverty among the working class in England at the end of the 19th century, there has developed a rich tradition of quantitative data analysis to answer empirical questions in the social sciences. The great advantage of survey data is that they facilitate quantitative analysis that allows for generalization to an entire population. This ability to generalize relies on the very powerful properties of sampling and statistical theory. The epistemological basis of quantitative analysis contrasts quite sharply with that of qualitative research methods, such as ethnography, which rely more on inductive logic and the researcher's ability to synthesize a complex array of multiple sources of information. As a result, the choice of quantitative versus qualitative methods often depends on the research question. Surveys by their very nature are designed to reach a large number of respondents, but they provide only limited information on each unit of observation. They are thus often ill suited for the study of nuanced questions related to identity, subjective experience, or historical causation. But surveys are well suited to studies of political opinions; social attitudes; economic decisions and outcomes; and easily observable social behaviors such as fertility, migration, living arrangements, or visits to the doctor.

For many research questions, there can be great advantage to combining quantitative and qualitative approaches. In fact, these inherent complementarities underlie the value of interdisciplinary research and area studies. Thus, scholars for whom generalization is not a priority should consider the possibility that survey data can be useful to their research. Similarly, those who consider generalization the primary objective of their work should not discount the importance of informing their analysis with less-structured interviews and observations.

How might the use of survey data complement qualitative studies? First, surveys can help frame questions or identify case sites for in-depth study. For example, if a researcher is interested in studying sites in both rich and poor regions, or in regions with both extended families and nuclear families, survey or census data can point to appropriate locations. Often, one will want cases that are reasonably representative of a certain typology or that exhibit multiple characteristics (e.g., industrial and ethnically diverse communities). While informants can steer you in the right direction, quantitative evidence documenting whether a case is representative may be more convincing to many audiences. Depending on the number of cases, it might be appropriate to use quantitative data as the basis for randomized selection of cases to be studied in greater depth.

Survey data can also complement qualitative work by providing context for or confirming the findings of qualitative work. For example, if interviews reveal that rural women complain about greater work burdens on the farm when husbands move to urban areas for temporary work, it could be useful to elaborate that finding with data from a quantitative study of the extent of migration in the region or changes in female participation in agricultural work in migrant and nonmigrant households. Such data may be available in household surveys.

Quantitative data analysis is becoming increasingly accessible to social scientists across the disciplines as more and better data sets become available, as advances in computing speed and user-friendly software make it possible to learn how to analyze survey data with reasonable time investments, and as methods of analysis become increasingly powerful.

Census and Survey Data

A census is a complete enumeration of a population. It can be considered a particular type of sample survey in which the sampling rate is 100%! Many national governments carry out a population census once every 10 years. This is an enormously expensive undertaking, but it provides valuable if limited information on the entire population. The very large scale of a census, and for that matter any large-scale survey, inevitably leads to problems of data quality. Certain populations, such as the illiterate or those who move frequently, may be difficult to enumerate, and the training of a large number of field staff may be difficult to regulate properly. Because they are undertaken infrequently, population censuses quickly become out of date for policy-making purposes. Of course, it is possible to conduct censuses on a smaller scale, for example by surveying all households in a village or all traders in a marketplace. However, for many research questions, social surveys that use probability sampling can provide a much more economical way to collect data since survey data enable one to make inferences from a small sample to a larger population.

Surveys may be conducted for a variety of reasons and by different types of individuals and organizations. Governments often carry out regular monitoring surveys to track outcomes of policy interest. For example, labor force surveys track changes in unemployment and other labor outcomes; income and expenditure surveys track changes in living standards, poverty, and inequality; and enterprise surveys monitor changes in investment and production. Government offices also keep administrative records of all types, usually based on reports made by lower-level government offices or other reporting units (e.g., tax payments, educational enrollment in schools, number of doctors and beds in hospitals). Such records can be a valuable resource for quantitative data analysis or for use as sampling frames for social surveys. However, both sampling error (a sample that is nonrepresentative of the population) and nonsampling error (reporting bias) may be major issues in interpreting administrative data.

In recent years, a large number of high-quality surveys have been conducted in developing countries throughout the world, and many of these data sources have become publicly available, often through the Internet. In fact, the first national general social survey in the world was established in a developing country in 1950—the Indian National Sample Survey. This fact should help allay concern that surveys cannot be conducted reliably in developing-country settings. The "Secondary Data Sources" section of the Bibliography following this chapter provides information on some useful places to begin searching for publicly available survey data from developing countries. The Inter-university Consortium for Political and Social Research, founded in 1962, has a large archive of well-documented, publicly available data sets from more than 130 countries. In 1980, the World Bank established the Living Standards Measurement Study (LSMS) to explore ways of improving the type and quality of household data collected by government statistical offices in developing countries. LSMS surveys have been conducted in 30 developing countries, and the data are publicly available on a website managed by the Bank's Development Research Group. Demographic and health survey data are available for 68 developing countries. These surveys build on a long history of active social surveys in the demography field (knowledge, attitudes, and practices, or KAP, surveys of fertility in the 1960s; the World Fertility Survey and Contraceptive Prevalence Surveys in the 1970s and 1980s). The Roper Center for Public Opinion Research maintains a data archive of opinion research in more than 30 countries. Finally, research institutes such as the International Food Policy Research Institute and RAND have directed surveys in many developing countries. The U.S. government, through the National Science Foundation and the National Institutes of Health (NIH), has also supported surveys in developing countries. The National Institute of Child Health and Human Development, an institute under NIH, maintains a website providing access to surveys it has supported in eight developing countries.

Increasingly, surveys are conducted explicitly for research purposes. For example, two longitudinal household surveys that have been very influential in development economics are the International Crop Research Institute for the Semi-Arid Tropics data set in India and the Indonesia Family Life Survey. Both have been the source of numerous research articles in the development literature. For low-budget surveys often conducted by academics, especially doctoral students, the feasible sample size may be much more limited. However, this limitation can be offset in many cases by the ability of the researcher to include original survey questions that address new and interesting questions. Many influential research papers across social science disciplines have been published using data sets with several hundred observations or fewer.

Using Survey Data Collected by Others ✳

If one is interested in examining survey data for a specific country, one should actively search for existing data sources on the Internet and at national and local government offices, libraries and archives, research institutes and universities, or even enterprises or other community organizations. The discovery of such information can alter one's research design. But be prepared to abide by stipulations governing data use or to be asked to pay for the data.

If one finds that an existing data set may be valuable, it is helpful to ask questions about the data to assess its quality, possible biases, and appropriateness for one's research question. First, who collected the data and for what purpose? Sometimes, the announced goal of a survey can influence the type of responses elicited. For example, businesses are likely to underreport revenue and profits to the tax authority. An evaluation survey of a project conducted by the implementing organization could be biased toward producing a positive assessment. Second, what sampling method was employed? Third, what was the response rate? Fourth, how are key questions worded or key variables defined? If the definitions are vague or nonstandard, or if the measurement is prone to error, one might think twice about relying on such data. Fifth, how was the survey conducted? Who developed the questionnaires, and how? Are the survey procedures well documented? How did training and supervision take place? Is there a substantial amount of missing data? Finally, who else has used the data? One can learn a great deal about the data by talking to other people who have used it.

If one decides to use survey data collected by others as a main part of one's research, it makes sense to invest in learning more about the data. It can be extremely informative to visit some of the surveyed areas and ask questions about topics that will be the focus of your study. This step can provide insights into local institutions, cultural practices, and social behaviors that may affect how you interpret the data. It is also a good idea to talk with researchers, government officials, or enumerators (the people who actually interviewed the respondents) involved in the survey. Ask them about their views of the strengths and weaknesses of the data. Sometimes you may learn that there were difficulties with the survey in some sites but not in others or difficulties with some sections of the questionnaire but not others. This is the type of information that one learns as a matter of course in running one's own survey but that can be obtained only through inquiry—and even then only to some extent—when using data collected by others.

Sometimes, extant data do not exist, or the questions you are trying to answer have not been asked in a survey. At this point, it may be important to consider conducting your own survey. In the next section, I briefly discuss various factors to consider when conducting a survey of your own design.

Conducting Surveys in Developing Countries

Should You Conduct Your Own Survey?

Conducting one's own survey in a developing country can be a major undertaking, and the costs of such a project in terms of both time and money should not be underestimated. The decision to conduct a survey is a decision to become not just a scholar but also a project manager, a fundraiser, a survey methodologist, and a motivator and supervisor of others. On the other hand, because one's own survey can be tailored to specific research questions and yield data never before analyzed by others, it carries high potential to yield truly new insights. There probably is no better way to develop reliable intuition about what issues are empirically (not just theoretically!) meaningful than to spend extensive time in the field conducting one's own survey. The experience of conducting a survey also provides insights that help one better evaluate the quality of empirical research conducted by others. Working with local colleagues on surveys strengthens collaborative relationships that can form the basis of future work. From this perspective, conducting a survey can yield long-term benefits to one's research that go far beyond the actual data collected. For good overall reviews of issues related to fieldwork in developing countries, see Bulmer and Warwick (1993) and Devereux and Hoddinott (1992).

Collaboration

Nearly all successful surveys in developing countries depend on the support of energetic, capable research collaborators from the host country who know how to get things done within the country's institutional, political, and social environment; are skilled at interacting with government officials and community leaders; have developed reputations within the country that build trust; and have valuable substantive insights into the research questions. On the flip side, collaborators pursuing agendas at cross-purposes with those of the researcher can easily frustrate research plans.

In some cases, researchers, and especially junior researchers, have limited ability to control either the organization or the individuals with whom they must deal. In such cases, it becomes critical to cultivate a positive working relationship. Part of this involves making sure that the collaborators perceive benefits to making the collaboration a success. The benefit bestowed can be intellectual—get them excited about the important contribution of the research; offer a course or lead a reading group on current research questions or methods; encourage collaborative research products; or help the collaborators realize their own intellectual goals (for example, through a visit to your institution). It can also be material—always provide adequate compensation for services, be as generous as possible to the host institution in the project budget. Finally, it might be personal—take the time to develop personal relationships, be helpful and friendly. In many cases, collaborators will be generous with their time and support, and it is important to reciprocate by sharing one's research results and giving back in other ways, especially by building research capacity in the host institution. However, if for any reason you lose trust in those with whom you are working, be proactive in changing your collaborators even if the change is awkward or costly.

Combining Surveys With Natural Experiments and Randomized Interventions

Recently, there has been growing interest in combining social surveys with natural experiments or randomized interventions to enable more convincing causal inference. Natural experiments are unusual circumstances with a random element that facilitates comparisons. For example, a new national policy such as universal health care or a major infrastructure investment program might facilitate a comparison between individual behavior before and after the introduction of the program. Or a lottery to determine whether one is drafted, wins money, or can send children to a new charter school can be used to compare treatment and control groups that have similar characteristics. Randomized interventions can also be incorporated directly into research designs (Duflo & Kremer forthcoming). Early studies of randomized health insurance policies (Manning et al. 1987) and randomized worker training programs (see LaLonde 1986 for a review) remain extremely influential. Recent examples in developing countries include the provision of education tuition subsidies for primary students in Mexico (Schultz 2004), the provision of school supplies such as flip charts and textbooks in rural Kenya (Kremer 2003), and the provision of iron supplementation to adults in Indonesia (Thomas et al. 2003). These projects are often partnerships between researchers and governments or nongovernmental organizations. Randomized interventions bring their own challenges. Members of control and treatment groups may react to the intervention in ways that are confounding (for example, individuals move from areas without interventions to areas with interventions), or the intervention may have spillover effects on the control group (for example, recipients of development project loans could have more funds to lend informally to nonrecipients).

Combining Surveys With Existing Surveys or Data Sets

If conducting one's own survey seems daunting or impractical, another model is to design a supplemental survey that can be combined with information from a survey that has already been completed or is ongoing. Whether this is a realistic option depends on whether one can find appropriate partner surveys and whether the project managers for those surveys are cooperative.

Joining forces often offers advantages to both sides. The most obvious is that with cost sharing, the sample size can be increased. Also, the researcher can benefit from the institutional capacity that has already been developed for the preexisting survey, while the manager of the partner survey may gain from the energy and expertise of the researcher. The disadvantage to the researcher is lost control over many key aspects of the survey, including timing, coverage, and content.

Because surveys are such major undertakings, it is wise to fully explore the possibility of collaborating with others. Even government monitoring surveys are fair game because many government organizations are keen to earn extra revenues or may be interested in your research topic and so might consider allowing you to add supplemental questions to a subsample of their survey. If a local research organization has already completed a survey with questions you find interesting, you might work with researchers at that organization to resurvey the same sample. The advantages of resurveys are the saved costs from using data that have already been collected and the possibility of collecting longitudinal data, which follow respondents over time. One disadvantage may be difficulty locating all the earlier respondents, leading to nonrepresentativeness caused by nonrandom attrition of the sample over time.

Keep in mind that collaboration is sure to involve many compromises. To ensure that such compromises are likely to be acceptable to both sides, each side should communicate its priorities and expectations clearly, especially regarding key survey-related issues such as sampling and monitoring.

Researchers should be attentive to the critical importance of being able to verify the quality of the survey (i.e., sampling, training, data collection, and monitoring). Agreements should be put in writing.

Sampling

Sampling is one of the most critical aspects of any survey because it forms the basis for the key claim of generalizability, which is the main strength of quantitative research. Sampling designs can be very complicated, depending on the goal of the research (Kish 1965 is a classic reference). For example, researchers can stratify the sample to ensure sufficient variation in an independent variable of interest (e.g., first divide the population into income groups and then sample randomly within each group). Members of specific groups of interest (e.g., the poor) may be oversampled, or sampling may be based on an outcome of interest (e.g., participants and nonparticipants in a program). The choice of sampling design often balances research goals and the costs of conducting the survey.

At the heart of sampling is the pursuit of representativeness through random selection. However, intuitions about sampling can be tricky. For example, one might randomly and with equal probability pick a set of villages in an area and then randomly sample a fixed number of households in each village. But if poor villages are systematically smaller in population than nonpoor villages, such a sampling scheme will overrepresent the poor. There are three possible solutions to this problem: (a) make sure the probability that a village is chosen is proportional to its population, and sample a fixed number of households per village; (b) sample a fixed proportion rather than an absolute number of households in villages selected with equal probability; or (c) use the above approach and record the population of sampled villages to create sampling weights that could be used to correct the bias when using statistical methods later.

The first step in sampling is to clearly define the population of interest, such as rural households in the country or region or those 60 years of age and older who live in a household with children. The next step is to develop a sampling frame, or a list of possible respondents. First, one should seek out appropriate census data or administrative records (e.g., village household registers). Be aware that outdated lists will underrepresent newly formed households or individuals. In many cases, unfortunately, preexisting lists are unavailable or require updating. In China, for example, rural migrants living in cities are notoriously difficult to study because they have left the countryside, are highly mobile, and often do not bother registering with local community offices in cities. In such cases, one must expend resources to create a sampling frame from scratch; that is, send enumerators to all households in the neighborhood or settle for a population slightly different from that of theoretical interest, such as registered migrants rather than all migrants.

A common approach to sampling is to first divide the population into geographical sampling units, such as villages. In a first stage, sample villages are selected based on existing village-level information about population, income, and so on. An individual sampling frame is then constructed only in the sampled villages. Statistics using data from multilevel, or clustered, sampling must adjust for the likely correlation in characteristics of observations drawn from the same cluster. Some surveys have also adopted spatial sampling approaches, often with the assistance of aerial or satellite maps. The unit of observation becomes a dwelling, and enumerators visit dwellings and interview whomever they find there. An application of this method using GPS technology in urban China, where unregistered migrant workers are numerous, is described in Landry and Shen (2005). GPS technology is also making it possible to collect, at reasonable costs, geographic data such as location, elevation, land size, and so on, as part of household village surveys.

Armed with a sampling frame, one can randomly select respondents to be surveyed. However, there is no guarantee that all the selected individuals can be found and will participate in the survey. Nonresponse can lead to an unrepresentative sample. Appropriate timing of visits can help increase the response rate (e.g., visit during evening hours if individuals work during the day, or visit on holidays, when household members are normally at home). Introductions by village or neighborhood leaders can help reduce refusal rates. A protocol should be developed to deal with nonresponse. Enumerators should be required to visit a respondent on several different days before giving up. If the respondent is replaced, the replacement should be randomly selected from a backup list sampled at the same time as the original sample. If the sampling frame provides information on the characteristics of the individual or household, one can choose replacements that resemble the original household, although this approach does not eliminate the possibility of bias.

Researchers must consider trade-offs among sampling error, nonsampling error, and cost in making decisions in the field regarding sample selection. For example, very remote villages may be inaccessible by vehicles, thereby substantially increasing survey costs. Similarly, some individuals may be illiterate and unable to answer the questions in the survey reliably or in a reasonable period of time.

Another important aspect of sampling is the choice of an appropriate sample size. Statistically, a larger sample makes it possible to measure the relationships between variables with greater precision. More formally, the outcome of statistical inference has four components: sample size; effect size;

significance level (required statistical confidence level, usually set at 95%); and power, or the odds that one will observe a treatment effect if it occurs. The minimum sample size necessary for precise estimation depends on the strength of the empirical relationship, which sometimes can be roughly approximated *ex ante* by making use of results from other studies. A useful reference for evaluating the power of statistical tests given a chosen sample size is Cohen (1988). In my experience, sample sizes of fewer than 200 observations often make it challenging to employ appropriate empirical methods or to produce results that are statistically significant.

Questionnaire Design

Clearly defining the research question is the first step in designing an effective questionnaire. One common mistake made by researchers interested in a specific issue area is to ask an exhaustive set of questions about everything that is important, unusual, or interesting about the issue without having a clear research question or methodology in mind. The result often is a long and unwieldy questionnaire that still omits critical information. Survey methodologists have shown that the quality of information that survey respondents provide declines significantly after more than 30 minutes, and the length of the questionnaire also dictates the amount of time enumerators must spend on each interview. Thus, there are costs in terms of both data quality and money if survey questionnaires are too long. Interesting but inessential questions should be eliminated.

In designing questionnaires, do not try to reinvent the wheel. Many smart people have spent a lot of time refining questions to study different topics, taking many factors into consideration. You should spend time finding out what other surveys have been conducted on the same or related issues, both in your country of interest and elsewhere. Ask for copies of questionnaires; most researchers or government officials are happy to provide copies of blank questionnaires. There are advantages in making questions comparable to surveys done elsewhere or to official statistical conventions used in the country; doing so can facilitate comparisons that will allow you to better contextualize or generalize your results. A particularly valuable resource for designing questionnaires for household surveys in developing countries is the edited volume by Grosh and Glewwe (2000), in which experienced experts summarize the current state of the art in questionnaire design for various topics (e.g., income and expenditure, agricultural production, self-employment, rural credit, education, health, etc.).

It goes without saying that questions included in survey instruments should be worded in culturally appropriate language. Active participation by local collaborators, informants, and study subjects is invaluable. Questions should be simple, direct, and familiar to respondents. Each question should be stated in a neutral, not a leading, manner and whenever possible should be written out completely to avoid misinterpretation. Because it is difficult to know what circumstances respondents will attribute to a hypothesized situation, hypothetical questions should be resisted. Two common criteria used to evaluate a question are reliability (whether the question produces a consistent response) and validity (whether the question is actually measuring what it was intended to measure). The former can be tested through pretesting, and one check of the latter is to translate and retranslate the questions. It takes a surprisingly long period of time and quite a few iterations to design an effective questionnaire. Some references that discuss more specific aspects of questionnaire design include Fowler (1995); Warwick and Lininger (1975); and Brislin, Lonner, and Thorndike (1973).

One common pitfall in questionnaire design is inadequate budgeting of time and resources for presurvey work, which often starts with open-ended interviews and ends in pretests of survey instruments to be used in the main survey. Often, time and resources to complete the project are limited, and researchers want to save resources to maximize the amount of data they can obtain from the main survey. However, the quality of the data is no better than the questionnaire, and many serious problems can arise if you do not do adequate pretesting in multiple survey sites. Seemingly straightforward questions may be interpreted by respondents in ways the researcher did not intend or predict.

Fielding a Survey and Managing the Data

Enumerators are the individuals responsible for interviewing respondents and so play a critical role in determining the quality of survey data. They can be university students (undergraduates or graduate students), research institute staff, or professional survey staff (e.g., those who work for a government statistical agency or other established survey organization). An advantage of using students is that they are usually bright, energetic, willing to follow the directions of supervisors, and relatively cheap to hire. The disadvantage is that they lack survey experience, are less socially mature, and may lose interest if the work is unusually difficult or tiring. The advantage of professional staff is that they are experienced, understand local circumstances and so are less likely to misinterpret questions, and have well-established relationships in local communities. The disadvantage is that they may be inflexible about their work procedures and motivated primarily by financial gain.

Training of enumerators should include basic interview techniques (e.g., polite, respectful behavior and attitude; how to avoid asking questions in a leading way); explanation of the goals of the research; and discussion of survey protocols, the meaning and purpose of each survey question, and protocols to follow when respondents do not understand questions or refuse to answer. A good training program should provide written materials that summarize key points and are easy to read (to serve as a reference for enumerators), include extensive practice interviews, and require that enumerators demonstrate competence through a formal evaluation exercise. Videotapes of positive and negative examples of enumerator behavior can serve as an effective teaching tool. When the survey starts, less experienced enumerators and experienced enumerators should visit households together for the first several interviews.

It is critical that the work of enumerators be monitored systematically. In surveys that I have directed, supervisors review completed questionnaires each evening and discuss problems with enumerators before the next day's work. After several days, the frequency of mistakes declines substantially. One can also ask enumerators to check each other's questionnaires. A written set of standard internal consistency checks (e.g., components add up to their sum, labor activities match up with reported income sources) should be provided to enumerators and be the basis of supervision checks. If the survey is occurring in several places at once, frequent communication during the earlier stages of the survey can ensure that issues that arise in the field can be addressed in a consistent manner.

It is important to revisit a subset of respondents to verify that enumerators actually interviewed respondents. If households have phones, such checks can be done by telephone. Usually, asking just a few questions from different parts of the survey instrument is sufficient to complete a check. Enumerators should be required to revisit any households with substantial discrepancies, and if one enumerator has multiple problem surveys, the enumerator should be fired, and all the households visited by that enumerator should be revisited by another person. Ideally, some monitoring should be done by individuals from an organization different from that of the enumerators. Both enumerators and their supervisors should be given incentives in the form of praise, bonuses, or prizes.

Once survey questionnaires have been completed, a number of decisions must be made about data entry and cleaning. Because entering data into computers is labor intensive, it is often cost effective to enter the data while in the host country. One can usually find staff of research institutes, university students, or private companies to do the work. The price should always be based on work completed (number of forms) rather than time spent. The contract should include financial incentives for fast completion, be based on quality standards evaluated by a method agreed on in advance, and stipulate final payment only after all the work has been completed.

If the questionnaire is short and relatively straightforward, spreadsheet software such as Excel can be used for data entry. However, in general, one will want to use a database program for which entry screens can be designed to look exactly like the questionnaires themselves (e.g., Access, dBase). The software should make it possible to enter range restrictions, such as not allowing months to be greater than 12, and internal consistency checks, such as requiring that children's ages be less than parents' ages or that total expenditures equal the sum of the components of expenditure. It takes some investment of time to learn the software and create the database structure and entry screens, so it may be a good idea to budget resources for an experienced programmer, if necessary. In developing countries, computers may have limited capacity, and recent versions of software requiring large memory may run slowly or not at all. I have had great success using an old version of a simple software program based on a disk operating system. The software provides essential functions but can run easily on even primitive computers.

If possible, data entry should occur in a fixed location with a supervisor familiar with the questionnaire always present to troubleshoot questions, such as how to deal with specific coding problems or use the software. Special codes should be used for different types of missing data (e.g., the respondent did not know the answer, the respondent refused to answer, the question was not applicable) since these distinctions can affect interpretation of results. If possible, data from each form should be entered twice, preferably by different individuals, and the two entries should be compared (this usually requires some programming). If double data entry is too costly, one must at least design an entry-checking protocol for manually checking the entered data against the questionnaires. Hard copies of questionnaires should be archived for future reference.

Some surveys now enter the data in the field, by means of notebook computers, so that problems can be discovered almost immediately and enumerators can make return visits to households without delay. While this practice can reduce the cost of revisits and improve data quality, it requires greater advance preparation and can increase costs because of greater hardware requirements and the need to support living expenses of data entry staff in the field. A usually prohibitively costly option is to equip enumerators themselves with notebook computers and bypass paper questionnaires altogether.

Analyzing Survey Data

Advances in statistical software, both in user friendliness and in the capacity to conduct various types of statistical analysis, make it increasingly easy to analyze empirical data with just a modest investment in learning new software. Among empirical economists and many other social scientists, Stata has become by far the most popular software for data management and statistical analysis, while SPSS (originally known as Statistical Package for the Social Sciences) remains a popular choice among sociologists and political scientists. These software packages now include excellent tutorials that make it relatively easy to summarize data (i.e., calculate sample and sub-sample means), produce tables and figures, and run regressions.

A good introduction to recent empirical methodologies for analyzing household surveys in developing countries is Deaton (1997). Another useful reference is Sadoulet and de Janvry (1995). Space constraints preclude a detailed discussion of the statistical analysis of survey data, but I will point out a few useful but frequently overlooked analytical tools that are easily implemented in many software packages:

- In reporting differences in the mean values of variables for two different groups, it is usually a good idea to test whether the reported differences are statistically significantly different from zero.
- The sampling design of the survey may require that sampling weights be used in statistical calculations. Multistage clustered sampling designs usually require that standard deviations and standard errors of regression coefficient estimates be adjusted for likely within-cluster correlations (Deaton 1997).
- Recently popularized nonparametric methods can produce revealing visual pictures of the distribution of a variable or the bivariate relationship between two variables that allow the slope relationship to vary over different parts of the distribution (Deaton 1997; Pagan & Ullah 1999).
- One common problem is estimating how x affects y even though y may also affect x, or some third factor may affect both x and y. Panel data (multiple respondents observed over multiple periods) can facilitate over-time comparisons that control for bias from many omitted variables (Hsiao 1986; Wooldridge 2002). If such data are combined with a natural experiment or a randomized intervention, one can compare the change that occurs in the treatment group with the change that occurs in the control group, the so-called difference-in-difference estimator (Wooldridge 2002). Another common statistical approach to identifying the effect of x on y is to use instrumental variables, which are variables that strongly affect x but do not affect y independently of x (for a clear explanation of this method, see Wooldridge 1999).

Final Thoughts on Research Involving Survey Data

Defining a research question is an iterative process. It often starts with a researcher's initial interest in a topic, stimulated by personal experience; the interest and encouragement of an adviser, mentor, or colleague; close reading of the existing literature in a particular discipline; or knowledge of an issue or circumstance in a specific region of the world. One useful question to ask one-self in choosing among potential research questions to be studied in a specific country or region is, "Why is this question of particular interest in this country or region?" This helps avoid a common mistake of mechanically deciding to address a currently popular question in the country of one's area expertise.

Once a question is chosen, the process of field research almost invariably alters the way in which the question is framed or posed, as well as the research design. All social scientists who have engaged in extensive field research in developing countries have a story to tell about how the substantive focus of a research project changed dramatically after they spent time in the field. Iteration frequently occurs when field research presents new insights into the question or reveals new opportunities for collecting information (e.g., the unexpected discovery of an archive; a useful informant or contact; a natural experiment; or an interesting social behavior, policy, or outcome). This circumstance may cause a rethinking of the research question itself or of the strategy for studying the question.

Many unexpected things can occur during field research, such as delays due to political events, natural disasters, institutional factors, and so on. The demands placed on you may change (e.g., demands for more money, restrictions on research activity), or you may find that your interests shift or your original idea proves infeasible. It is a good idea to think about contingency plans for accomplishing your research goals well ahead of time, just in case things do not go as planned.

In the old days, when costly transport and communications isolated the researcher in the field for months at a time, many of these judgments had to be made alone. In the new world of cheaper air flights, long-distance calling cards, and the Internet, it is possible for researchers to iterate between field research and academic reflection and consultation while residing at their home institution or in the field. Such an approach is strongly recommended because it is easy for researchers to lose perspective when fully immersed in field research. Udry (2003) argues that surveys themselves can be designed to incorporate iterative learning and that such a design, while costly in time, can allow survey researchers to be more creative and more responsive to surprises.

The goal of this chapter has been to provide a general introduction to the use of survey and census data in social science research in developing countries. I have argued that the collection or use of such data can be a useful component of many field research plans and research designs, whether one plans to rely primarily on quantitative or qualitative methods. The increasing availability of data sets and the rapid advances in the ability of computing software to manage and analyze data make it more feasible than ever before to use survey and census data in one's research.

However, conducting surveys in developing countries can be challenging, and numerous factors at every stage of the survey process, from sampling to questionnaire design to data entry, can affect the quality of the data and so the quality of the research. Much of this chapter has been spent pointing out potential pitfalls in the collection of one's own data and issuing warnings about quality issues in survey data produced by others. I hope that social scientists across the disciplines will feel confident in using survey data in their research and will find such data a valuable component of their research methodology.

Supplemental References

Booth, Charles. (1889). *Labour and Life of the People.* London, UK: Macmillan.

Brislin, Richard, Walter J. Lonner, and Robert M. Thorndike. (1973). *Cross-Cultural Research Methods.* New York: John Wiley.

Duflo, Esther and Michael Kremer. (Forthcoming). "Use of Randomization in the Evaluation of Development Effectiveness." In *Proceedings of the Conference on Evaluating Development Effectiveness, July 15–16, 2003.* Washington, DC: World Bank Operations Evaluation Department.

Kremer, Michael. (2003). "Randomized Evaluations of Educational Programs in Developing Countries: Some Lessons." *American Economic Review* 93(2), 102–106.

LaLonde, Robert. (1986). "Evaluating the Econometric Evaluations of Training Programs with Experimental Data." *American Economic Review* 76(4), 604–620.

Manning, Willard, Joseph Newhouse, Naihua Duan, Emmett B. Keeler, and Arleen Leibowitz. (1987). "Health Insurance and the Demand for Medical Care: Evidence From Randomized Experiment." *American Economic Review* 77(3), 251–277.

Schultz, T. Paul. (2004). "School Subsidies for the Poor: Evaluating the Mexican Progresa Poverty Program." *Journal of Development Economics* 74(1), 199–250.

Thomas, Duncan, Elizabeth Frankenberg, Jed Friedman, Jean-Pierre Habicht, Mohammed Hakimi, Jaswadi, Nathan Jones, Gretel Pelto, Bondan Sikoki,

Teresa Seeman, James P. Smith, Cecep Sumantri, Wayan Suriastini, and Siswanto Wilopo. (2003). "Iron Deficiency and the Well-Being of Older Adults: Early Results From a Randomized Nutrition Intervention." Unpublished paper. Retrieved November 2, 2005, from http://72.14.207.104/search?q=cache: w4Gd_5ly1FUJ:emlab.berkeley.edu/users/webfac/emiguel/e271_s04/friedman. pdf+Iron+Deficiency+and+the+Well-Being+of+Older+ Adults:+ Early+Results+ From+a+ Randomized+ Nutrition+Intervention&hl=en

Udry, Christopher. (2003). "Fieldwork, Economic Theory and Research on Institutions in Developing Countries." *American Economic Review* 93(2), 107–111.

Bibliography: Surveys and Secondary Data Sources

1. Overview and Essentials

Alreck, Pamela and Robert Settle. (1995). *The Survey Research Handbook: Guidelines and Strategies for Conducting a Survey*. Chicago, IL: Irwin Press.

Babbie, Earl. (1990). *Survey Research Methods*. Belmont, CA: Wadsworth.

Bulmer, Martin and Donald Warwick. (1993). *Social Research in Developing Countries: Surveys and Censuses in the Third World*. London, UK: University College London Press Limited.

Caldwell, John C. (1985). "Strengths and Limitations of the Survey Approach for Measuring and Understanding Fertility Change." In *Reproductive Change in Developing Countries*, edited by John Cleland and John Hobcraft. Oxford, UK: Oxford University Press.

Devereux, Stephen and John Hoddinott, eds. (1992). *Fieldwork in Developing Countries*. New York: Harvester Wheatsheaf.

Fink, Arlene. (1993). *Evaluation Fundamentals: Guiding Health Programs, Research and Policy*. Newbury Park, CA: Sage.

———, ed. (1995). *The Survey Kit Series*. Thousand Oaks, CA: Sage.

Freedman, Ronald. (1987). "The Contribution of Social Science Research to Population Policy and Family Planning Program Effectiveness." *Studies in Family Planning* 18(2), 57–82.

Grosh, Margaret and Paul Glewwe. (2000). *Designing Household Survey Questionnaires for Developing Countries: Lessons From 15 Years of the Living Standards Measurement Study*, 3 vols. Washington DC: World Bank.

Hess, Jennifer, Jennifer Rothgeb, and Andy Zukerberg. (1998). "Developing the Survey of Program Dynamics Survey Instruments." Statistical Research Division Working Papers in Survey Methodology, no. SM98/07, U.S. Bureau of the census. Retrieved September 8, 2005, from www.census.gov/srd/www/byyear.html

Hess, Jennifer and Eleanor Singer. (1995). "The Role of Respondent Debriefing Questions in Questionnaire Development." Statistical Research Division Working Papers in Survey Methodology, no. SM95/18, U.S. Bureau of the Census. Retrieved September 8, 2005, from www.census.gov/srd/www/byyear.html

Michigan Program in Research Methodology, Institute for Social Research at the University of Michigan, accessed September 8, 2005, at www.isr.umich.edu/gradprogram/

Oksenberg, Lois, Charles Cannell, and Graham Kalton. (1991). "Strategies for Pretesting New Questions." *Journal of Official Statistics* 7(3), 349–365.

Rea, Louis M. and Richard A. Parker. (1997). *Designing and Conducting Survey Research: A Comprehensive Guide.* San Francisco, CA: Jossey-Bass. See Chapter 1 ("An Overview of the Sample Survey Process"), Chapter 2, Chapter 3, Chapter 4 ("Administering the Questionnaire," in particular, sections on "Precoding the Survey Instrument" and "Editing the Completed Questionnaire"), Chapter 5, Chapter 6, Chapter 7, and Chapter 8.

Rossi, Peter, James D. Wright, and Andy B. Anderson. (1983). *Handbook of Survey Research.* Orlando, FL: Academic Press.

Schutt, Russell L. (1998). *Investigating the Social World.* Thousand Oaks, CA: Pine Forge.

Sudman, Seymour and Norman M. Bradburn. (1982). *Asking Questions: A Practical Guide to Questionnaire Design.* San Francisco, CA: Jossey-Bass. See Chapter 2, "Asking Non-Threatening Questions About Behavior"; Chapter 3, "Asking Threatening Questions About Behavior"; Chapter 4, "Questions for Measuring Knowledge"; Chapter 5, "Measuring Attitudes: Formulating Questions"; Chapter 6, "Measuring Attitudes: Recording Responses"; Chapter 7, "Using Standard Demographic Terms" (skim); Chapter 8, "Order of the Questionnaire"; Chapter 9, "Format of the Questionnaire"; and Chapter 10, "Designing Questions for Mail and Telephone Surveys."

Warwick, Donald P. and Charles A. Lininger. (1975). *The Sample Survey: Theory and Practice.* New York: McGraw-Hill.

Weisberg, Herbert and Bruce D. Bowen. (1977). *An Introduction to Survey Research and Data Analysis.* San Francisco, CA: W. H. Freeman.

2. Planning, Proposing, and Sampling for Survey Data

Cohen, Jacob. (1988). *Statistical Power Analysis for the Behavioral Sciences.* Hillsdale, NJ: L. Erlbaum Associates.

Grosh, Margaret and Paul Glewwe. (2000). *Designing Household Survey Questionnaires for Developing Countries: Lessons From 15 Years of the Living Standards Measurement Study,* 3 vols. Washington DC: World Bank. See associated website: www.worldbank.org/lsms/index.htm

Kish, Leslie. (1965). *Survey Sampling.* New York: John Wiley.

Krathwohl, David. (1988). *How to Prepare a Research Proposal: Guidelines for Funding and Dissertations in the Social and Behavioral Sciences.* Syracuse, NY: Syracuse University Press. See Chapter 8, "A Checklist for Critiquing Proposals."

Landry, Pierre and Mingming Shen. (2005). "Reaching Migrants in Survey Research: The Use of the Global Positioning System to Reduce Coverage Bias in China." *Political Analysis* 13(1).

Ross, Kenneth N. (1992). "Sample Design Procedures for a National Survey of Primary Schools in Zimbabwe." In *Issues and Methodologies in Educational Development no. 8*. Paris, France: International Institute for Educational Planning, UNESCO.

Singleton, Royce A., Bruce C. Straits, and Margaret Miller Straits. (1993). *Approaches to Social Research*. New York: Oxford University Press. See Chapter 6, "Sampling."

3. Qualitative Inquiry in and Beyond the Design Process

Bunte, Pamela A., Rebecca M. Joseph, and Peter Wobus. (1992). "The Cambodian Community of Long Beach: An Ethnographic Analysis of Factors Leading to Census Undercount." United Cambodian Community, Inc., and Center for Survey Methods Research, Bureau of the Census. Ethnographic Evaluation of the 1990 Decennial Census Report no. 9. (EV92/09). Retrieved September 9, 2005, from www.census.gov/srd/www/byyear.html

de Vaus, David A. (1996). *Surveys in Social Research*. London, UK: University College London Press. See Chapter 1, "The Nature of Surveys"; Chapter 2, "Theory and Social Research"; Chapter 3, "Formulating and Clarifying Research Questions"; and Chapter 4, "Developing Indicators for Concepts."

Fuller, Theodore, John Edwards, Sairudee Vorakitphokatorn, and Santhat Sermsri. (1993). "Using Focus Groups to Adapt Survey Instruments to New Populations: Evidence From a Developing Country." In *Successful Focus Groups*, edited by David L. Morgan. Newbury Park, CA: Sage.

Massey, Douglas. (1987). "The Ethnosurvey in Theory and Practice." *International Migration Review* 21(4), 1498–1521.

Newby, Margaret, Sajeda Amin, Ian Diamond, and Ruchira T. Naved. (1998). "Survey Experience Among Women in Bangladesh." *American Behavioral Scientist* 42(2), 252–275.

Rynearson, Ann M., Thomas A. Gosebrink, and Leslie A. Brownrigg (with Barrie M. Gewanter). (1990). "Barriers to Censusing Southeast Asian Refugees." Bureau of the Census Ethnographic Exploratory Report no.10 (no. EX90/10). Retrieved September 9, 2005, from www.census.gov/srd/www/byyear.html

Trochim, William M. (1999a). "Sampling." In *The Research Methods Knowledge Base*, 2d ed. Cincinnati, OH: Atomic Dog Publishing.

———. (1999b). "Language of Research." In *The Research Methods Knowledge Base*, 2d ed. Cincinnati, OH: Atomic Dog Publishing.

4. Developing Good Questions: Fundamental Concepts

Converse, Jean and Stanley Presser. (1986). *Survey Questions: Handcrafting the Standardized Questionnaire*, Series No. 07–063. Beverly Hills: Sage.

Fowler, Floyd. (1995). *Improving Survey Questions: Design and Evaluation*. Thousand Oaks, CA: Sage.

Freedman, Deborah, Arland Thornton, Donald Cambum, Duane Aiwin, and Linda Young-DeMarco. (1988). "The Life History Calendar: A Technique for Collecting Retrospective Data." *Sociological Methodology* 18, 37–68.

Kalton, Graham. (1983). "Introduction to Survey Sampling." *Sage University Paper Series on Quantitative Applications in the Social Sciences, Series No. 07–035.* Beverly Hills, CA: Sage.

Sudman, Seymour and Norman M. Bradburn. (1982). *Asking Questions: A Practical Guide to Questionnaire Design.* San Francisco, CA: Jossey-Bass. See Chapter 1, "The Social Context of Question Asking," and Chapter 11, "Questionnaire from Start to Finish."

Sweet, James, Larry Bumpass, and Vaughn Call. (1988). "The Design and Content of the National Survey of Families and Households." *University of Wisconsin Center for Demography and Ecology NSFH Working Paper no. 1.* Madison: University of Wisconsin. Retrieved September 9, 2005, from www.ssc.wisc .edu/cde/nsfhwp/

5. Pretesting: Rationale and Overview of Field Techniques

DeMaio, Theresa, Jennifer Rothgeb, and Jennifer Hess. (1998). "Improving Survey Quality Through Pretesting." Statistical Research Division Working Papers in Survey Methodology, no. 98/03. Washington, DC: U.S. Bureau of the Census. Retrieved September 9, 2005, from www.census.gov/srd/papers/pdf/sm98–03.pdf

Foddy, William. (1998). "An Empirical Evaluation of In-Depth Probes Used to Pretest Survey Questions." *Sociological Methods and Research* 27(1), 103–134.

Schechter, Susan, Johnny Blair, and Janet Vande Hey. (1996). "Conducting Cognitive Interviews to Test Self-Administered and Telephone Surveys: Which Methods Should We Use?" University of Maryland Survey Research Center Working Paper.

6. Data Precoding, Coding, Cleaning, and Management

de Vaus, David A. (1996). *Surveys in Social Research.* London, UK: University College London Press. See Chapter 14, "Coding."

Ross, Kenneth, T. Neville Postlethwaite, Marlaine Lockheed, Aletta Grisay, and Gabriel Carceles Breis. (1990). "Improving Data Collection, Preparation and Analysis Procedures: A Review of Technical Issues." In *Planning the Quality of Education: The Collection and Use of Data for Informed Decision-Making,* edited by Kenneth Ross and Lars Mahlck. Paris, France: UNESCO.

7. Administration

Biemer, Paul P., Robert M. Groves, Lars E. Lyberg, Nancy A. Mathiowetz, and Seymour Sudman, eds. (1991). *Measurement Errors in Surveys.* New York: Wiley.

de Vaus, David A. (1996). *Surveys in Social Research.* London, UK: University College London Press. See Chapter 7, "Administering Questionnaires."

Jenkins, Cleo R. and Don Dillman. (1995). "Towards a Theory of Self-Administered Questionnaire Design." Statistical Research Division Working Papers in Survey Methodology, no. SM95/06. Washington, DC: US Bureau of the Census. Retrieved September 9, 2005, from www.census.gov/srd/www/byyear.html

Lyberg. Lars E. and Daniel Kasprzyk. (1991). "Data Collection Methods and Measurement Error: An Overview." In *Measurement Errors in Surveys,* edited by Paul P. Biemer, Robert M. Groves, Lars E. Lyberg, Nancy A. Mathiowetz, and Seymour Sudman. New York: Wiley.

Weeks, Michael. (1992). "Computer-Assisted Survey Information Collection: A Review of CASIC Methods and Their Implications for Survey Operations." *Journal of Official Statistics* 8(4), 445–465.

8. Fieldwork in Principle and Practice

Billiet, Jacques and Geert Loosveldt. (1988). "Improvement of the Quality of Responses to Factual Survey Questions by Interviewer Training." *Public Opinion Quarterly* 52(2), 190–211.

Current Population Survey Interviewers Manual. US Bureau of the Census. Retrieved September 9, 2005, from www.bls.census.gov/cps/bintman.htm. An example of an interview, examples of training, and interview manuals.

Fowler, Floyd J. (1993). *Survey Research Methods.* Newbury Park, CA: Sage. See Chapter 3, "Nonresponse: Implementing a Sample Design."

Frey, James H. and Sabine Mertens Oishi. (1995). *The Survey Kit Volume 4: How to Conduct Interviews by Telephone and in Person.* Thousand Oaks, CA: Sage. See Chapter 3, "Interviewer Selection and Training."

Hua, Haiyan et al. (1997). "Field Supervisor's/Enumerator's Manual." In *Girls' and Women's Education Project Documentation.* Katmandu: World Education Nepal. Examples of training and interview manuals.

———. (1997). "GWE/Nepal Literacy Study Hypotheses and Indicators." In *Girls' and Women's Education Project Documentation.* Katmandu: World Education Nepal.

———. (1997). "GWE Survey: Program and Site Selection Information." In *Girls' and Women's Education Project Documentation.* Katmandu: World Education Nepal.

Igoe, Lin Moody, ed. (1993). *China Economic, Population, Nutrition and Health Survey 1993 Work Manual.* Beijing, China, and Chapel Hill, NC: Chinese Academy of Preventive Medicine and Carolina Population Center.

Examples

Rea, Louis M. and Richard A. Parker. (1997). *Designing and Conducting Survey Research: A Comprehensive Guide.* San Francisco, CA: Jossey-Bass. See Chapter 4, "Administering the Questionnaire."

Watkins, Susan Cotts (with Naomi Rutenberg, Steve Green, Charles Onoko, Kevin White, Nadra Franklin, and Sam Clark). (1995). "'Circle No Bicycle': Fieldwork in Nyanza Province, Kenya, 1994–1995." University of Pennsylvania Population Studies Center, Social Networks Project. Retrieved September 9, 2005, from www.ssc.upenn.edu/Social_Networks/Level%203/Papers/PDF-files/Circle-No-Bicycle.doc

Weinberg, Eva. (1983). "Data Collection: Planning and Management." In *Handbook of Survey Research*, edited by Peter H. Rossi, James D. Wright, and Andy B. Anderson. New York: Academic Press, Inc. Focus on pp. 350–358.

9. Analysis of Survey Data

Deaton, Angus. (1997). *Analysis of Household Surveys.* Baltimore, MD: Johns Hopkins University Press for the World Bank.

Hsiao, Cheng. (1986). *Analysis of Panel Data.* Cambridge, UK: Cambridge University Press.

Pagan, Adrian and Aman Ullah. (1999). *Nonparametric Econometrics.* Cambridge, UK: Cambridge University Press.

Sadoulet, Elisabeth and Alain de Janvry. (1995). *Quantitative Development Policy Analysis.* Baltimore, MD: Johns Hopkins University Press.

Wooldridge, Jeffrey M. (1999). *Introductory Econometrics: A Modern Approach.* Cincinnati, OH: Southwestern College Publishing.

———. (2002). *Econometric Analysis of Cross Section and Panel Data.* Cambridge: Massachusetts Institute of Technology Press.

10. Secondary Data Sources

International Labor Office

International Labor Office: http://laborsta.ilo.org/

United Nations

United Nations Development Programs. [Annual]. *Human Development Report.* New York: Oxford University Press, various issues, also see www.hdr.undp.org/

World Bank

World Bank. [Annual]. *World Development Report.* New York: Oxford University Press.

World Bank Data and Statistics Division, accessed September 9, 2005, at www.worldbank.org/data/

World Bank, Living Standards Measurement Survey, conducted throughout the world; accessed September 9, 2005, at www.worldbank.org/html/prdph/lsms/

Some Recent Surveys Available Online

African Ideational Diffusion Project, accessed September 9, 2005, at www.acap
.upenn.edu/

Demographic and Health Surveys, accessed September 9, 2005, at www.measuredhs.
com/

Indonesia Family Life Survey (IFLS) longitudinal survey of 30,000 individuals living in
13 of the 27 provinces in the country, RAND-directed surveys in 1993/94, 1997,
1998, and 2000, accessed September 9, 2005, at www.rand.org/labor/ FLS/IFLS/

International Crop Research Institute for the Semi-Arid Tropics (ICRISAT) Village
Level Study Panel Data, accessed September 25, 2005, at www.econ.yale.edu/~
egcenter/special.htm [available through the Yale Economic Growth Center
Center for Data Sharing by request].

International Food Policy Research Institute, accessed September 9, 2005, at www
.ifpri.org/

Inter-university Consortium for Political and Social Research, accessed September 9,
2005, at www.icpsr.umich.edu/

Latin American Migration Project, accessed September 9, 2005, at lamp.opr.princeton
.edu/

Mexican Migration Project, accessed September 9, 2005, at www.pop.upenn.edu/
mexmig/

Nang Rong Surveys, accessed September 9, 2005, at www.cpc.unc.edu/projects/
nangrong/

National Institute of Child Health and Human Development, National Institutes
of Health, accessed September 9, 2005, at www.nichd.nih.gov/about/cpr/dbs/
res_ss_large.htm

RAND, accessed September 9, 2005, at www.rand.org/services/databases.html

RAND Family Life Surveys from Indonesia, Malaysia, Bangladesh, and Guatemala,
accessed September 9, 2005, at www.rand.org/labor/FLS/

Roper Center for Public Opinion Research, accessed September 9, 2005, at
www.ropercenter.uconn.edu/

South African Household and Livelihood Survey, accessed September 9, 2005, at
www.worldbank.org/html/prdph/lsms/country/za94/za94home.html

World Fertility Surveys, accessed September 9, 2005, at opr.princeton.edu/archive/wfs/

7

Combining Qualitative and Quantitative Tools

Qualitative Research: Does It Fit in Economics?

Michael J. Piore

This chapter focuses on qualitative research, particularly in economics. It is largely a reflection on my own work. Thomas Kuhn argues that science has to be understood first as social practice and only afterwards as an intellectual endeavor. A scientific discipline is a social community, and people enter it through a process of initiation and imitation (Kuhn 1970). What we learn in the university is not scientific theory and certainly not a theory of how to do science. We are exposed to practices: the practices of our teachers in the classroom and laboratory and the practices they admire, which we read about in the articles they assign us. The theory of how science

AUTHOR'S NOTE: A version of this paper was originally prepared for presentation at the conference *Do Facts Matter in Elaborating Theories? Cross Perspectives From Economics, Management, Political Science and Sociology*, at Centre de Recherche en Gestion-Ecole Polytechnique, Paris, in October 2002, and will be published in similar form in the conference volume.

should be done is almost never taught. And even the theory that explains the practices and articles to which we are exposed and that gives the discipline some coherence is constructed after the fact. It is not always taught directly, is always incomplete, and is often internally contradictory. Kuhn's view of science is, of course, very much contested (Sardar 2000). But it certainly captures how I came to do what I am doing.

I.

I will begin with a characterization of my own research, which has centered around particular policy problems and focuses on particular domains of activity. Using a research "methodology" centered on unstructured, open-ended interviews with economic actors, I have addressed a range of issues, including labor markets, migration (Piore 1979a), adjustment to trade (Piore 1998), technological change (Piore 1968), and trade union decline (Piore 1983).

I began looking at the internal labor markets of large manufacturing firms in order to understand the impact of technology on employment and entered the debate in the 1960s about structural unemployment (Piore 1969; Doeringer & Piore 1971). I turned quickly to the contrast between these jobs and low-wage work in what we came to view as the secondary sector in order to understand the problems of black workers and the failures of employment and training policy to successfully address them (Piore 1968). I am currently working on the shift in labor market "regulation" from collective bargaining driven by economic identity to legal regulation driven by political mobilization around social identities such as race, sex, and ethnicity, and on the organization of product design and development as a window into new forms of business organization.

Despite the variety of subjects, however, my research approach has been fairly consistent. It is often described as a case study approach (Chapter 2 in this volume), and in a way it is. But case studies as practiced in the social sciences tend to be viewed as essentially offering empirical results. I have used my "case study" findings, however, not as empirical evidence but as inputs to the construction of theory. In principle, I could be building tight mathematical (or symbolic) models conventional in economics—and increasingly in other social sciences—out of the material drawn from the case studies. And several of my students over the years have in fact done so. The results could be tested empirically, but not by replicating the case studies to achieve a larger n. However, I chose to develop that theory in a narrative form instead, reinforcing the "qualitative" flavor of the research, which I conceive of as a question of style (a style which I will not try to justify here) rather than of substance.

This is not an approach to research that I chose deliberately or self-consciously. I stumbled into it in my dissertation research in a way that I have described elsewhere (Piore 1979b). It was in part a considered reaction to the limitations and failings I discovered when I tried to apply the more conventional research approach. The courage to react in this way came, as Kuhn suggests, from the example of my thesis adviser, John Dunlop: I found most interesting and original the work that grew out of his practical experience as a labor arbitrator and mediator and from the contrast between the world he encountered through those experiences and the world of economic theory (Dunlop 1957, 1958; Livernash 1957). I continued doing it because it was interesting and fun and seemed to yield insights into problems I considered it important, socially and morally, to solve. Miraculously, what I was doing attracted enough interest and attention that I got tenure anyway, despite my research approach. It has been only recently, when I reached an age august enough that people could believe—mistakenly—that the canons of the profession were very different when I was a young researcher, that I have felt a need to justify what I was doing back then.

II.

The use of open-ended interviews as a research technique depends on the ability to draw out of the interview material something that is interesting and meaningful. It depends, in other words, on the ability to "read" the interviews or, to use a term that is perhaps more apt (but in this context also more ambiguous), to "interpret" the interviews. For me, interpreting interviews has always been at least as much a matter of intuition and instinct as of systematic methodology; one has the feeling of flying by the seat of one's pants. That feeling makes the research process exciting (and scary) relative to standard theoretical or econometric approaches. Nonetheless, it depends on an appreciation for the open-ended interview as a research instrument. For me, this appreciation emerged only gradually through practice over time.

Initially, I saw the open-ended interview as preliminary to the interview proper. It was the idle conversation you engaged in with the respondent—the social amenities—before you got down to the "real" business of posing specific questions. To my surprise, I found these interviews substantively more interesting than the answers I got in response to the questionnaire, and occasionally—more than occasionally, I must confess—I indulged myself and the respondent by prolonging the interview even though I had the sense that it was not part of the real research process. But I also discovered rather quickly that many of the same respondents who were easy to engage in the preliminaries did not tolerate the formal questions well. I could not seem to get them to answer my questions directly or in the right order. When I followed the formal interview format too tightly, they clammed up or provided answers that seemed designed to get me out of the office as quickly as possible. Truth and honesty became very secondary considerations. What worked in interviews was letting the respondents tell their stories. Indeed, I came to believe that this was the only thing that worked consistently. It seemed as though people agreed to be interviewed in the first place only because they had a story to tell, and the formal questions I asked basically became an excuse to let them tell that story. When I tried to forestall the story, I lost the interview.

One can generally reconfigure the interview material into a questionnaire format after the fact, although in principle, the questionnaire should be designed before the interview. One of the advantages of open-ended interviews is that the respondents often answer questions you would not have thought to ask. An elementary textbook in sample survey analysis will tell you that data generated in this way are subject to all sorts of biases because questionnaire results are sensitive to the precise wording of a question and the order in which questions are asked. This is not an insurmountable problem in survey research, where the biases are consistent. They are unlikely to be consistent in reconfigured open-ended interviews. But it is not clear that responses to a formal questionnaire that are driven by the respondent's wish to be rid of the whole thing would be any less biased.

What open-ended interviews do yield, and yield consistently, are stories the respondents tell. The story is the "observation." The stories are basically narratives. The question is thus what to do with the stories. Typically, stories are not analyzed as statistical data; stories are "interpreted." I have used the stories not as data points but to suggest particular revisions in theory.

III.

The problem plaguing open-ended interviews as inputs into the reconstruction of theory is that they appear to be so personal and idiosyncratic. They depend on the capacity of the individual researcher to generate surprises, to recognize patterns, and to organize those patterns to form a theory. It is difficult and potentially counterproductive to delegate the task of interviewing to a colleague or a research assistant because one never quite knows in advance what will turn out to be important. It is even difficult to delegate the task of transcribing the interviews because what turns out to be important is not necessarily the direct response to a question but rather the background detail or the apparently random aside that the question provokes in the respondent. The interpretation can depend on a detail far removed from the goals or substance of the interview, a detail of which the researcher is not even aware at the moment it presents itself. The interpretation emerges through a chain of factoids that come together, often in an epiphany, at some odd moment when the material lies dormant in the back of one's mind.

An example of such a chain is the clues to the origins of the Italian industrial districts in central Italy that Chuck Sabel and I visited, which ultimately led us to develop the argument of *The Second Industrial Divide* (Piore & Sabel 1984). Our trip to Italy was motivated by a completely different research project: undocumented immigration to the United States and the inability to find an underground labor market, which the extralegal status of the immigrants had led us to expect. We went to Italy to find out what such a market would look like once it emerged. We thought we might find it in New York City, but we missed it there because we did not know—or thought we did not know—what to look for. In any case, we expected to find in Italy a set of markers that would signal its development in advance if it had not had time to develop. We were surprised by what we found. The first surprise was that many of the supposedly underground, retrograde firms were, in fact, open, aboveboard, and technologically dynamic and that even the underground firms (of which there were many) seemed to be moving in this direction. This discovery would never have led to a theory of the end of mass production, however, had Sabel and I not already been engaged in a debate with each other about the division of labor, a debate that we conceived of as completely separate from and independent of the immigrant project that had brought us to Italy in the first place.

An important factor in the emergence of these dynamic, small firms was a complex intergenerational effect. The founders of these firms were skilled craftsmen with extensive practical knowledge but no formal education. They had acquired their skills in large companies and had been laid off in one of the several waves of Italian labor militancy that, as the aristocracy of the working class, they tended to lead; they had founded their own companies with the large severance payments that their employers were obliged by law to pay. These older workers had transferred their practical knowledge to their children, who worked with them in the family business after school and during vacations. But the children—unlike their parents—also had a formal education, which provided technical knowledge and exposure to the wider world and its markets. The children had planned to take that education and move with it into large firms and government bureaucracies in what they (and we) thought of as the modern sector. But the economic and social rigidities of Italy in the 1970s, the rigidities that their parents' militancy had created, manifested themselves in very high youth unemployment. These upwardly mobile, educated children were unable to find work when they left school and were forced back into their parents' firms. It was these kids who created what we called "flexible specialization," combining advanced technology, to which they gained access through their formal education, with their practical knowledge in traditional industries to cater to niches for specialized products in world markets. The clue to all this was the old men who took us on tours of the family factory because their children were too busy managing the enterprise to take us. When you visit a manufacturing plant—whether it is a family shop making high-fashion wedding dresses or a 2,000-worker factory assembling jet engines—there is always a factory tour (the factory tour is part of the ritual of this kind of research). You would never think to make a note of who gave you the tour or where the tour guide stood in the management hierarchy or what role he or she had played in the history of the enterprise. You invariably have to make conversation with your guide, but you do not think of the conversation as an "interview." A formal interview with our factory tour guide in Italy would not have captured the pride of the father in his son's accomplishments, because that pride was conveyed by the tone of his voice and the look in his eyes as much as by the substance of what he was saying. And yet that pride, remembered months later in an idle moment, was the clue to the role of intergenerational transition in the emergence of the Italian industrial districts.

What can one do to stimulate epiphanies of this kind? Does it all depend on luck and personal intuition? One sure way of broadening the interpretive process is to work in teams. It is difficult to delegate the interviews, but they can be shared by having a colleague or a research assistant present during your interview, hearing the same things you hear, "seeing" the same gestures, the hesitations and fumbling that cannot be captured in the transcript or on tape. It is no accident that *The Second Industrial Divide* was a collaborative endeavor. The team works to best advantage when its members discuss what they have seen and can bring different perspectives to the situation because they come from different backgrounds.

This approach is actually captured in our case studies of product design. It is one of the ways in which designers work. For example, each year, Levi Strauss sends a team of its designers, accompanied by people from the textile houses that provide its materials and the laundries to which it subcontracts its finishing operations, to Europe to "look." They spend their days walking the streets, watching what people wear, shopping in stores, and listening to people talk to each other about the clothes on the rack. Then they come back to the hotel at night and sit around comparing notes and arguing with each other about what they have seen and what it implies about the possible directions in which fashion might evolve and how Levi Strauss might lead it (Lester & Piore 2004).

IV.

In point of fact, existing theory can play a role similar to that of the design team. It sits in the back of your mind as you ruminate about the interview material. Because the theory is so strong and so demanding, it is as if a team of your colleagues were there beside you arguing about what the interviews mean. It is like being engaged in a continual debate with the rest of the profession about what you are finding and what it means.

The use of theory to stimulate the interpretation of interviews should be possible in any social science discipline. But it seems to me, the hostility of my colleagues notwithstanding, that it is both easier and more important to do in economics because it plays off two characteristics of economics as a discipline. First, economics is highly structured. Second, the discipline has a strong normative disposition. Economics is structured in the sense that it operates from a very tight body of theory and an equally tight, and theoretically grounded, set of empirical techniques. Economics is normative in the sense that it seeks to evaluate economic arrangements and prescribe improvements. The high theory is structured around the notion of Pareto optimality, which defines normative criteria in a very precise way. Applied economic research is directed at the solution of a set of specific, and in the end well-specified, social problems. The theory itself is built around the idea of rational individuals pursuing their self-interest in a competitive market, where they interact indirectly with each other through price signals. The theory seeks to produce as its outcome a stable equilibrium; normative judgments are derived by comparing alternative equilibria.

The vulnerability of economics is that it is addressing problems in the world. When the solutions it proposes do not seem effective, the theoretical apparatus is challenged. But that apparatus is so tightly woven that it has great difficulty responding to that challenge in a systematic way. You could question any one of the assumptions on which the basic model is built, but there is no guide as to what alternative assumption to put in its place. In addition, when you actually try to think through the relationship between the necessarily simplified and abstract theory and the real world in which the problems that theory addresses arise, there are so many assumptions to reconsider that even if you knew how to select alternatives, it would be hard to know which ones to reconsider.

In this sense, what my case study methodology has amounted to is using the material from open-ended interviews to identify the assumptions of conventional theory that seemed to be wrong and the alternative assumptions to put in their place. The research "worked" because it was problem oriented: The problems were real and important, people were looking for solutions to them, and the prescriptions derived from conventional theory were not working. I have to say that it "worked" for a second reason as well: Because it drew on the actors themselves and their actual motivation and behavior (or what they told me were their motivations and behavior), the actors recognized themselves in the theories I was constructing and thus "certified" my "results." Whether a theory needs to be built around "realistic" assumptions and whether the actors should be able to recognize themselves in a theory are, of course, much-debated methodological issues (Friedman 1953; Machlup 1946; Lester 1946). I have no special wisdom to offer on this score. Personally, I have always felt more comfortable with theories of this kind and certainly more comfortable with this kind of theory than with theories that actors themselves reject as characterizations of their behavior. But this is probably because I tend to judge theory (especially theories that we use to make policy) as a story or narrative; people who have an aesthetic that gives primary weight to logical coherence and consistency—a criterion that, incidentally, I also think is important—tend not to care about the storyline in this sense. But whatever its methodological validity, the fact that the actors certify the theory gives it enormous legitimacy in the face of an overtly hostile profession. My work on low-income labor markets has benefited especially from this legitimation. The dual labor market hypothesis suggested that workers and employers in the secondary sector behaved differently from those in the primary sector. Although this hypothesis violated the strong presumption in economics that there is a unified theory of behavior, workers and employers recognized themselves in the distinction. My work on migration, in which the conventional assumption regarding economic man was limited to first-generation migrants, was intuitively plausible to government officials working in migrant communities and to employers who hired these migrants, as well as to the migrants themselves.

More to the point, the problem of how one goes about revising theory is central to research within the discipline of economics, whatever one thinks of my own particular solution to it. The most systematic approach to this problem in the discipline at the moment is the newly emergent field of experimental economics, which derives both the conventional assumptions it questions and the alternatives it puts in their place from controlled (and, one might argue, contrived) psychological experiments. The broader field of behavioral economics seems to be defined by a general willingness to try out alternative behavioral assumptions. Another approach has been to focus on a particular set of assumptions and to introduce apparently ad hoc alternatives (ad hoc in the sense that they have no empirical content) in their place. An example of this second approach is the focus on the assumption of perfect information by the group of economists awarded the Nobel Prize in 2002 (Akerlof 2002; Stiglitz 2002). Joe Stiglitz traces his preoccupation with information to experiences in Kenya in his early career that are a somewhat less systematic version of my own case studies. However, one suspects that his preoccupation is also due to the analytical tractability of this problem in the profession as a whole. That tractability derives, I believe, from the fact that econometrics, the empirical branch of economics, is essentially a theory of rational inference from incomplete information. Neither behavioral economics nor, Stiglitz aside, the approach focusing on a particular set of theoretical assumptions is motivated by policy concerns (although of course they have implications for policy). The innovations in economic theory that grew out of the great depressions—particularly Keynesian economics—are counterexamples; it was the policy problem that created both the motivation and the space within the discipline for an alternative theory to emerge. But the particular assumptions on which the new theories focused and the alternative assumptions around which they were built are not so obvious. Still another approach—the one that is generally offered in textbook science—is the conflict between theory and empirical results. But the empirical branch of economics does not lend itself to this role. I take it as an empirical fact that it does not; why it does not is a much more profound question. It has always seemed to me that the reason it does not stems from an interaction of two factors. On the one hand is the strength of our attachment to economic theory. On the other is the empirical theory, which is extremely complex and sophisticated relative to the techniques that are actually used in practice to analyze data. As a result, the empirical analyses always seem inadequate. When theory and empirics conflict, it has proven easier to question the empirics than to question the theory.

The use of case studies for the construction of theory is not limited to economics (see Chapter 2 in this volume). Indeed, in my own use of case studies, for the most part, economics has provided a hard set of theoretical expectations against which to react. My own research has been less a reaction to theory in the strict sense and more a reaction to my surprise at hearing what the actors were telling me. And when I tried to identify the source of the expectations that led to that surprise, I found it to be the story about the world that economic theory seems to tell. Hence, I ended up trying to track down systematically the "surprise" that violated my expectation—the part of the story that created the expectations and thus the way those expectations were embedded in the more formal and parsimonious version of economic theory. Any discipline creates a series of expectations; ultimately, those expectations derive from theory. Thus, the "methodology" of looking for the surprise in the interviews, tracing its source in theory, and then trying to identify how the theory might be amended to incorporate the surprise is as applicable to social science in general as it is to economics.

Economics does present a special problem, however. Among the social sciences, the discipline of economics is unique in conveying the sense of a system of *interactive* elements. It leads one to be skeptical of the responses given by individuals, but not because we assume the actors are lying, which would present a different sort of problem. Rather, economics encourages skepticism because it assumes that outcomes are not generally affected by the actions of any single individual and instead reflect the interactions among many individuals. Thus, abstracting the behavior of individual actors from interviews is only the first step in "modeling" the process at issue. It can nonetheless be a critical step.

V.

The revision of theory is an especially acute problem in economics, but it is an issue in any scientific discipline. Using interview material to revise theory poses the same problem raised by using empirical data, that is, whether to challenge the theory by parsing the material into a set of theoretical categories or by using the narrative directly as the "observation." And it leads to a distinction between what I will call a minimalist approach and a more radical approach to this kind of research. To make this point, I need to briefly discuss the structure of conventional economic theory.

The theory has two components: a theory of individual behavior and a theory of how, given their behavior, individuals interact and cohere to form a larger economic system. I could illustrate my point with either of these components, but I will focus on the theory of individual behavior. Behavior, in that theory, is understood as a series of discrete acts. Each act is self-conscious and deliberate, the outcome of a specific decision. The decision is *instrumental*, meaning the decision maker is presumed to make a sharp distinction between means, ends, and a causal model connecting the former to the latter. Decisions are rational in the sense that the decision maker organizes the means so as to maximize the ends, given his or her understanding of the underlying causal relationships.

The minimalist approach to the use of open-ended interviews would take each step in the decision-making process as a potential point of entry into the revision of the theory. Thus, one might infer from these interviews the means available to the actors, the ends, or the causal models used to solve the problems. This approach tries to parse the material collected in narrative form into the standard set of theoretical categories. In this sense, it is the theoretical analogue of the approach that parses the answers in a formal questionnaire and uses them to generate data for empirical research.

A different approach is to take the narrative itself as the observation. This is—at least in my understanding—what statistical theory would suggest. What might that mean? It could mean that the narrative itself becomes a functional part of the working of the system. For example, I have recently been studying identity groups based on race, sex, ethnicity, and the like, within the engineering profession. Many of these groups meet regularly to "network" but also to hear a speaker, generally a member of the identity community, talk about his or her career. The speaker's talk is invariably presented in narrative form. These narratives, one can argue, create models or pathways through the labor market in an economy in which careers are no longer based on well-defined professions or the lines of progression in bureaucratic organizations (Arthur & Rousseau 1996). Thus, they come directly to influence behavior in the economy. Treating the narrative as an observation in this way is clearly different from breaking the narrative into a series of components, which are then abstracted from the narrative context itself. It actually contravenes a component of the aesthetic of economic theory that I have not talked about: the notion that the variation among individuals is smooth and continuous and not lumpy and discontinuous. But one is still interpreting the narrative material in terms of the basic categories of instrumental decision making.

A second approach to treating the narrative as the unit of observation is to analyze it in terms of its characteristics as a narrative. There is a literary tradition about interpreting narratives with an enormous theoretical literature that seems potentially helpful here. I cannot claim to have mastered this literature. Indeed, it is so vast that I have not even tried. I have, however, read around in it. And although I still have the hope that the key article is just over the horizon, I have not found this literature very helpful. The problem is that it focuses on a set of abstract characteristics like the structure of the plot or the use of time, which do not map in any obvious way to the structure of economic theory (Lieblich, Tuval-Mashiach, & Zilber 1998).

The focus on the narrative itself as the unit of observation leads to a still more radical departure from the conventional framework (and, incidentally, one in which the literary tradition of narrative analysis could come to play a role): The narrative may be taken as a marker of a pattern of cognition and behavior totally different from that hypothesized in economics and in rational choice behavioral models more broadly. Here, the key assumption of the economic view of behavior is not that it is instrumental or rational but that it consists of a series of discrete acts, each of which is deliberate and hence motivated. An alternative is to think of behavior as ongoing in time, moving in a particular direction or toward a particular object, but deflected (or redirected) by situations the actor encounters along the way (Dreyfus 1991). Because narrative links together actions in time and highlights the kind of encounters that redirect action, it reflects the way in which the actors think about behavior of this kind. Their understanding of others is an "interpretation" of such narratives, and their own behavior is conceived in terms of a similar narrative in which they imagine themselves to be acting. In the hands of the German philosopher Martin Heidegger and the hermeneutic theory, which develops this idea of behavior, the key is not just the narrative but the meanings that are ascribed to it. (Hermeneutics is also discussed in Chapter 3 of this volume.) Those meanings are in turn developed through interaction between people in a process that resembles conversation and in the way in which language evolves through conversation. This interaction complicates the open-ended interview because it suggests that the observation in the interview is not actually the narrative itself but the *interpretation* of the narrative. Moreover, because the act of interpretation is conversation-like, the interviewer becomes implicated in the process as an interlocutor with the respondent in the interpretive process.

Because this is so far from the conventional model, it is hard to see exactly what its implications for economic analysis are. At the Industrial Performance Center at MIT, we have been addressing the problems of industrial design and product development in a series of case studies in terms of this view of behavior. We are trying to understand economic processes through a dual perspective that uses both the conventional approach of behavior as rational decision making and the alternative, hermeneutic approach, and we are using the material of open-ended interviews as yet another window into economic activity (Lester & Piore 2004).

From my early work on internal labor markets, for example, I gained the insight that workers saw their wage rate as an end in itself and not as a means either to efficient resource allocation in the enterprise or to higher levels of consumption (as is presumed in conventional theory). But I also discovered that workers understood causal processes in production very differently from the way an engineer or a manager understood those processes, even though everybody in the shop used the same vocabulary. Another example is the use of the equivalent of open-ended interviews with corporate management to argue that the firm maximizes growth rather than profits

(Marris 1968; Galbraith 1972) or that managers are not rational (but only boundedly rational).

Pursuing this approach to interpreting interviews, one can make a number of additional points. I will make three here. First, in most narratives the actors' behavior can be explained by a combination of several analytical models. Respondents also include in the narratives events that they do not understand analytically; they use the mere proximity of events in space and time as a substitute for an analytical model (Bruner 1990). As the researcher thinks through the interview material, the goal should be to separate these different elements, which is not easy. Second, one is ultimately looking for analytical models because that is what we, as social scientists, use to think about social problems. Thus, the narratives contain several different kinds of information. For example, they offer us analytical models of the behavior of actors themselves. These models can be important in and of themselves, and hence a plausible theory should be able to account for them. As noted earlier, these models are of tremendous forensic value in the policy-making process since the actors are attracted by arguments in which they recognize themselves (which is not to deny the forensic importance of models that present actors not as they are but as they would like to be). Third, the actors' own models of their behavior are clues to the way the larger social system behaves. That behavior cannot, of course, be inferred directly. But since actors operate within that larger social system, one can ask what social system would be consistent with the actors' own models of their behavior. What would the social system have to look like for it to allow actors to hold and believe in the models they carry around in their heads?

To my mind, it is on this last point that social science, and particularly economics, has been most deficient. The deficiency lies in the failure to give sufficient importance to the distinction between information and the framework in which the information is processed and understood (Piore 1995). There is not even a standard vocabulary for making this distinction, although sometimes it seems to be conveyed by the distinction between information and knowledge. In econometrics, it is the distinction between data (observations) and a structural model. The key question is, What alternative models are used to analyze the same data and where do they come from? The supposition is that at the very least, the models that the actors use are consistent with their experiences.

A final point: In interpreting interviews, I do not think sufficient attention is ever given to the possibility that the world is really chaotic; it doesn't fit anybody's models, not those of the social scientist and not those available to the actors. Sometimes the actors themselves recognize this, as when they link together events that do not actually have a causal relationship, using proximity in time and space as a kind of pseudocausality. The great movement toward decentralization of power in large enterprises in the 1980s is a case in point. We tended to see this trend as a deliberate effort to adapt to a newly unstable and uncertain environment in which local knowledge had achieved much greater importance than it had in the past. I still believe that the movement was largely defined by this development. Nonetheless, it is hard to distinguish what one might call principled decentralization from a kind of de facto decentralization that occurs when the center loses confidence in its understanding of the situation and simply leaves decisions to be made at lower levels of the hierarchy, by default.

Supplemental References

Akerlof, George A. (2002). "Behavioral Macroeconomics and Macroeconomic Behavior." *American Economic Review* 92(3), 411–433.

Arthur, Michael B. and Denise M. Rousseau. (1996). *The Boundaryless Career, a New Employment Principle for a New Organizational Era.* New York: Oxford University Press.

Bruner, Jerome Seymour. (1990). *Acts of Meaning.* Cambridge, MA: Harvard University Press.

Doeringer, Peter and Michael J. Piore. (1971). *Internal Labor Markets and Manpower Adjustment.* New York: D. C. Heath.

Dreyfus, Hubert L. (1991). *Being-in-the-World: A Commentary on Heidegger's Being and Time, Division I.* Cambridge, MA: MIT Press.

Dunlop, John T. (1957). "Wage Contours." Pp. 127–139 in *New Concepts of Wage Determination*, edited by George W. Taylor and Frank C. Pierson. New York: McGraw-Hill.

———. (1958). *Industrial Relations Systems.* New York: Holt.

Friedman, Milton. (1953). *Essays in Positive Economics.* Chicago, IL: University of Chicago Press.

Galbraith, John Kenneth. (1972). *The New Industrial State.* New York: New American Library.

Kuhn, Thomas. (1970). *The Structure of Scientific Revolutions.* Chicago, IL: University of Chicago Press.

Lester, Richard A. (1946). "Shortcomings of Marginal Analysis for Wage Employment Problems." *American Economic Review* 36, 63–82.

Lester, Richard A. and Michael J. Piore. (2004). *Innovation—The Missing Dimension.* Cambridge, MA: Harvard University Press.

Lieblich, Amia, Rivka Tuval-Mashiach, and Tamar Zilber. (1998). *Narrative Research: Reading, Analysis, and Interpretation.* Thousand Oaks, CA: Sage.

Livernash, Robert E. (1957). "Job Clusters." Pp. 140–160 in *New Concepts of Wage Determination*, edited by George W. Taylor and Frank C. Pierson. New York: McGraw-Hill.

Machlup, Fritz. (1946). "Marginal Analysis and Empirical Research." *American Economic Review* 36(3), 519–554.

Marris, Robin L. (1968). *The Economic Theory of "Managerial" Capitalism.* New York: Basic Books.

Piore, Michael J. (1968). "Impact of the Labor Market Upon the Design and Selection of Production Techniques Within the Manufacturing Plant." *Quarterly Journal of Economics* LXXXII(November), 602–620.

———. (1969). "On the Job Training in a Dual Labor Market: Public and Private Responsibilities in On-the-Job Training of Disadvantaged Workers." Pp. 101–132 in *Public-Private Manpower Policies: Industrial Relations Research Association Research Volume*, edited by Arnold Wever, Frank H. Cassell, and Woodrow L. Ginsburg. Madison, WI: IRRA.

———. (1979a). *Birds of Passage: Migrant Labor and Industrial Societies.* Cambridge, UK: Cambridge University Press.

———. (1979b). "Qualitative Research Techniques in Economics." *Administrative Science Quarterly* 24(4), 560–569.

———. (1983). "Can the American Labor Movement Survive Re-Gomperization?" Pp. 30–39 in *Proceedings of the Thirty-Fifth Annual Meeting of the Industrial Relations Research Association.* Madison, WI: Industrial Relations Research Association.

———. (1995). *Beyond Individualism.* Cambridge, MA: Harvard University Press.

———. (1998). "Trade and the Social Structure of Economic Activity." Pp. 257–286 in *Imports, Exports, and the American Worker*, edited by Susan M. Collins. Washington, DC: Brookings Institutions Press.

Piore, Michael J. and Charles Sabel. (1984). *The Second Industrial Divide: Possibilities for Prosperity.* New York: Basic Books.

Sardar, Ziauddin. (2000). *Thomas Kuhn and the Science Wars.* Duxford, Cambridge, UK: Icon Books.

Stiglitz, Joseph. (2002). "Information and the Change in the Paradigm in Economics." *American Economic Review* 92(3), 460–501.

Bibliography on Study Design and Quantitative Methods

1. General Issues in Study Design

Abbott, Andrew. (1988). "Transcending General Linear Reality." *Sociological Theory* 6(2), 169–186.

Johnson, Allen. (1978). *Qualifications in Cultural Anthropology: An Introduction to Research Design*. Palo Alto, CA: Stanford University Press.

Johnson, Allen and Orna Johnson. (1990). "Quality Into Quantity: On the Measurement Potential of Ethnographic Fieldnotes." In *Fieldnotes: The Making of Anthropology*, edited by Roger Sanjek. Ithaca, NY: Cornell University Press.

Lieberson, Stanley. (1985). *Making It Count: The Improvement of Social Research and Theory*. Berkeley: University of California Press.

Marini, Margaret M. and Burton Singer. (1988). "Causality in Social Sciences." *Sociological Methodology* 18, 347–410.

McCloskey, Deirdre N. and Stephen T. Ziliak. (1996). "The Standard Error of Regressions." *Journal of Economic Literature* 34(1), 97–114.

Ragin, Charles C. (1987). *The Comparative Method: Moving Beyond Qualitative and Quantitative Strategies*. Berkeley: University of California Press.

———. (1994). *Constructing Social Research: The Unity and Diversity of Method*. Thousand Oaks, CA: Pine Forge Press.

———. (2000). *Fuzzy Set Social Science*. Chicago, IL: University of Chicago Press.

Sudman, Seymour and Norman M. Bradburn. (1982). *Asking Questions*. San Francisco, CA: Jossey-Bass.

2. General Texts for Statistics and Econometrics

Berndt, Ernst. (1991). *The Practice of Econometrics, Classic and Contemporary*. Reading, MA: Addison-Wesley. Includes useful tutorials in how to apply statistical methods in specific contexts.

Freedman, David, Robert Pisani, Roger Purves, and Ani Adhikari. (1991). *Statistics*, 2d ed. New York: W. W. Norton.

Greene, William. (1990). *Econometric Analysis*. New York: MacMillan.

Hoel, Paul. (1984). *Introduction to Mathematical Statistics*, 5th ed. New York: Wiley.

Krueger, Alan B. (2001). "Symposium on Econometric Tools." *Journal of Economic Perspectives* 15(4), 3–10.

Mirer, Thad. (1988). *Economic Statistics and Econometrics*, 2d ed. New York: MacMillan.

Ramanthan, Ramu. (1992). *Introductory Econometrics with Applications*, 2d ed. New York: Harcourt Brace Jovanovich College Publishers.

Rudd, Paul. (2000). *An Introduction to Classical Econometric Theory*. Oxford, UK: Oxford University Press.

3. Specific Quantitative Methods and Concerns

Angrist, Joshua D. and Alan B. Krueger. (2001). "Instrumental Variables and the Search for Identification: From Supply and Demand to Natural Experiments." *Journal of Economic Perspectives* 15(4), 69–86.

Atkinson, Anthony B. and Andrea Brandolini. (2001). "Promise and Pitfalls in the Use of 'Secondary' Data-Sets: Income Inequality in OECD Countries as a Case Study." *Journal of Economic Literature* 39(3), 771–799.

Bollen, Kenneth. (1989). *Structural Equations With Latent Variables*. New York: John Wiley.

Bowden, Roger and Darrell A. Turkington. (1984). *Instrumental Variables*. New York: Cambridge University Press.

Box, George E. P., Gwilym M. Jenkins, and Gregory C. Reinsel. (1994). *Time Series Analysis: Forecasting and Control*, 3d ed. San Francisco, CA: Holden Day.

Brownstone, David and Robert Valletta. (2001). "The Bootstrap and Multiple Imputations: Harnessing Increased Computing Power for Improved Statistical Tests." *Journal of Economic Perspectives* 15(4), 129–142.

Bryk, Anthony S. and Stephen W. Raudenbush. (2001). *Hierarchical Linear Models*. Thousand Oaks, CA: Sage.

Chay, Kenneth Y. and James L. Powell. (2001). "Semiparametric Censored Regression Models." *Journal of Economic Perspectives* 15(4), 29–42.

DiNardo, John and Justin L. Tobias. (2001). "Nonparametric Density and Regression Estimation." *Journal of Economic Perspectives* 15(4), 11–28.

Engle, Robert. (2001). "GARCH 101: The Use of ARCH/GARCH Models in Applied Econometrics." *Journal of Economic Perspectives* 15(4), 157–168.

Godfrey, Lesley G. (1988). *Misspecification Tests in Econometrics: The Lagrange Multiplier Principle and Other Approaches*. New York: Cambridge University Press.

Hamilton, James D. (1994). *Time Series Analysis*. Princeton, NJ: Princeton University Press.

Hansen, Bruce E. (2001). "The New Econometrics of Structural Change: Dating Breaks in U.S. Labor Productivity." *Journal of Economic Perspectives* 15(4), 117–128.

Harvey, Andrew. (1990). *The Econometric Analysis of Time Series*. New York: Philip Plan.

Hausman, Jerry. (2001). "Mismeasured Variables in Econometric Analysis: Problems From the Right and Problems From the Left." *Journal of Economic Perspectives* 15(4), 57–68.

Heck, Ronald and Scott Thomas. (2000). *An Introduction to Multilevel Modeling Techniques*. Hillsdale, NJ: Lawrence Erlbaum Associates.

Hoddinot, John, Lawrence Haddad, and Harold Alderman, eds. (1997). *Intrahousehold Resource Allocation in Developing Countries: Models, Methods and Policy*. Baltimore, MD: Johns Hopkins University Press.

Horowitz, Joel L. and N. E. Savin. (2001). "Binary Response Models: Logits, Probits and Semiparametrics." *Journal of Economic Perspectives* 15(4), 43–56.

King, Gary, Christopher J. L. Salomon, Joshua A. Murray, and Ajay Tandon. (2004). "Enhancing the Validity and Cross-Cultural Comparability of Survey Research." *American Political Science Review* 98(1), 191–207.

Koenker, Roger and Kevin F. Hallock. (2001). "Quantile Regression." *Journal of Economic Perspectives* 15(4), 143–156.

Maddala, G. S. (1983). *Limited-Dependent and Qualitative Variables in Econometrics*. New York: Cambridge University Press.

McKenzie, David J. (2001). "Estimation of AR(1) Models with Unequally Spaced Pseudo-Panels." *Econometrics Journal* 4(1), 89–108.

Signorino, Curtis S. (1999). "Strategic Interaction and Statistical Analysis of International Conflict." *American Political Science Review* 93(2), 279–298.

Stock, James H. and Mark W. Watson. (2001). "Vector Autoregressions." *Journal of Economic Perspectives* 15(4), 101–115.

Tuma, Nancy Brandon and Michael T. Hannan. (1984). *Social Dynamics: Models and Methods*. New York: Academic Press.

Wasserman, Stanley and Katherine Faust. (1994). *Social Network Analysis: Methods and Applications*. New York: Cambridge University Press.

Wooldridge, Jeffrey M. (2001). *Econometric Analysis of Cross Section and Panel Data*. Cambridge, MA: MIT Press.

Bibliography: Study Design & Quantitative Methods

PART II

Essentials for the Conduct of Research

In Part II of this volume, we offer five essays that reach across methods and pertain to the essential aspects of starting and conducting a field-based research project. Stevan Harrell and Andrew Schrank provide snapshots of two methodological techniques discussed at greater length earlier in the volume that are essential aspects of social science fieldwork: ethnography and case studies. By choosing to do fieldwork, social scientists across the disciplines necessarily assume the mantle of these two approaches: They choose to speak with an ethnographic voice and argue for their particular case. In doing so, they create the texts bridging disciplines and deepening our understandings of places, people, and methods. Social scientists returning from, or departing for, the field will find in these essays touchstone references and ideas for reflection that will amplify and perhaps elucidate their own experiences.

Harrell provides a historical perspective on ethnography and suggests ways to approach the literature and method. His suggestions invite reflection about how and what to write and on the stance one takes as a social scientist and an individual in the field, gender dynamics, the fluidity of meaning and findings in the field, and the ethics of fieldwork. Schrank offers an argument for the case study as a source for causal inference. In his argument, he provides the critical justification for why social scientists, especially those trained to do large-n studies, are encouraged to do fieldwork. His essay also provides essential material for social scientists needing to develop the merits of their case.

The remaining three essays consider the challenges of initiating a project (Michael Watts), the ethical dimensions of research (Sara Curran), and the necessity of maintaining perspective throughout (Shrank). Watts provides a witty, irreverent, but nonetheless serious perspective on the importance of getting started early, seeking frequent feedback from different experts, revising once and revising yet again, preparing through language study and background research, anticipating problems, and developing backup plans and alternatives. He uses his essay to acknowledge how graduate training typically shortchanges "what it means to do 'independent research,'" especially field-based research. Drawing on his own experiences, his years as an outstanding mentor to numerous graduate students, and his service on many scientific review panels, he offers tangible examples for any social scientist, whether a new graduate student or a well-established scholar.

In her essay on research ethics in cross-cultural settings, Curran considers first the history, emergence, and role of institutional review boards. She offers examples from her own experiences to suggest what to expect from and how to interact with these boards. In the second part of her essay, she briefly summarizes ethical concerns that go beyond regulatory control, also mentioned by other authors in this volume, especially Gottlieb, Giles-Vernick, Harrell, Schrank, and Watts.

The concluding essay in this section offers a retrospective reflection by Schrank on his own fieldwork experience as an International Predissertation Fellowship Program fellow. Here he offers up sage advice for keeping academic work and the fieldwork experience in perspective. His dramatic and honest narrative brings to life the angst and worry, as well as the sense of accomplishment and independence, that come from having worked hard and persevered through a research project in another cultural setting. His very personal narrative reiterates and powerfully summarizes the numerous lessons offered by the other authors in the volume.

Finally, the bibliographies in this section include texts considered essential by the contributors to this volume and then some.

8

Essentials for Ethnography

Ethnographic Methods

Stevan Harrell

T he process of doing ethnographic research was a kind of insider infor
mation until about 1970, when Peggy Golde edited and published
Women in the Field. Until then, the prevailing wisdom was that fieldwork
was something individual and idiosyncratic to be learned by doing and
therefore not teachable. There were accounts of fieldwork, to be sure, but
their role was primarily to enhance the mystique of the heroic anthropologist braving unfamiliar customs, suspicious natives, and horrible hygiene in
order to add to the Science of Man. Once you had done it, you could sit and
drink beer and swap stories by the hour. But fieldwork was like combat in
that you had no idea what it was like until you had done it. What was written in those days was a series of research narratives about how it was done
but not about how to do it, about the information that was gathered as
opposed to an analysis of how it was gathered.

Since 1970, everything has changed, and the process of fieldwork has been
scrutinized repetitively (and sometimes repetitiously) from many angles. The
stimuli for this scrutiny seem to be two: the realization that we can learn
from each other and in fact have an obligation to share information, and the
troubling thought that fieldwork, as an unsystematized process, embodies
biases that we hardly realize are there. Thus, two rather different but related

literatures have sprung up: one on how to do it (techniques) and one on what it is really doing (critiques). Techniques are covered in more detail elsewhere in this volume. In this essay, I concentrate on the narratives and the critiques.

One can read just about any ethnographic monograph from the "classic" era between the two World Wars (and some of the more modern literature) and find an account of what the anthropologist did in the field. Particularly enlightening, not only about the methods employed by the old masters, but also about their attitudes toward their work, are the introductory sections of several works written when ethnographic methods were just becoming popular. These include introductory material in works of British social anthropology in Oceania: Bronislaw Malinowski's *Argonauts of the Western Pacific* (1922) and Raymond Firth's *We, the Tikopia* (1936); and in Africa: E. E. Evans-Pritchard's *The Nuer* (1940); as well as the introduction to a later American work whose field circumstances were nevertheless quite similar: Napoleon Chagnon's *Yanomamö, the Fierce People* (1968). Perhaps the most introspective and thus most valuable of the works dealing with this early period are the chapters on fieldwork from Margaret Mead's autobiography, *Blackberry Winter* (1975), which describe her experiences in the Pacific from the late 1920s through the 1940s. All these works share a fine command of English prose, a firm belief in the worth of the ethnographic endeavor, and, at least in the case of Mead and Evans-Pritchard, just a hint of self-doubt about how good the work might actually be. They cover a stretch of time when ethnographic fieldwork was a daring and often dangerous adventure, when a lone ethnographer went to a faraway and difficult-to-reach place, was out of touch for weeks or months at a time, had to self-medicate when he or she got sick, and was usually dealing with a language known to very few outsiders. It was easy for the anthropologist to act the hero then, at least in retrospect. In addition, there was no point in questioning the accuracy of the information collected, because there was no way to check on it. And the "natives," the objects of the field research, were usually illiterate and unable to evaluate what was being written about them. Combine this with the general attitudes of racial or at least cultural superiority among Europeans and Euro-Americans at that time, and the complexity of fieldwork was really reduced to two elements: how to get it done, physically and emotionally, and how to negotiate the barriers of language and custom that prevented understanding. It is easy to see how the heroic narrative of the anthropologist was established in these kinds of circumstances. They are so different from even today's most remote field situations, which are nevertheless reachable by satellite phone and where local residents usually know all about research and anthropology. But much of the psychic or emotional experience is the same: Our self-doubt, loneliness, suspicion, and frustration, and even the sense of triumph or just accomplishment when the job gets done, are probably not very different from what Malinowski or Mead or Evans-Pritchard experienced.

More accounts of what it was like, written just at the beginning of the era of methodological and critical scrutiny of the fieldwork process, can be found in Golde's *Women in the Field* (1970). Beginning with Laura Bohannan's lightly fictionalized *Return to Laughter* (1964/1986), written under the pseudonym Elenore Smith Bowen, a different genre emerges: the book written primarily to narrate the field experience itself rather than just to use the field experience to establish the bona fides of the anthropologist. Paul Rabinow's *Reflections on Fieldwork in Morocco* (1977) and Jean-Paul Dumont's *The Headman and I* (1978) are influential early examples of this genre. Another outstanding personal account, with a purpose of narrating the process rather than validating the results, is Alma Gottlieb and Philip Graham's *Parallel Worlds* (1994). In these works, the story is no longer necessarily triumphalist or self-congratulatory. Rather, the works are pervaded with a kind of epistemological self-doubt, a worry about what, if any, real knowledge might come out of the ethnographic encounter. One can see in this kind of work an implicit critique of the process of knowing gained through ethnographic research, but the critique in these books stays implicit; rather than spelling out what might be wrong or just worrisome about this way of collecting information, the authors narrate the process and leave the reader to draw conclusions.

Reading narratives, of course, does not tell one much about how to actually do ethnography, but if one is interested in technique, there are plenty of manuals, almost all published in the 1970s and 1980s. These include works by Robert Burgess (1982), Werner Schoepfle (1987), R. F. Ellen (1984), Pertti Pelto and Gretel Pelto (1978), and James Spradley (1979, 1980). All these are full of useful tips about how to gather information. And when read in conjunction with the narratives described above and the critiques described below, they can provide a useful balance to too much soul-searching, as well as a helpful guide when one does not have the luxury of just reading and thinking about ethnography but actually needs to do it. But manuals do little to still the critique of ethnographic methods.

The general critique of anthropology as a politically and socially embedded endeavor, rather than an objective science, began in earnest with two edited books published in 1973/1974: Talal Asad's *Anthropology and the Colonial Encounter* and Michelle Rosaldo and Louise Lamphere's *Woman, Culture, and Society*. The first questioned the colonial roots of the discipline, the other its implicit and unexamined gender bias. This general critique of the discipline's epistemological groundings and social biases quite naturally carried over into the literature on the fieldwork process; this critique demoted and quite possibly enriched ethnography from positivistic science to literary endeavor that may or may not be scientific. The most influential collection in this vein has been James Clifford and George Marcus's *Writing Culture* (1986), which was heavily influenced by the post-structuralist literary criticism and philosophy of that time and whose message can be oversimplified to say that there are questions about whether anthropology is a science at all and about whether ethnography can produce scientific results. Therefore, we should see ethnography as a particular kind of literary text with no particular scientific validity. The slightly more optimistic volume by Marcus and Michael Fischer, *Anthropology as Cultural Critique* (1986), offered ethnographers more of a way out, showing how such literary texts might still be very useful in understanding how human cultures and societies worked and how anthropology might serve just as usefully as a mirror of our own predicament as it would as documentation of cultural diversity. Also noteworthy (and shorter, easier, and wittier) is Clifford Geertz's *Works and Lives* (1988), which takes anthropology as literature very seriously and shows how some of the pioneers we have met before, particularly Evans-Pritchard, made very effective use of certain kinds of ethnographic writing to validate their own results.

Recently, there have been attempts to combine critical with methodological thinking, to extract anthropologists from the epistemological bind created by the early critiques. Both Tony Larry Whitehead and Mary Ellen Conaway's *Self, Sex, and Gender in Cross-Cultural Fieldwork* (1986) and Roger Sanjek's *Fieldnotes* (1990) contain many valuable pieces; the latter work in particular is noteworthy because it deals with the way observations become notes that, in turn, become analysis.

It is almost certainly true that, despite the extensive literature on ethnographic methods, narratives, and results that has been published in the past 30 years, all of it makes much more sense to those who have done ethnography than to those who are planning to do it but have not had the experience. But if one is determined to get a vicarious taste or a reassuring preview, there are some useful exercises one might perform. One might begin by reading the introduction to Evans-Pritchard's *The Nuer* (1940), in which he details the travails of a British anthropologist in what was essentially enemy territory, living with a group that the British colonial authorities were having a hard time trying to subdue. One could follow this up with critiques of Evans-Pritchard's approach in Clifford Geertz's *Works and Lives* (1988), in James Clifford's "On Ethnographic Authority" (in his *The Predicament of Culture,*

1988), and in Renato Rosaldo's "From the Door of His Tent," in Clifford and Marcus's *Writing Culture* (1986). Then ask yourself if you feel like doing ethnography. If so, how would you do it?

Go on to read two articles on the relationship between qualitative and quantitative methods: John J. Honingman's "Sampling in Ethnographic Fieldwork," in Burgess's *Field Research: A Sourcebook and Field Manual* (1982), and Allen Johnson and Orna Johnson's "Quality Into Quantity: On the Measurement Potential of Ethnographic Fieldnotes," in Sanjek's *Fieldnotes* (1990). Feel any better? Why or why not? Does the definiteness of quantitative methodology make you feel better about the validity of the enterprise?

Another useful exercise begins with Napoleon Chagnon's *Yanomamö, the Fierce People* (1968) and *Studying the Yanomamö* (1974), both of which contain autobiographical accounts of very difficult fieldwork, written by a master of English prose. Chagnon's books about his field adventures in the South American rain forest are the most popular texts ever written in anthropology because of the captivating narrative. But then read the popular critique in Patrick Tierney's *Darkness in El Dorado* (2002), which accuses Chagnon and others of all sorts of unethical acts in the service of information gathering. At that point, surf the net for critiques of the critique in the Web pages of the American Anthropological Association (AAA) and several universities. Among these are the AAA El Dorado Task Force Report: www.aaanet.org/edtf/index .htm; the statement from the University of Michigan provost: www.umich .edu/~urel/darkness.html; and the preliminary report from the University of California, Santa Barbara: www.anth.ucsb.edu/ucsbpreliminaryreport.pdf; as well as the thoughtful review by David Stoll in *The New Republic*. (See also Bibliography on Ethnography in this volume.) The questions here are not so much epistemological as ethical, and they are certainly not limited to ethnography: What actions are justified in the pursuit of knowledge?

As a final exercise, you can return to the Old Mistress herself. First, read Derek Freeman's attack on Margaret Mead in *Margaret Mead and Samoa* (1996), which claims that Mead, a naïve young woman at the time of her Samoan work, was basically hoodwinked by mischievous informants and her own gullibility. Then, go back and read the original work by Mead, *Coming of Age in Samoa* (1928). Finally, read the special issue of the *American Anthropologist* in 1982, in which several area specialists discuss the question of the scientific value of Mead's findings. At the end, do you stand with or against Mead? Or is it impossible to tell anymore, given the thick haze of time and criticism enveloping her original work?

Ethnography has moved from being ideally intuitive, individual, and purportedly inspirational to being public, methodological, and critically scrutinized. This may or may not mean that young ethnographers—no longer armed only with the notebooks, antimalarials, and exhortations of old, but now with tomes of theory and reams of critique—are better prepared for their adventures in the field than were their founding grandmothers. They may or may not gain insight or even useful tips from all that has been written about their craft. As mentioned above, I think the material is much more useful after one's field experience, when one can use it to reflect on that experience, rather than beforehand, when all one has are expectations and anxieties. There is still no substitute for doing ethnography. In addition, after one has done it, one craves information on someone else's experience to compare, to evaluate, and to observe critically. I suspect that the number of pints drained in this exercise has not diminished as the amount of ink spilled has increased, but a lot of the material is worth reading for the retrospective insight it can provide.

As ethnographic methods move increasingly out of anthropology and into other academic disciplines, it is also worthwhile to consider the extent to which they are useful to those trained in different theoretical paradigms and expectations. Political scientists or historians who have become ethnographers have so far written little about their experience but have produced notable works of ethnographic reporting. Perhaps reading about anthropologists doing ethnography provides a good bridge until we can begin to hear about the ethnographic experiences of colleagues in other disciplines.

9

Essentials for the Case Study Method

The Case Study and Causal Inference

Andrew Schrank

Though everyone who writes about case studies defines a case study differently, the *Oxford English Dictionary* offers a suitable working definition, describing it as an "attempt to understand *a* [my emphasis] particular person, institution, society, etc., by assembling information about his or its development."[1] The information can be either qualitative or quantitative or a combination of the two. It can be collected by an individual or a team. It can consist of interviews with key informants, surveys of representative populations of actors, archival materials, observations by participants (ethnographies), or any other widely accepted source. And it can be analyzed using one or more of a wide variety of analytical methods, including, but by no means limited to, close reading, historical interpretation, the construction of "analytical narratives," and even the use of inferential statistics. Consider, for example, Robert Putnam's study of "civic traditions in modern Italy" in *Making Democracy Work,* which relies on surveys, key informant interviews, secondary sources, and the statistical analysis of subnational political performance. For the most part, however, case studies are distinguished from other social scientific methods by the indefinite article "a" in the afore-mentioned definition. A case study investigates *a* person, institution, or society rather than people, institutions, or societies more broadly.

The case study is the unappreciated workhorse of the contemporary social sciences. It has made—and continues to make—enormous contributions to every social scientific discipline. The classic works of sociology and political science involve case studies. Anthropologists, geographers, and historians use the approach all the time. And mainstream economists are quick to underscore the virtues of a well-designed case study, at least when it suits their rhetorical or polemical purposes.[2]

Nevertheless, the methodological literature on the case study is for the most part defensive rather than instructive (Feagin, Orum, & Sjoberg 1991; Levi 2000). For every book or article offering insight into the practice of case-based research, one finds a half dozen books or articles debating the very merits of the approach—and most of those works, by the way, are critical.

Nor does the asymmetry end with books and articles. Think about it: We extol the virtues of works like Charles Tilly's *The Vendée* (1964), Guillermo O'Donnell's *Modernization and Bureaucratic Authoritarianism* (1973), and Chalmers Johnson's *MITI and the Japanese Miracle* (1982) in our thematic seminars, but we deride their research designs—and therefore, at least implicitly, their authors—in our methodology classes. They have selected their cases on the dependent variable. They have omitted potentially relevant control variables. And they have "degrees of freedom" problems that just won't quit. Any reasonably well-trained third-year political science, sociology, or geography graduate student can effortlessly recite the list of method-ological transgressions—and that, in a sense, is the problem.

Our methodology classes tend to discourage students from pursuing the types of projects they come to admire in their "substantive" classes: well-informed, detailed inquiries into the interests, ideas, and behaviors of real people in real places at decisive historical conjunctures. One wonders whether dissertations like Seymour Martin Lipset's *Agrarian Socialism* (1950), Nora Hamilton's *The Limits of State Autonomy: Post-Revolutionary Mexico* (1982), or William Reno's *Who Really Rules Sierra Leone?* (1985) would be proposed—let alone welcomed—in our own departments. Increasingly, I fear, the answer is "no."

Don't get me wrong. Truly exceptional work will always rise above momentary fads and fashions, and I, for one, feel no need to challenge Margaret Levi's assertion that the first books of "such distinguished contemporary comparativists as Robert Bates or David Laitin or Sidney Tarrow" would, if written today, "still be published by a major university press" (Levi 2000, p. 20). In fact, I would go even further and say that if they were written today, they would still be classics in their respective fields. But I am not at all sure that they would be written today, for many graduate students in some disciplines have been turning their backs on the detailed, single country (or community, region, firm, movement, etc.) case study for more than a decade now in a potentially misguided effort to meet a uniform, textbook standard of methodological rigor that holds that quantitative data are necessarily better than qualitative, large samples are necessarily better than small, and deduction is necessarily better than induction.

In fact, the prevailing view of the case study owes much to the critique offered by Donald Campbell and Julian Stanley in their classic exposition of *Experimental and Quasi-Experimental Designs for Research* in 1966. According to Campbell and Stanley, the "one-shot case study" entails the observation of a "single group" that has allegedly been exposed to "some agent or treatment presumed to cause change" (Campbell & Stanley 1966, p. 6). If X is the treatment (e.g., the "deepening" of import-substituting industrialization described by O'Donnell in *Modernization and Bureaucratic-Authoritarianism,* 1973) and O is the outcome (i.e., the onset of authoritarian rule), X is allegedly responsible for O.

The limits to the one-shot case study are by now well-known. Absent either a baseline measure of the outcome variable (e.g., an assessment of the political situation prior to the process of deepening) or a control group (e.g., data on countries that failed to deepen their industrial structures), one can neither be certain that a change in the status of the outcome variable has actually occurred nor attribute the alleged change to the ostensible cause with any degree of certainty. As a result, the case study methodology suffers from "such a total absence of control," in the words of Campbell and Stanley, "as to be of almost no scientific value" (1966, p. 6).

A number of well-known analysts have responded to Campbell and Stanley's critique by undertaking "comparisons between or among a small number of cases," in Bennett's terminology, and thereby increasing their sample sizes.[3] The most commonly used small-n approaches derive from John Stuart Mill's "method of difference" and "method of agreement." The former (Table 9.1) looks for two or more cases that are similar in all critical respects except for a dichotomous outcome variable and a dichotomous independent variable, which is assumed to be the "cause" of the outcome in question.

The latter (Table 9.2) looks for two or more cases that differ in all critical respects except a dichotomous outcome variable and a dichotomous independent variable that is therefore assumed to be the "cause" of the outcome in question.

Table 9.1   Mill's Method of Difference

Case	Outcome	Independent Variable	Control Variable 1	Control Variable 2
1	Yes	Yes	Yes	No
2	No	No	Yes	No

Table 9.2   Mill's Method of Agreement

Case	Outcome	Independent Variable	Control Variable 1	Control Variable 2
1	Yes	Yes	Yes	Yes
2	Yes	Yes	No	No

According to Theda Skocpol, perhaps the foremost contemporary practitioner of small-n comparative research, the comparative method is nothing more than "that mode of multivariate analysis to which sociologists necessarily resort when experimental manipulations are not possible and when there are 'too many variables and not enough cases'—that is, not enough cases for statistical testing of hypotheses" (Skocpol 1976, p. 177; Skocpol & Somers 1980).

Nevertheless, Mill's methods have been criticized on a number of grounds. They are vulnerable to selection bias, measurement error, and curve fitting. They rely on an epistemologically untenable, deterministic notion of causality. And they are confounded by interaction effects, omitted variables, identical patterns of concomitant variation (i.e., situations in which multiple predictors exhibit the identical pattern across cases), and multiple causes of the same outcome. Consequently, Stanley Lieberson, perhaps the foremost contemporary critic of small-n causal analysis, holds that "the fundamental underpinnings of the Mill methods are indefensible."[4]

Lieberson's critique is powerful but not unassailable. While the case study is by no means the appropriate research design for each and every social scientific problem and is indeed ill suited to traditional, probabilistic causal analysis, it is anything but useless. After all, Campbell himself concluded—in a "partial recanting" published years after his magnum opus had become the industry standard—that the case study offers more control than his previous "caricature" would have implied, for the authors of case studies frequently find that their prior beliefs are untenable when they reach the field—an unlikely outcome in the absence of at least some form of control (Campbell 1975).

When might a case study be appropriate? A number of situations exist:

- When it promises to yield fundamental insight into a rare but important process or event that offers no obvious point of comparison (March, Sproull, & Tamuz 1991; Adams, Clemens, & Orloff 2005).
- When it addresses an ambiguous, obscure, or otherwise inhospitable population that is difficult to reach through traditional methods (Geis 1991).
- When it explores a crucial, deviant, or negative case that will shed light on an established theory (Stinchcombe 1968; Lijphart 1971; Emigh 1997).[5]
- When a case study approach is used in conjunction with a large-n statistical study to flesh out underlying causal mechanisms (King, Keohane, & Verba 1994; Ragin 1987; Skocpol & Somers 1980; Paige 1975; Romer 1993; Kurtz & Barnes 2002).
- When it is combined with a small-n comparative approach to assess necessary causal conditions or conditional theoretical statements (Dion 1998; Paige 1999).
- When it can be evaluated against an established body of theory that offers multiple observable implications (Campbell 1975, pp. 181–183).
- Or when no adequate body of theory exists, and the relevant hypothesis or control group is therefore unclear (Walton 1992).

Any or all of these situations would justify the use of case-based methods, regardless of whether they would foster valid causal inferences in the narrow sense of the term. For ongoing discussions about the approach, see the websites for the Consortium on Qualitative Research Methods (www.asu .edu/clas/polisci/cqrm/) and the American Political Science Association's Qualitative Methods Section and associated newsletter (www.asu.edu/clas/ polisci/cqrm/QualitativeMethodsAPSA.html).

It took me a long time to realize that small-n researchers and large-n researchers could profit from mutual dialogue. Large-n researchers have to compromise nuance for generalizability; small-n researchers compromise generalizability for nuance. In both cases, the goal is mostly to understand social processes and their implications, and both methods are fraught with fundamental study design concerns that allow only partial answers. But in mutual dialogue, the two methodological enterprises can yield more complete insights into social processes.

Notes

1. Oxford English Dictionary, 2d ed. (1989). Oxford, UK: Oxford University Press. Retrieved September 23, 2005, from dictionary.oed.com/cgi/entry/50034022/50034022se53?single=1&query_type=word&queryword=case+study&first=1&max_to_show=10&hilite=50034022se53.

2. The latter point is perhaps best illustrated in Srinivasan and Bhagwati (2001) in the Bibliographies at the end of Part II.

3. Bennett, Andrew. (2001). "Case Study: Methods and Analysis." Pp. 1513–1519 in *International Encyclopedia of the Social and Behavioral Sciences*, edited by Neil J. Smelser and Paul Baltes. Amsterdam, The Netherlands: Elsevier. Quotation is from p. 1516.

4. Lieberson, Stanley. "More on the Uneasy Case for Using Mill-Type Methods in Small-N Comparative Studies." *Social Forces* 72(4), 1225–1237. Quotation is from p. 1236.

5. Examples of the various stages would include Barrett and Whyte (1982), Barnett (1990), and Emigh (1998). See the Bibliographies at the end of Part II.

10

Essentials for Research Design

In Search of the Holy Grail:
Projects, Proposals, and Research
Design, but Mostly About Why Writing
a Dissertation Proposal Is So Difficult

Michael Watts

> *There is too little emphasis [in the U.S. academy] . . . on what it*
> *means to do independent research.*
>
> —William Bowen and Neil Rudenstein,
> *In Pursuit of the Ph.D.* (1992)

AUTHOR'S NOTE: A version of this chapter was delivered at the International Predissertation Fellowship Program (IPFP) Annual Fellows Conference in October 2002. I am grateful to the participants, to Ellen Perecman in particular, and to the army of IPFP fellows who have struggled with the sorts of questions I try to raise here. More critically, much of what I have to say here has emerged from 15 years of running dissertation workshops at the University of California, Berkeley (globetrotter.berkeley.edu/DissPropWorkshop/), a system focused on proposal writing that emerged in the careful hands of David Szanton while at the Social Science Research Council.

The art of writing a research proposal is a curious and paradoxical exercise. It is indisputably a foundational moment in graduate student training and professional formation. Indeed, it is arguably one of the most difficult and exacting tasks confronting students. And yet it is one of the great curiosities of academia that proposal writing, and research design and conduct more generally, is so weakly institutionalized within the university and within graduate programs throughout the social sciences. This is precisely what Bowen and Rudenstein (1992) gesture to in their rather extraordinary, but nevertheless sadly accurate, claim that universities lay too little emphasis on what it means to do "independent research," in other words, what we would all take to be the bedrock of the academic enterprise. The same claim might be made of fieldwork, so often a constituent part of the research design on which any good proposal rests. Whether "the field" is a village in northern Uganda, a barrio in Los Angeles, a legal firm in Paris, or an archive in Pittsburgh, the actual conduct of independent research in the field is an exemplary case of what Bruno Latour (1987) calls "black boxing." Fieldwork, which typically has a central place in the social scientific study of the developing world, has the aura (and anxiety) of any rite of passage. But with a difference. It is a learning-by-doing ordeal for which there is presumed to be no body of preparatory training (i.e., course work) and for which the measure of success is Darwinian in nature: Those who succeed return; those who do not presumably were not good at fieldwork and were bound for academic extinction.

It is perhaps for all these reasons that Bowen and Rudenstein, in their important book *In Pursuit of the Ph.D.* (1992), characterize the period between the end of graduate course work and the engagement of a dissertation topic as one of the most fraught and difficult in graduate formation. The selection of a topic, they say, is "a formidable task," and students must be encouraged to engage with their dissertation projects in the first and second years of study at the graduate level. In practice, they rarely are so encouraged in the social sciences or in the humanities, and the transition from course work to dissertation project, from writing nifty critical literature reviews on organization theory or poststructuralism to "the research question"—another rite of passage—is often paralyzing. There is no obvious road map to facilitate this transition or the discovery of a robust, credible, interesting, and original project. And the fact that students have been swimming along merrily in a sea of high theory—hegemony practices, disciplinary discourses, or transaction costs—does not necessarily help much either. ("How exactly am I going to 'operationalize' my Foucauldian study of the microphysics of political power in San Francisco's credit unions?") The discovery and articulation of a compelling research project and robust research design are often a source of radical bewilderment and anxiety. It is, after all, about making fundamental choices: Brazilian social movements and not schooling in Oregon, an engagement with neo-Weberian theory rather than rational choice, and so on. And not least, it necessitates decisions that engage the intellectual with the personal: Can I take my companion and child to Tierra del Fuego for a year and a half? Can I really hack it in Calgary for two winters? All this talk of emotion and reason may sound terribly West Coast-ish in tenor, but we cannot ignore the truth that in their most demanding form, research and writing require a state of mind and a way of being that most people in the world spend their lives trying to avoid: withdrawal, obsession, panic. This is the stuff of the research enterprise, and yet it is surprising how many classic monographs cover their tracks and obfuscate the mistakes, errors, and panic of how the book emerged, ignoring the lived realities of working in the field. It is interesting to reflect on why the research proposal or research design has become a sort of "public secret" on campuses and indeed why, in my view, it has all too often not been an object of serious scrutiny in the past few decades. Perhaps the poststructural skepticism toward method and truth and the attraction of the conditions under which knowledge is produced have contributed to a sort of flight from research design.

I want to introduce a number of issues pertaining to research design and proposal writing and to lay out in broad terms the kinds of concerns and knotty problems that enter into the long and complicated process of framing, designing, conducting, and obtaining funding for a researchable project.

The Funding Regime

Before I turn to the nuts and bolts of the proposal-writing process, let me say a few words about the political economy of funding and proposal writing. Some readers may wish to consult some interesting work by the anthropologist Don Brenneis, who has conducted ethnographic work on the proposal review process (see Brenneis 1994), posing questions such as the following: What actually transpires in the course of peer group assessment? What sort of normalization transpires as multidisciplinary or theoretically contrary academics "review" a proposal? What indeed is the canon that defines the "good proposal"? Students depend on a variety of funding sources: federal agencies, such as the National Science Foundation and the Fulbright Program of the Institute of International Education; private foundations, such as the Ford Foundation, the Carnegie Foundation, and the MacArthur Foundation; small donors, such as the American Association of University Women; and nongovernmental organizations (NGOs), such as the Aspen

Institute and the Social Science Research Council (SSRC). These organizations have quite different interests, forms of governance, and review and may require markedly different sorts of proposals (a 2-page précis vs. an elaborate, 20-page research proposal). Such variability in the interests and foci of funding programs points directly to a need to consider and reflect on the institution (the funder), the program (the substance), and the process (review and evaluation). Let me begin with several self-evident, but nonetheless important, starting points for thinking about the relation between the intellectual project and the mundane need to bankroll it:

- Identify the panoply of organizations that might consider funding your project; the Foundations register (a listing of all foundations, available through www.nootherfoundation.org) and university research offices are obvious places to begin.
- Be creative and flexible in reading the rubric of a funder and of the specific grant program in question and consider the ways in which you might package your interests (take note: not compromise your interests) in order to be eligible for funding through a particular program. A funder may have a program on peace and security or technological innovation that precisely rests on the desire to think expansively and in cross-disciplinary ways about such issues and may readily encompass what you do.
- Excavate background information on the funding agency to learn, for example, what sorts of projects it has funded in the past, who the members of the selection committee are, and whether they have privileged or encouraged certain sorts of approaches or problems.
- Take careful note of the deadlines and requirements of each application to give yourself time to prepare a proposal; two weeks or even two months will not do. The process is long, iterative, and time consuming. Any proposal that leaves the author's desk without having been read by a large number of people and subjected to rigorous critical feedback is, almost by definition, vulnerable.
- Recall that all research competitions are competitions! Getting support is competitive and is becoming more so. The consequences are rather obvious. You have to submit a proposal that represents your best effort; you cannot submit a wildly disorganized and incomplete project proposal just because the deadline comes around and hope that something is better than nothing. Experts in your field will be judging what you write.
- Your project will be (for better or worse) assessed relative to others'. Research monies are tight, and competition is intense. A reviewer or

screener might be reading 30 proposals and have to eliminate 20. To stand a chance, your proposal must not simply be solid; it must jump out of the pile. It must, in other words, excite the reader. There are several ways in which a proposal can achieve this distinctiveness. One is to have three typos in the first line. Another is to bury the hypothesis in the trivial details of a footnote on page 8. I would not recommend either of these strategies. Your proposal must *grab* the reader: a tight, compelling, well-written, and clever opening paragraph does wonders.[1] A meandering "fishing expedition" or a poorly articulated alleged association between modernity and protest will ensure that your proposal is headed for the wastebasket. Crude and harsh, perhaps, but these are the conditions under which your project is reviewed, and accordingly, they demand some serious reflection.

- Because you have only one chance for success and most (although not all) programs have one deadline per year, allow yourself time to think, write, and plan for the deadline. You simply cannot begin too early. I would suggest the first day of graduate school.

Primary Objectives and Parameters

For the purposes of this chapter, I am making a number of assumptions about the construction of a research proposal as an exemplar of research design. I do this because I am assuming that most readers are in the process of drafting a research proposal or are thinking about dissertation projects and that they intend to conduct something like fieldwork, namely, a process by which they generate evidence. There is, in my view, something like a canon of what a good proposal looks like and what properties and qualities the reviewers of proposals, or dissertation committee members for that matter, look for and privilege. I propose a walk through the process of designing a research proposal as a way of flagging issues that we all need to think about because the process is so difficult, so demanding, and so drawn out. In passing, I shall draw on my own experiences conducting research in West Africa (Nigeria and Senegambia), in South India (Kerala), and in California (the Sacramento Valley), which, like most everyone else's, reflect a combination of systematic, contingent, accidental, and occasionally ridiculous human practices. My interests have focused, in particular, on peasants, rural transformation, social movements, and a variety of agrarian issues, including household dynamics and gender questions. These interests shape the sorts of examples I provide here, but the principles I seek to emphasize are as valid in the humanities and social science professions (law, public health).

Let me immediately say that this chapter will not be a primer on the problems of research design. This is not an occasion for a crash course in designing surveys, training assistants, thinking about respondent bias, or working through the problems of evidence or a genealogy of hermeneutic theory (other chapters in this volume explicitly address such questions). Neither should this chapter be construed as a treatise challenging or even questioning the theoretical or disciplinary approaches one might adopt as an economist, anthropologist, or historian. Of course, I have my own biases, and in the interests of full disclosure, I will try to make them explicit now. First, I take seriously the notion that one should consider a variety of methodological approaches to a research problem and look into multiple methods (an exemplary case would be Paul Lubeck's book *Islam and Urban Labor in Northern Nigeria*, 1987). Second, I will emphasize some key moments in research design and proposal writing (for example, linking evidence to a particular question) as a way of driving home the point that you need to be as clear, as self-conscious, and as explicit as possible in explaining *how* you will conduct your project (e.g., you have arrived in rural Idaho with your U.S.-made pickup truck and gun rack to study the militias. Now what are you going to do?). A good research design makes research life in the barrios of Los Angeles or Bogota much easier. Given all the unknowns associated with doing fieldwork and collecting data, a research proposal is a sort of security blanket. By definition, a proposal pushes you to construct something more deliberate than a fishing expedition ("I'll go and poke around and see what is there"). A well-thought-out research proposal provides you with an identifiable problem; a tentative hypothesis, claim, or proposition; a road map of necessary evidence; and at least some ideas about how and where that evidence can be located or generated. To leave the warm and cuddly academic groves of Berkeley or Cambridge for "the field" without having thought carefully through all such matters is to invite catastrophe, or at least more confusion and anxiety—the state most people are in when they start thinking about a dissertation topic. We can all do with less of this. A proposal, then, has the merit of identifying a hypothesis or a hunch or an argument or a paradox to be explained. How else could one begin? There is something worse than a bad hypothesis, idea, or proposition, and that is no hypothesis, idea, or proposition at all.

Let me briefly define a research proposal as a text that links—in a more or less formal way—theory, method, and evidence (Burawoy et al. 1991). A more elaborate definition would be that a research proposal presents a question or problem theorized in such a way that it generates a claim or argument (a hypothesis, if you wish), attached to which are evidentiary needs on the one side and a series of means (methods) for generating, locating, and assessing evidence on the other. How these pieces are articulated or linked—for example through a comparative study of three country cases using a large-n sample—represents what I would call the research design. As I have already implied, different funders impose different requirements and organizational templates, and the institutional culture of disciplines may vary with regard to how formal (let us say, how amenable the evidence should be to statistical interpretation) such proposals should be. In some disciplines, the language of hypothesis testing may seem remote or outright anachronistic. But all the social sciences and humanities have to grapple with the intellectual and practical problems of conducting independent research, namely, that some evidence is theory laden, that some questions have particular evidentiary demands, and that some methods may not be appropriate for answering certain questions or for generating certain sorts of information. Researchers are in the business of writing narratives of differing sorts. Some sustain arguments and propositions; others provide different explanations and understandings of social life.

Put it this way, independent research seems straightforward and, perhaps, pedestrian. But, of course, it isn't. It is the most difficult thing you will do, even more difficult than writing the dissertation. There are very good reasons why Bowen and Rudenstein (1992) emphasize anxiety and paralysis in their account of the genesis of a research project. The process is loosely institutionalized; it is often confounded by bad advising and poor training; and it is certainly made no easier by the profound arbitrariness of arriving at a topic. How can something predicated on logic and reason so frequently be so contingent or accidental? Why on earth did I choose beer-brewing cooperatives in Burundi and not national dental organizations in Des Moines? Is beer or teeth more or less likely to get me a job? There really is no avoiding this reality. Selecting and designing a research project is hard, exhausting, and unsettling; it is also thrilling, exhilarating, and exciting.

But the difficulty of designing and writing a good research proposal is unquestionably compounded by the fact that students come to it relatively late in their graduate careers. Because of highly structured course work and the impending nightmare of qualifying exams, when a student steps into the field, the planning horizon for dissertation research is typically the immediate and the short term rather than three years down the way. Graduate training can sometimes seem like permanent crisis management (perhaps not unlike Trotsky's account of capitalism). But it is, in fact, impossible to start thinking about a research project too early, for several reasons. First of all, the identification of a place and a problem—household dynamics and commercialization in northern Kenya, for example—carries with it enormous implications as regards the skill set required to carry out the research: fluency in the local language, an area studies background, and training in large-scale social survey design, to say nothing of training in theory, which is the bread and butter of graduate formation. Starting as early as you can is key to building into your graduate formation a series of integrated needs for conducting a project. (It is rather difficult to pick up Chinese late in the game.) Second, the process of writing a research proposal is deeply and profoundly recursive. The proposal can change radically between the sixth and the tenth drafts, which take into account feedback from your committee, friends, and peers. To expect this process to take anything less than six months is myopic. Proposals undergo radical change from the first to the tenth draft; if you look at the University of California, Berkeley, Dissertation Proposal Workshop website (globetrotter.berkeley.edu/DissPropWorkshop/), you will see examples of precisely what is entailed in this recursive process of framing, reframing, refining, sharpening, and so on. Third, the practical start-up demands of a project are time consuming, particularly when the project is to be conducted in a non-native environment. There is ideally a need to make regular predissertation visits to establish scholarly contacts, affiliations, and academic networks; there is a need to scout out possible field research sites and perhaps improve language skills; and most of all, there is a desire to test one's primitive ideas on the local scholars who are familiar with the subject at hand. To ensure such preplanning requires time and flexibility.

The great value of a research proposal carefully crafted early on in one's graduate training is that it acts as a foundation on which a program of work can be constructed. It provides an intellectual and methodological road map. For example, you may want to study the ways local transnational organizations shape the agendas and practices of local green groups—perhaps a case study of the relations between local Ecuadorian environmental NGOs and U.S.-based transnational environmental organizations that fund them—and such a project generates immediate demands for graduate training. In other words, it requires that you put yourself in the best possible position both to secure funding for the project and to complete a well-organized and effective field project. Quite specifically, one might anticipate that you will identify the following as (minimally) necessary:

- Spanish language training, and perhaps training in a local vernacular as well, should the Ecuadorian NGOs be representative of indigenous peoples
- Theoretical work on transnational organizations and transnational networking
- Methodological training in interviewing, ethnography, and participant observation
- Conceptual work on interorganizational behavior, management, and practice

- Background work on environmental movements and organizations, including funding, structure, and governance
- Literature searches on Ecuadorian green movements
- Affiliations and contacts with organizations in the United States and Ecuador that will provide the case studies for the study

What makes for a good and compelling research proposal? A 10–15 page research prospectus that includes sections on theory, method, design, and plan of work will typically be required by the funding organization, and this template will provide the basis for my discussion below. There is no one way, one narrative structure, or one proposal organization to link problem, theory, method, and evidence. But I would say that there are some generic demands ("principles") that any compelling proposal must respond to, namely:

- Transparency
- Clarity
- Methodological precision
- Theory-driven expectations
- Plan of work ("doability")

By transparency, I mean that the logic by which theory, evidence, and method are connected must be explicit. This implies two things. The reader must be able to understand, first, the design of your project and, second, why you have chosen this particular approach to your problem or question. If you are proposing to study the nature of social and economic differentiation among peasants in northern Thailand in relation to the neoliberal reforms since 1985, then it must be clear how you are going to measure differentiation (what criteria, how many people), what means you will use to collect data appropriate to the measures you have chosen, and how you plan to separate the effects of the neoliberal reforms on differentiation from other "causal" forces (say, farming ability and household size). Transparency, then, is simply the legibility of the process by which you construct a problem, pose a hypothesis or question, and explore the evidentiary needs of your research and validity of your results. The implications of transparency are that a reader must be able, without effort, to understand clearly how you link a theorized problem with a claim, with evidence, and with method.

Clarity refers to the need to strike a balance between the specialized lexicon of theory and discipline and the need to be able to "walk" a reader through a proposal in such a way that the reader fully and easily grasps the internal logic or architecture of the study. The demand for clarity does not imply a linguistic or expressive dilution (a dumbing down) but rather highlights the dangers of obfuscation (what exactly is this proposal suggesting?), ambiguity (how many people will the researcher be interviewing?), and a lack of sufficient information (what exactly is the researcher proposing to do in the name of ethnographic fieldwork, or "hanging out" in the village?). The clarity question can quite easily be tested by asking two or three people to read your proposal and explain to you, in a few sentences, the central problem and central claim. Let me assure you, this is always a rather humbling experience.

Methodological precision asserts the importance of focusing on the "how" question. Typically, funders scrutinize with particular care the part of the proposal that addresses the knotty problems of evidence and data collection, yet students fudge that very part or gloss it over. How large must the sample be? How will the sample be selected, especially in view of the total absence of any reliable survey data? Is representativeness an issue? How can one confidently assume that data on peasant credit relations will be reliable? How exactly can evidence be collected on state espionage? The key point I wish to make here is that there are lots of exciting and creative and innovative questions that we as scholars can pose but that generate evidentiary demands that cannot be met (e.g., they might presuppose that we have access to the internal records of large transnational oil companies or require taking up arms and fighting for a liberation movement in a small African country). This may sound perfectly obvious in the abstract, but all proposals must be able to convince a reader that reliable, valid, and quality information appropriate to the question can be collected under the conditions of fieldwork in an ethically responsible way.

The demand that the proposal meet certain expectations derived from theory is perhaps counterintuitive and somewhat controversial. It reflects the idea that the ways in which you couch your problem—the theoretical tradition in which you have chosen to operate—provides something more than a context for the research to which you gesture in a literature review. It is theoretical precisely because it leads us to expect certain outcomes or to generate specific hypotheses. One can argue over the extent to which theory predicts or overdetermines the research process. But theory must be useful. As Gilles Deleuze (1993) put it, it is a sort of toolbox that you have decided to deploy, and to this extent, it leads you to a hunch about what is going on, what you expect to find. The hunch may be wrong—your research will discover this—but a proposal must contain such a hunch and, through the principles outlined, convince a reader that your proposition is plausible and worth exploring. A compelling proposal cannot stop at the point where you pose a question; you must have something to say about it (a claim, an argument, a hypothesis), and this is what theory does for you (see Pryke, Rose, & Whatmore 2003).

Doability highlights practical considerations that will shape the "fundability" of the proposal—and indeed, your ability to pull off the project! It is one thing to have a theoretically brilliant and well-designed study of financial markets and transnational capital flows; it is another to have the time, money, and resources to analyze vast data sets and complete the analysis in several months. Typically, driven by a sort of data insecurity, most proposals vastly overestimate both the quantity of evidence that they need and their capacity to generate or collect it. That is why one of the most common responses to the first draft of a research proposal is, "Interesting, but this is a lifetime's work!" I remember vividly one of the first proposals I read in 1980 for the Dissertation Fellowship Competition of the SSRC Africa Committee. It was a project on peasant differentiation in Kenya with a sample of 4,000 households, which the applicant hoped to interview in three months. Another applicant hoped to explore the problem of runaway children in Nigeria using police records. Comparisons often confer great explanatory power, but the costs in terms of time, skills, and practicality are accordingly enhanced. The doability question is both practical and epistemological in nature.

In adhering to these principles, the reader of a proposal should be fully able to appreciate the nature of the problem, how the researcher is approaching the study, and how it is to be conducted (when, where, how). In this way, a good proposal offers the reader a clear answer to the following three questions:

- What will we learn that we do not already know?
- Why is it worth knowing?
- How will we know whether the findings are valid?

All these questions are in some measure shaped by field and by discipline. For example, validity may be one thing for a rational choice analysis of collective action and something rather different for an ethnographic analysis of a social movement. But you must always keep these three questions in mind because they represent an important set of criteria by which your project will be assessed and evaluated. It is always a useful exercise to put yourself in the position of someone reading and evaluating a proposal. For this reason, a Dissertation Proposal Workshop on the SSRC model, which turns everyone into a reviewer, can be a powerful learning experience.

At this point, let me say a word about the construction of a proposal in relation to the reader—or more precisely, reviewers, screeners, and selection committees—and in relation to its assessment. I have already stressed the competitiveness of the selection process and its political economy, for want of a better phrase. One can, of course, become almost immobilized by the prospect of second-guessing what funders need or are looking for. Nevertheless, there are a number of narrative devices, tricks of the trade, and obvious dos and don'ts that bear reiteration.

• Powerful opening: Get straight to the point; do not drift around in some aimless way. The opening paragraph is your first salvo. You must have a way of encapsulating what this project is about in a few sharp, snappy sentences.

• Freshness or originality: There is no simple way to make a proposal stand out, and the process of crafting a research project must not be an excuse for showiness, fashion, or superficial cleverness. Nonetheless, one way of giving a project some panache is to construct your study around a puzzle, a paradox, or a conundrum. Consider the following illustration: The rise of political Islam has been associated with particular social patterns of recruitment and a rejection of certain liberal ideals; case X in Jordan, however, stands as a striking contrast. Why? Or, my theory would lead you to expect that people would vote in one way, but in practice they did the opposite. Why? Or, why does Y movement in Nigeria that attacks ethnic politics as a stain on the Federation have ethnic identification as its basis for political mobilization? Paradoxes, exceptions, crises, and comparisons are powerful ways of making a scholarly statement.

• Candid attitude toward ignorance or sensitivity: Even the best plans and early proposal writing can come up short, and the best plans are confounded by unexpected crises and risks. A student preparing to conduct fieldwork in Chiapas in 1994 or in lower Manhattan in mid-September 2001 obviously had to confront unexpected political and practical difficulties. The point is that there will always be absences and deficiencies in one's training and knotty practical and ethical difficulties to be confronted. Never bury these problems or attempt to hide them. Respond to them directly. If your language skills are not terrific, explain your plans to improve them. If you are working in a sensitive war zone, explain why you think you can conduct work there safely without endangering your life or the lives of others. If you are collecting large-n data of a social-survey sort but have no training in survey design, explain how you intend to acquire these skills. You might consider a summer intensive course at the University of Michigan's Institute for Survey Research, in which case you should say so and include it in the budget! A reviewer of a proposal will fully understand that one cannot know everything in advance and that all questions cannot be answered at the time of writing, but these inevitabilities are no excuse for sloppiness or inexactitude. What the reviewer wants is evidence that at the very least you have thought about these things and have something to say about them.

- Security in ambition: Conducting a project is always anxiety provoking, given the unknowns and insecurities. How could it be otherwise? One common response to the combination of practical and personal insecurities (Am I the person to do this? Am I up to it?) is to add more wood to the research fire, such as by adding questions, expanding the theme (do I have enough?), and adding more data (a sample of 800, not 80). Insecurity breeds ambition. But this response can work against doability. One of the most common refrains of the dissertation adviser or the screener is, "It's just too big."

- Self-promotion: Never be reticent about making clear why you are the person to do this project. You are fluent in the necessary language(s), have work experience and personal connections in the region, and have made several predissertation trips. Explaining why you are the person to do the project is imperative.

- Say, don't fudge: There will always be unknowns in any project. Which village will I select? How will I select my snowball sample? Can I interview people on sensitive issues like credit? The tendency is to defer judgment on these issues ("I'll figure it out when I get there"). There are good reasons, perhaps, for improvisation in fieldwork. Sometimes, things do not work out, or local contingencies shape outcomes and choices. But such logic can breed either complacency or a sense in the proposal that you have not thought through (as best you can) what you might do. Give it your best-reasoned shot; don't obfuscate, don't fudge. Convince a reader that you have thought about these questions in the context of not knowing all the relevant details and that you have plausible and credible answers.

- No shopping: A research design cannot be a reconnaissance trip or a shopping expedition. A huge shopping list of generally unstructured questions does not make a proposal.

- Specificity (or, You can rarely be "too specific"): Any adviser would rather read a proposal that has all the details in place (even if not justified!) and all the specifics addressed than a proposal that is full of vague historical associations and fuzzy speculation.

Entry Points and Using Evidence

At this point, let me step back a little and reflect on how we identify a researchable problem or question (what I shall call points of entry) and the ways in which such a question or problem can be framed (what I shall refer to as logics of inquiry). I have taken this language and the discussion that follows from an, alas, unpublished book project, *Epistemology and Social Science* (1985), by professors Paul Lubeck and Bob Alford, of the University of California, Santa Cruz. I am grateful to Paul Lubeck for sharing this work with me. A similar approach is outlined in Andrew Sayer's *Method in Social Science* (1992). Often we start with an ill-defined interest that takes the form of an association or a broad relationship, ill-specified and general in its articulation. For example, we might be interested in the relation between migration and intrahousehold dynamics or between Hindu nationalism and neoliberal reforms or between armed struggle and forms of democratization. Just how and why we get to these entry points really does not matter, and we should not spend too much time figuring out why we are drawn to violence or gender or class conflict (though these might be interesting topics for us and our therapist). These entry points are all important, but they do not address critical middle-level questions and specifics: What are the local forms of armed struggle? What are the specific aspects of neoliberalism, and how do they have causal efficacy? What sort of evidence would we need to identify this or that variable?

Entry points, then, usually take the form of a particular sort of question or query, and their goal is to identify the right research question. Often, this process is treated as one of individual choice or as a curious process of osmosis, in which the field of knowledge is transmitted to the researcher or emerges inexorably from the data. In practice, there is, of course, a complex tacking back and forth between theory, question, and data. One cannot overemphasize the importance of struggling to formulate a coherent—that is to say, conceptually integrated and empirically grounded—research question. The question does ultimately commit or obligate the scholar in key ways: to mastering literatures, to identifying with a theory, and to plowing through sources of data. All this effort is likely to lead to dead ends and paralysis unless you are explicit and self-conscious about the theoretical and empirical decisions you have made.

Whatever the entry point, you will need at some stage to generate a specific question rooted in empirical circumstances and with a particular design and scale (perhaps a large-n, perhaps a national comparison, perhaps a single-village case). Each entry point typically generates a different sort of question and may provide the groundwork for the elaboration of a research program. Practical questions might emerge from a student's experience working in a nonprofit, the Peace Corps, or a government agency. How can an Indian NGO deliver better family planning advice to south Indian women in deeply patriarchal households? How might organic grape growers in the Napa

Valley improve their market share? Why the hell do the farmers who are at the tail end of the irrigation system never get water? One's practical concerns must be located with respect to a theoretical framework and within a logic of inquiry if they are to qualify as action research. By action research, I mean a theorized and scholarly program of work with direct practical implications emerging from the object of study.

Another entry point or research question is empirical. Empirical questions can also take a variety of forms: Some are abstract (How is class consciousness shaped by social interactions among persons of equal status?), some are concrete (Were Catholics more involved than Muslims in the genocidal activities in Rwanda in 1994?), and some are historical (How did the discourse of the 1946 rebellion in X differ from the rebellion in 1978?). And finally, some questions are theoretical: Does bureaucratic authoritarianism reduce the legitimacy of rule? Under what historical circumstances does social integration increase? How do members of militant movements construct beliefs about the meaning of life that justify suicidal acts?

The question then becomes how to push this question forward, develop and refine it, and convert a hunch into a research proposal. There are several immediate responses to this impulse. One is to figure out a conceptual tool kit that can help you refine your question but can also generate hypotheses or propositions to be tested or evaluated. Another is to identify the sort of evidence that is appropriate to the questions and the means by which valid evidence can be collected. A third is to try to understand how a particular approach to linking evidence and theory is shaped by practical considerations: limited time, energy, and resources. In quality research institutions, much time is rightly spent on teaching students a road map of theory appropriate to the discipline and to the selection of concepts relevant to the research project. Often, much less attention is given to the perhaps banal and pedestrian questions of evidence, both what constitutes evidence for a particular approach to a problem (and why) and the mundane issues of acquiring such evidence, however constituted. As I have already mentioned, it is customarily the methods section of the research proposal that is weakest, and it is often weak because it is underspecified—for example, "I shall engage in participant observation." But it may also be weak because the connections—the rules—by which evidence is linked to theory or theorized claims are often opaque.

Let's take three projects for illustrative purposes. One is a study of a farmer's movement in India, with a focus on the question of the meanings of being identified with the movement. Another examines the particular historical conjuncture out of which the Mafia was born in mid-19th-century Sicily. A third is an analysis of strike action in relation to rational choices made by different actors.

One might categorize these questions, which, incidentally, could be approached through differing sorts of theoretical tool kits, into one of three "logics of inquiry": phenomenological, historical, and causal. Such logics provide ways of linking theory and evidence. They do not help you answer your questions but rather highlight the choices that have to be made given the fact that working with one set of tools limits what can be pursued as well as the manner in which it can be pursued. Logics of inquiry offer the opportunity to formulate and reformulate a question within different approaches and to see the choices available to you regardless of the content of the question.

Let me examine each of these logics, drawing on Lubeck and Alford and on Sayer as a way of showing how the logics of the different rules linking theory and evidence confer different options.

Causal Logic: One broad class of procedures attempts to distinguish the relative importance of different causal factors, to discover the causal structure that explains variation in the social world. It explains variations in the attributes of different units of analysis by deploying a multivariate analysis. In order for evidence to be recognized by theory (whether Marxian, rational-choice, or neoclassical), it must be transformed into variables. This approach is frequently grounded in, and draws strength from, positivism. The model for this logic is the natural sciences, which assume that the world is knowable, real, and divisible into autonomous parts; that observations can be replicated; and that bias can be controlled. The most important variables cannot be manipulated by investigators. Rather, they must assume that classification into subgroups substitutes for experimental manipulation and that one can draw data from a sample and measure the variables of interest without rupturing the actual social relations among individuals and groups from which the data are drawn. A survey is the most typical quantitative example of multivariate analysis. A survey is appropriate when some degree of independence of the independent variables can be defined. (See Chapter 6, this volume.) Objectivity requires the careful specification of variables and their measures and the reporting of all relevant data and how they were gathered. The observer is assumed to be at some distance from the observed. A basic task is obviously to reduce interview bias and measurement error. A model of causal logic might be Emile Durkheim's study of suicide (1897/1997).

Phenomenological Logic: This is an interpretive logic of inquiry. The various theories that make use of it assume that social reality is constructed by and through symbolic and cultural interpretations, webs of meaning, and signification built and used by human actors. It is typically based on a phenomenological philosophy and is customarily associated with field observations of real-life situations, participant observation, and ethnographic methods and secondarily with the interpretation of key texts. Within this logic, there is a sort of causal connection between categories in the actor's mind and his or her actions, between the roles being played and the rules of the game. But, as Lubeck and Alford note, the open-ended, negotiated, self-conscious character of social interaction means that causation is not linear; relations are contingent and subject to continual change. Meaning symbols and discourses are the theoretical categories that identify and locate relevant evidence for analysis. Observations of actual interactions, events, movements, and gestures would typically be qualitative data. Participant observation is the method that links phenomenology to interpretive theory and to qualitative field notes as the form of evidence (see Burawoy et al. 1991; Burawoy et al. 2001). Objectivity results from self-conscious checking of the observer's perceptions and his or her relations to those observed. The researcher participates in social life, and categories of observation cannot be separated from those activities. While questions of meaning—for example, which symbols in the discursive political struggles of a particular expression of political Islam are problematic sources of conflict and differing interpretations?—are associated with cultural theory and the humanities, there is no a priori reason why surveys might endeavor to collect systematic data on some symbolic questions. A model of interpretive logic might be Michael Gilsenan's *Recognizing Islam* (1990) or, in a different register, Clifford Geertz's account of thick description in *Interpretation of Cultures* (1973).

Historical-Dialectical Logic: This approach is based on a historicist philosophy and draws strength from the observation and belief that contingent sequences of events take place within an interdependent historical totality. Evidence is primarily, but not wholly, textual, and the method is to construct a narrative sensitive to conjunctures, contingencies, and contradictions. Historical analysis assumes that all relationships and processes are interdependent and change over time in relation to one another. The essential concepts are totality (a single case changing over time), conjunctures (overdetermination, and multiple factors changing together), and chronology (sequences of concrete events). Historical events are discrete moments in time that can stand in for a variety of forces at work within a totality. Theoretical categories that identify empirical units of observation are, for example, the Depression, the Great War, and the New Deal. They sum up the meaning of a particular period, and each of these events is a complex totality that derives its meaning from a larger context but also becomes the mechanism for gathering and interpreting specific historical data. According to Lubeck and Alford (1985), the ideal example of the historical logic of inquiry focuses on a single case seen as a totality of interdependent elements that constitute each other and cannot be separated from their relations with each other. Blok's (1974) account of the genesis of the Mafia in 19th-century Sicily is a case in point. The sequences of events are contingent outcomes that cannot be attributed to separable causes; the process is, in other words, dialectical. A search for patterns and changes is the method linking philosophy of history to historical theory, and the unit of analysis is the global, societal, or subsocietal entity that constitutes a whole. The interplay between structural forces and conjunctural or contingent events is an intrinsic theoretical issue within the historical logic of inquiry. There is a sort of causation at work here, too, but causes are neither linear nor independent; they are interdependent and dialectical. A model might be Karl Marx's *The 18th Brumaire of Louis Bonaparte* (1960).

The descriptions of these logics that I have provided above are abbreviated and stylized, but I want to refer to two key points about them. First, each type of evidence for a project located with respect to one of these logics must be converted to a form recognized by the theory in order to be defined as appropriate for explanation. A causal theory recognizes only primary data that can be converted into a variable. Texts or narratives of events are key to historical logics. They must be converted into variables through some sort of coding if they are to be deployed by causal logic, although this coding may be qualitative as well as quantitative. Interpretive theory may use field notes, but within the historical logic, they are a text, and for causal analysis they must be rendered into multivariate form. Second, in practice, a research project may deploy two or more of such logics of inquiry—great works typically do—and a research program may indeed involve using specific data in a variety of ways (if possible) to make it appropriate for different types of analysis. Whether and how, for example, a historical text can be converted into a variable is an important and complex question. Analyses of quite different sorts located in different theoretical traditions may all locate their study in one of these logics. Marxist, neoclassical, and institutional analyses of household economic behavior may all adopt a causal analysis by deploying similar sorts of multivariate data. Similarly, a Marxist analysis could be located in theory in any of the logics of inquiry (though there will be a ferocious debate over whether causal logics are consistent with some versions of Marxian political economy). The key point, however, is that focusing on these various logics makes clear the sorts of choices that are available once a question has been formulated.

Once you have made your choices, for example, a Marxian analysis of the culture of work in south Indian textile factories or an institutionalist analysis of the *ejido* reforms in Mexico, you can begin to seriously explore the sorts of evidence you need and the knotty questions of validity and reliability and so on. This is not the place to work through these complex issues. But I would, in passing, take note of a number of issues that are typically lost sight of in many projects falling within the international studies arena.

National Accounts: Virtually all dissertations addressing some aspect of development typically refer to and make use of macroeconomic and national accounts data (even if the object of scrutiny is the village or the household). Yet anyone who has worked in Africa or Indonesia is acutely aware of deep problems associated with the most basic economic data. For a period in the 1980s, for example, the Nigeria Central Bank published no financial and monetary data; the disparities in estimates of Malian staple food output made by the World Bank, the Food and Agriculture Organization of the United Nations, and the U.S. Department of Agriculture can be, and often are, enormous. Clearly, the epistemology of numbers warrants more attention than is customarily granted to the duplicated World Bank table or the U.N. Development Programme statistical roll.

The Archive: The use of historical sources deployed by the social sciences, such as colonial archives, missionary archives, and business archives, has also become an almost standard part of field research in many parts of the world. But how can you be confident that you can derive the sorts of data you need from historical texts? This question is not only one of textual interpretation but also one of whether such information was indeed collected and whether and how it can be located! Simply because you are interested in prostitution in colonial Nairobi or communal violence in colonial South India does not mean that the archive is laid out in a fashion that will expedite the discovery (a colonial file entitled "Prostitution" waiting for your arrival), or indeed the interpretation, of the information you need. To invoke the archive as a source of evidence is simply a beginning, not an end. As Luise White points out in her book on prostitution in Kenya, *The Comforts of Home* (1990), one needs in some way to understand the social and epistemological organization of the archive—the "colonial mind"—in order to figure out where certain sources of information might be located.

The Assistant: Many dissertation projects have quite limited budgets, but the use of assistants in conducting surveys or as interpreters is ubiquitous. Much has been made in anthropology of the deployment of the assistant (or the "key informant," who may be in effect an assistant). I simply want to raise here the practical dimensions of using enumerators and assistants, the dull details of employment, and the hermeneutic complexities of a sort of intellectual intermediation, of obtaining information twice removed. What kind of people does one recruit as assistants? From where? With what background? With what local understanding and connection? How are they to be trained? And what is their contractual or other relation to you, the principal investigator (PI)? What salaries and benefits should they receive? Whether all this needs to be documented in a research proposal is an open question. But to simply indicate in a methods section that you will make use of interviewers can only raise flags if these issues are not addressed.

The Survey: Survey design is an art in itself, and any project involving large-n samples and a survey designed by the PI must establish that the PI has the training to undertake such a project. Surveys generate substantial amounts of data, and a proposal must therefore be able to address the demands and resources associated with large-scale data collection, management, and analysis. Saying that you have put in the budget a $5,000 request for a new powerful laptop will not suffice! Finally, some sections of the social sciences and the humanities shy away from using survey data ("I do not collect that sort of data," "I prefer ethnography," and so on). Given the value of multiple methods in research design, I would encourage the use of surveys in research even if they are not a central data collection device because they are a powerful tool for scanning, probing, and assessing the landscape in which your study will be located. In other words, spillover and synergistic effects and insights can be derived from the collection of data in a rather mundane baseline survey. It has also been my experience that the need for systematic data— which can be generated only by a survey—may emerge in the course of a project whose need for such data was not anticipated. Being prepared for such eventualities then has a particular payoff.

Violations, Pathologies, and Eyes on the Prize

It is precisely because these principles of proposal writing are so intractable and demanding that one can better understand certain "pathologies" or violations that attend the crafting of a research proposal: the flight into high theory (to avoid the demands of "operationalization") or the descent into data and empiricism (to circumvent the demands of theorizing a problem). All this in turn feeds the necessary and inevitable panic and self-doubt associated with a first cut at thinking about a dissertation project. One would have thought that opportunities—formal or informal—to share these anxieties and to benefit from collective experiences of others would have been institutionalized in some way in every department. And yet, they rarely are. It all seems to be ad hoc and word of mouth. On the Berkeley campus, for example, it is almost impossible to find a course on fieldwork, ethnography, or writing a proposal. The moral of the story is clear: Create such opportunities, seminars, and courses in your own program! Organize! Organize!

Let me turn to one final issue. The research proposal that you craft is ultimately a "big hypothesis." I mean this in at least two senses. First, you may discover in the course of your research that things are not quite what you expected: The problem of out-migration is less significant than you thought, or the ease with which you can study domestic violence has been greatly exaggerated. Second, the world—and the world of your research site— changes. You may find yourself in a war zone; you may get sick for long periods of time; you may simply be unable, for reasons of sensitivity, to approach a problem because of shame or embarrassment or the threat of violence. All these sorts of contingencies constitute the necessary and inevitable risks and uncertainties of doing research. They drive home the point that no matter how theoretically brilliant and methodologically sound the proposal is, it may—and often does—confront a real world and lived experience, including your abilities to do what you think you can do. When it does, it will demand flexibility, improvisation, and an ability and willingness to go back and think again, or tweak the research, or perhaps, at its worst, abandon the project. All of which is to say that the research process is dialectical and recursive; there is a complex feedback between the document you prepare (and may have received funding for) and the risks, unknowns, and contradictions of actually "doing research." Perhaps none of us can be prepared for such eventualities. But even the best-laid research plans cannot— and should never—be cast in stone. It is, for this reason, that good advisers (and funders) constantly reinforce the need to write regular reports on what you have achieved, how things are going, and the ups and downs of data collection, as well as the need for a return trip from the field at some point during your research. Standing back from the day-to-day grind of what you are doing—seeing the forest instead of the trees—is a key requirement for conducting a research project and for having the vigilance and self-reflection to see where and how you might be going off the rails.

To emphasize the contingencies of research and of research in action takes me far from where I began. The same can be said for the completion of data collection and the long and arduous process of making sense of field notes, surveys, and interviews and, not least, for writing the dissertation (Zerubavel 1999). Here is not the place to reflect on how to organize our field notes, how to prepare for our return to the university after a spell in Africa or France, or how to begin the arduous process of writing. But they are all part and parcel of this complex thing called "doing research." Writing a research proposal is, of course, a foundational moment in this process, and this chapter is by no means intended to generate panic or massive depression. But I would be the first to acknowledge that intellectual and academic work must necessarily engage with the emotions. It is perhaps inevitable that making explicit the silences and absences in graduate training programs—of actually talking about and taking seriously the business of doing independent research—raises the bar and, by definition, makes clear the challenges that we all face.

Note

1. I speak from the bitter experience of having read at least 100 proposals a year throughout the 1980s and 1990s for the SSRC, the National Science Foundation, and other funders.

11

Research Ethics are Essential

Ethical Considerations for Research in Cross-Cultural Settings

Sara R. Curran

S tories from the field frequently involve varying degrees of ethical angst among researchers. The angst will sometimes appear directly in publications or documents, in conversations among researchers, or as words of wisdom to the next generation. Sometimes, the angst can be observed between the lines in the recorded or observed behaviors and attentions a researcher bestows on subjects, respondents, or communities during and

AUTHOR'S NOTE: This essay benefited from my tenure on the selection committee for the SSRC/ACLS's International Predissertation Fellowship Program. In addition, I have drawn heavily on numerous discussions during my ethics seminar, "Ethics of Research Practice in the Social Sciences," required of all Ph.D. students at the Woodrow Wilson School for Public and International Affairs at Princeton University. From 2002 through 2004, my coinstructor, Harold Shapiro, and the 30 students who took the course at various times have provided valuable insights and perspectives. I am grateful for research assistance from Sarah B. Martin and editorial assistance from Melanie Adams.

after the fieldwork. Ethical angst in the field is inevitable when the work involves others—whether they are colleagues, respondents, assistants, or people in positions of authority. Research is not a solo enterprise, and social relationships are invariably imbued with many different meanings entailing responsibilities, obligations, and entitlements that may or may not be obvious at any one time and certainly evolve as a research project progresses. These social aspects of research mean that participants in a research project have varying interests, which sometimes coincide and at other times collide. Such conflicts of interest are at the heart of most ethical dilemmas.

Preparing for the possibility of ethical dilemmas, learning how to get disentangled from them, or resolving them is not easy. Compounding these difficulties is the fact that social science graduate training about the ethics of research is frequently haphazard. Often, training in the ethics of research or the profession includes at least one of a number of episodic moments, but it is rarely sustained or revisited. For example, researchers and students may be required to take an online human subjects research training module, their faculty mentor may informally advise them about ethical issues, a methodology course may address ethical issues during one week of a semester, or they may be required to attend one or two hours of a seminar on the topic. Although it is difficult to prepare for ethical dilemmas that may arise during fieldwork, and there may be instances that could not have been anticipated with any amount of training, there is now a large and rapidly growing collection of work that addresses ethical issues in social science research. This corpus of work can be found in books, edited collections, specialized journals, as well as special issues of journals and online. Throughout this essay, I will refer to some of that material, but I can only scratch the surface because the ethics literature is growing at such a rapid rate. Rather than provide a complete ethical guide to fieldwork practices, I offer some basic guidelines that I hope will sensitize researchers to potential ethical concerns. This essay is no substitute for regular visits to virtual or real libraries and conversations with experts in this area.

If there is one message that shines brightly through the essays in this volume, it is the message about transparency. Whether it is transparency in the exact methodological procedures or whether it is the more hermeneutic transparency revealed through delineating how one's feelings affected the outcomes of an interview or the interpretation of events, many of the authors in this volume consistently reiterate the importance of revealing the complexities of the data-gathering process. In so doing, they argue, the researcher furthers science writ broadly. The emphatic attention to this concern leaves the reader with an ethical obligation and responsibility that come with the entitlements of being a social science researcher.[1]

The first half of this chapter addresses issues concerning human subjects and institutional review boards (IRBs). One of my goals is to briefly explain the history of the IRB, the reasons for IRB scrutiny in social science, and its limitations for social science researchers and to provide some perspective on how best to interact with local IRB panels. I show how IRB scrutiny goes only so far, that is, that social science fieldwork can result in ethical dilemmas that are not covered by enforced regulations.

The second half of the chapter goes beyond regulations to discuss issues that occur outside formal regulatory scrutiny: how one recognizes an ethical dilemma, the kinds of contexts in which ethical dilemmas arise, and some particular examples of ethical concerns in the field and afterward. I conclude by suggesting implications contemporary research practices may have for future research practice and ethical dilemmas.

Ethics in a Regulated Environment

In early spring of 1990, I had just joined a team of social scientists conducting research on community contexts and contraception in Thailand. I was a graduate student at the time, and my involvement in the project included helping manage a database, creating variables, conducting analyses, and writing internal reports and memos to assist the principal investigators. By the summer of 1990, we had discovered interesting patterns of contraceptive prevalence across the 50 villages. Survey data from all the women in these villages, who were between 15 and 49 years old, indicated village-based clusters of particular kinds of contraception. In some villages, the predominant method was the pill. In other villages, the predominant method was the IUD. In still other villages, the predominant method was sterilization. The research team was surprised and puzzled and decided to go into the field to investigate this phenomenon. By the fall of 1990, plans were under way to conduct, with the collaboration of colleagues in Thailand, a series of focus groups in select villages. These focus groups were designed to discuss family planning, access to health care, sources of information about contraception, and perceptions about contraception. The focus groups were to be limited to married adults, and discussions with men and women were to be conducted separately.[2]

Prior to going into the field, though, one of the lead investigators suggested that we request human subject approval. She took the lead and duly submitted a request to conduct the research, including information about the questionnaire guideline and the study design and protocols, to our university's IRB.

Our request was rejected. It was a stunning moment. The rejection meant our study could not go forward under university regulations. The reason for the rejection: Our topic was too sensitive to be discussed in a group setting. With that response, the investigators regrouped. I was sent off to the library to find ethnographic references and evidence from previous studies about family planning and contraception in Thailand. Our Thai colleagues were asked to write letters of support (at that time, their institution did not have an IRB) and provide explanations about the feasibility of the study design and its cultural appropriateness in the Thai context. Armed with local knowledge and background materials explaining the discursive norms and cultural context in Thailand, the lead investigator provided further justification for our study design and resubmitted our application to the IRB. In addition, the lead investigator discussed concerns with the IRB members during a formal meeting, answering many of their questions. In the end, the study was approved.

This was my first encounter with the power of the IRB, and at the time, it seemed more like a barrier than a research aid. Although it appeared to be an appropriate venue for vetting research that involved invasive procedures in psychology or biology, I had the distinct impression that it was not appropriate for social science. Of course, at the time, I was not aware of the precedents in social science necessitating IRB scrutiny. I have since come to better appreciate the value and limitations of the IRB.

Since my first exposure to the IRB, I have had several professional affiliations in different academic institutions and watched how various individuals, centers, and departments struggle to relate to the IRB and prepare their graduate students for interactions with it. In general, there is reluctant compliance and the widely held perception that this is a bureaucratic hoop not particularly relevant to well-intentioned social science researchers. On the other hand, I have also witnessed the proliferation of IRB panels in nonacademic social science organizations and in many academic institutions around the world. Increasingly, funding sources outside the public sector are also requiring IRB approval prior to allocating funds. A rise in interdisciplinary research also exposes more social scientists to research practices in the medical and biological fields, where human subject research protection is a matter of course. And finally, a growing number of scientific journals are requiring formal indication of official human subject approval before they will publish study results. Globalization and the forces of isomorphism mean that whatever one's personal opinion about the relevance of IRB panels for social science research, they are likely here to stay and will become a routine aspect of the research process for all social science research.

Our current regulatory environment primarily stems from concerns about biomedical research that can be traced back to the 19th century (Faden & Beauchamp 1986; Katz 1972). Most concerns about this research derive from invasive procedures that harmed subjects. But some cases are recognized because they violated rights to privacy or because research participants were coerced or deceived (King, Henderson, & Stein 1999). It was not until the middle of the 20th century that formal guidelines and codes were developed. The development of these guidelines was spurred by the egregious findings from the Nuremberg trials and resulted in the recognition of the Nuremberg Code of research ethics (circa 1947–1949).[3] Despite the Nuremberg Code, U.S. researchers continued to use protocols that raised serious ethical concerns. Several of these cases have now become touchstones.

The U.S. Public Health Service's Tuskegee syphilis study,[4] the Jewish Chronic Disease Hospital case,[5] the Willowbrook study,[6] Milgram's obedience study,[7] and the Stanford Prison Experiment[8] were highly publicized studies that took place from the 1930s through the early 1970s. These cases all imposed serious physical and psychological harm on subjects and involved either incomplete consent or deception. These improprieties were exposed publicly during the late 1960s and early 1970s, coincident with growing civil rights consciousness in the United States (King, Henderson, & Stein 1999). During the same period, the Wichita Jury Study and Humphrey's "tearoom trade" study (for more details, see Faden & Beauchamp 1986) were also condemned, not because they imposed physical harm on subjects, but because they purportedly violated the rights and interests of subjects.

As a result of the publicity surrounding these projects, the National Commission for the Protection of Human Subjects of Biomedical and Behavioral Research issued the *Belmont Report* in 1979.[9] In the *Belmont Report,* three moral principles are put forth to guide research practice: respect for persons, beneficence, and justice. Derived from a principlist paradigm that emerged from the European Enlightenment, these moral principles were subsequently codified in the United States by the *Common Rule* in 1991.[10] The *Common Rule* describes the research that is to be regulated, the procedures and the institutions that regulate the research, and the guidelines for upholding the principles established by the *Belmont Report.* It was the *Common Rule* that required the establishment of an IRB panel within any research organization receiving federal funding.

The assumption that a modified biomedical model for standard ethical review can and will fit all purposes is increasingly recognized as problematic and limited in its effectiveness as a tool for monitoring and compliance in social science research (King, Henderson, & Stein 1999; Lederman 2004).

At the same time, social science researchers also need to teach IRBs about the different conventions and contexts of social science research so that the boundaries of appropriate, bureaucratized reviews are better defined in the interests of researchers, the subjects of research, and researchers' institutions.

An IRB panel is usually composed of representative scientific peers and community members. Every university or college structures its IRB differently, and it behooves researchers to be well aware of the composition of the panel. Depending on the size of a university or college and whether it has a medical or public health school, scientific peers may include research clinicians from biomedical disciplines, as well as psychologists and other social scientists. Smaller universities or colleges without large medical research programs are likely to have IRB panels composed of scientists from disciplines spanning the spectrum from biomedicine to economics. In larger universities, some IRB panels are convened specifically for social science research. Community members vary across IRB panels; often there is a standing member, but ad hoc members can be invited on a case-by-case basis for particular types of projects. It is to an IRB that a researcher files a human subject approval request. In addition, each IRB must publish its guidelines defining the kinds of research included in and exempt from review.

Common Rule regulations are periodically revisited, and over the past 20 years, social scientists have marshaled several efforts to redefine what kind of research is covered by the *Common Rule* and what kind of research might be exempt.[11] Suffice it to say that the main tenets of the regulations are unlikely to change dramatically. But the scope of research covered by the *Common Rule* is likely to change, and the ways in which individual IRB panels enforce their guidelines may also vary to some extent. Keep in mind that since most research conducted under the auspices of an academic institution is considered the property of that institution, the *Common Rule* holds those institutions responsible for research misconduct and proper implementation of the regulations, particularly if those institutions are recipients of federal monies (even if the study at hand is not federally funded).

The three principles—respect for persons, beneficence, and justice—have also yielded a standard set of adherent practices.[12] Respect for persons recognizes that individuals are autonomous agents who can enter a research project only voluntarily and with adequate information about the consequences of the research to evaluate their decision to participate. Greater protection is required for persons with diminished autonomy (typically defined as children or the incapacitated, including prisoners). The adherent practice for the principle of respect for persons is informed consent, which has three components: information, comprehension, and voluntarism. Information to convey to respondents includes a statement informing the individual about the research project's purpose, procedure, risks, and anticipated benefits; a statement offering the individual the opportunity to ask questions and to withdraw at any time from the research; an explanation of how participants are selected; and identification of the person responsible for the research.[13] Ensuring a potential respondent's comprehension includes consideration of the manner and context in which the information is conveyed, including the organization or pace at which the information is conveyed. If the subject cannot comprehend what is being said, someone who can comprehend and who is responsible for the well-being of that individual must be found and should be allowed to observe and to decide whether to withdraw the subject from the study. Voluntarism is observed with a formal agreement to participate in research and acknowledgment that the decision was made voluntarily. It requires conditions free of coercion and undue influence. Coercion occurs when an overt threat of harm is intentionally presented by one person to another in order to obtain compliance. Undue influence, by contrast, occurs through an offer of an excessive, unwarranted, inappropriate, or improper reward or other overture in order to obtain compliance. Also, inducements that would ordinarily be acceptable may become undue influences if the subject is especially vulnerable.[14]

Beneficence is an obligation to make an effort to secure respondents' well-being. It has two aspects: the duty to do good and nonmalfeasance, or the duty to refrain from causing harm or increasing harm. Beneficence in the research context governs both the design and the conduct of research, including not only immediate risks and benefits to subjects but also consideration of whether the research is "worth doing" in light of long term expected results and their societal implications. There are some aspects of research that can clearly be evaluated based on harm and benefits, but assessing long-term benefits is always more difficult than assessing immediate harm and benefit.

Justice is the least-developed principle as applied to research and has a variety of formulations. Its purpose is to eliminate biases against groups of people. It is meant to fairly distribute the benefits and burdens of research among cultural, social, gender, racial, and ethnic groups (King, Henderson, & Stein 1999, p. 9). In recent years, the justice principle has gained more attention because it forces consideration of respondents as members of communities with identities and concerns that may be quite independent of the individual participant's. It is not easy to adjudicate researchers' obligations and responsibilities against the entitlements of the community or the respondent. Simultaneously bringing the community and individual into focus requires attention to issues of power and its distribution in the past, present, and future. This focus on justice and the distribution of power can generate an internal inconsistency with the earlier principle of respect for persons and for individual autonomy. Most recently, these issues have become particularly salient with regard to research about HIV/AIDS in developing countries. In these circumstances, "Researchers are increasingly questioning their positions of privilege and their relationships with powerful others, such as funders, policymakers, and their academic community, causing them to rethink what research they are willing to do and to pay much closer attention to how they ought to do it" (King, Henderson, & Stein 1999, pp. 9–10).[15] Some extreme examples from HIV/AIDS research in developing country settings are worth considering. Benatar (2002), for example, points out how the descent of a large team of biomedical researchers into the homes of villagers can be disruptive for community relations and possibly compromise individual members' position within a community. Even if HIV/AIDS were not a stigmatized disease within that setting, cultural norms may privilege the community over individuality. Getting permission from the community leaders may be culturally appropriate but may also compromise an individual's health (Benatar 2002).

When researchers apply to an IRB for human subject approval, they typically complete a questionnaire based on the three principles. This questionnaire asks about the purpose of the study, the anticipated risks and benefits, the study protocols (sampling procedures and the conditions of participation), the way informed consent will be ascertained, and the way subjects will be protected (whether there will be anonymity and how the data collected will be cared for to protect participants' privacy).

In social science research, there are some red flags that cause IRB panels to pay special attention to the study. These red flags are the following:

- Any indication that participants will be deceived.
- Topics that are perceived to be sensitive and to put respondents at some emotional or mental distress.
- Potential that respondents might be vulnerable (besides children, prisoners, and mentally challenged respondents, other vulnerable populations might be victims of violence, refugees, or respondents participating in illegal activities).
- Nonwritten forms of consent (see Fluehr-Lobban 1994 for suggestions)
- Unusually large gifts in exchange for participation in the research or inducement rewards for recruiters of subjects, which unintentionally coerce respondents' participation.

By highlighting these red flags, I do not mean to suggest that one should never pursue sensitive topics or give gifts and so forth. Instead, researchers need to do their homework ahead of time and prepare the necessary justifications, given the validity of the study design and the benefits of the research.

On this latter point, in my experience, although IRB panels rarely critique a project's scientific study design, they will evaluate the merits of the study and decide whether the merits include significant benefits. If it appears to them that the study design is so poor or that the benefits of the research are not enough to merit wasting participants' time, then they may fail to approve a project.

To minimize red flag reactions from an IRB panel, especially when one is about to set off to do research in a very different cultural or legal context, it is critically important to allocate enough time to prepare and receive approval before departure. IRB approval is not a "last minute" hoop to jump through. Collect extant information about the data collection approach you will use to demonstrate prior risks and benefits. Find former panel members to advise you on whether there are potential red flags and how to address them. Talk to other researchers who have been to the field and, even better, those who have been to your site. Read ethnographic and historical material on your site and document the cultural context that supports the research approach without undo harm or risks to participants. Contact your on-site collaborators (individuals and institutions) to at least get their feedback and formal approval (especially if there is a local IRB).[16] Most important, do not obfuscate the study design. Be as transparent as possible. Panel members are scientists. They know how to evaluate study designs and will reject projects that are not clearly described.

In sum, IRB panels are here to stay, and it behooves researchers to be prepared when submitting an application. Doing so reduces the possibility of delays in research schedules. And because IRBs are a given, make the most of the experience by approaching it as an opportunity for exchange and learning, in which the researchers are teachers as much as panel members are evaluators. IRB panels and their jurisdiction and rules are not fixed in stone. At the very least, by treating the encounter as an opportunity to enlighten the panel on the method and its appropriateness in a particular context, you are providing a public service to other social science researchers in the future. Finally, in as much as the encounter with an IRB can be the first time ethical considerations about a project are considered, the exercise can be worthwhile, especially as attention to issues of justice becomes increasingly important for IRB panels and for social science research more generally.

There are several limitations of IRB panel procedures and human subject approval. First, follow-up is rare, and subsequent required reporting to the IRB panel is limited. Second, the scope of ethical considerations does not completely address the nature of social science research, especially if the project is of some duration, the initial approach is exploratory and open-ended, and the social dimensions of the project are complicated. As research projects lengthen and relationships with those in the locale deepen, the research may become richer, but the burdens on the individual respondents and the community may be taken for granted. Or if the research is exploratory, there may be heightened concerns about whether the research procedures will really reveal anything new or open up possibilities for taking research in unanticipated directions that may have subsequent ethical considerations warranting some ethical review. But even more important, social science research is necessarily socially interactive, and by definition, ethical stances and expectations will be invoked in the development of trustworthy relationships between researchers and those in the research site. Thus the weight of ethical responsibilities lies with the researcher and the coping skills gained through disciplinary training (Lederman 2004).

For other formal guidance on ethical concerns that exist within the regulatory domain and beyond it, researchers can sometimes turn to their disciplinary codes of ethics. These, however, vary dramatically across disciplines, and for some disciplines they are nonexistent. Anthropology, sociology, history, political science, and psychology have well-publicized codes.[17] Each of these disciplines offers guidelines about the ethical issues pertaining to its methodological approaches as well other dimensions of the profession and discipline.

Other Ethical Considerations: Before and After Regulatory Approval

Going into the field and being in the midst of fieldwork can frequently call into question the assumption that the ethical stance outlined in the first half of this essay is universally true and applicable. Inevitably, the social science researcher comes face to face with the possibility of a relativist paradigm that presumes shifting positions and relationships rather than a principlist and universal paradigm. This is because our studies include individuals and groups, are context-based (studying gender, culture, race or ethnicity, place, others), are likely broad rather than narrow, have significant duration involving longstanding social relationships, and evolve during their course (King, Henderson, & Stein 1999, p. 15).

For example, one moment during my fieldwork seems relatively minor with the perspective of time but has stayed with me for many years. It encapsulates, in particular, the importance of entrée, the inevitable and sometimes necessary reshaping of relationships, and the need for reflective engagement throughout a research project. In 1992, I had been living in a small Thai village for three months, learning Thai through immersion, and working with a research assistant to conduct a household census. My research assistant was a university student studying for her master's degree in medical anthropology.

I had hired her to help me do the census, and she was ideal, having come from the region (albeit from an urban center in the region) and being fluent in the local dialect. But she was also a very urbane young woman in dress and manner. After finishing the household census, she returned to her studies while I remained behind to begin more in-depth observation. Shortly after her departure, I was casually discussing my research with my host family one night after dinner when the conversation suddenly began to reveal several misconceptions about who I was and what I was doing in the village. The first was that I was working for my research assistant. The second was that she was working for a local NGO that had a relationship with the villagers that was not entirely positive. I was stunned. As I proceeded for the next few months, it became clear that my host family was not the only group of villagers to hold these misconceptions.

The revelation forced me to reshape and clarify my relationships with the villagers, my research assistant, and the local NGO. It called into question the preceding months' conversations, which may have been affected by these perceptions and therefore represented more guarded observations than I had initially assumed. In the process of repositioning myself within the community, I also had to acknowledge that there were lots of anomalies about me that were hard to reconcile within the local context and that I had to negotiate in my everyday relationships and in the context of my research. These anomalies were fundamental to villagers' ways of establishing my relative status in a society that values status distinctions. For example, I was married but still in school. I had been married for four years but had no children. I was studying for a doctorate but was only barely literate in Thai script. I was cagey about my income and did not seem to be working, but I always seemed to have enough money. And I dressed more casually and more like them than any other university person they had encountered. On reflection, I realized that I had defied many gender and social status categorizations and that my doing so meant members of the community had had trouble reconciling my presence there. Along many dimensions, I could not be put in a neat social box, making it difficult for them to situate me comfortably in relation to themselves. This partially explained the ease with which they had come to the conclusion that this was not my research.

The other part of the explanation resided with my mode of entrée. The presumed association with the local NGO was the result of my having been driven to the village initially by one of the NGO staff members in the NGO car (with the label of the NGO prominently displayed on the car's side panel). During those first few months, that NGO staff person made a point of frequently stopping by to "check-in" on Pui (my research assistant) and me. There was another, younger American woman volunteering at the NGO headquarters who also came to visit Pui and me once. Our entrée and the apparent connection to the NGO were all too apparent to villagers. All this despite the fact that each of the household heads in the village was informed about my project through a written informed consent form and a verbal discussion. The perceived association with the NGO heightened my concerns about my apparent power over and access to resources that would distinguish and separate me from villagers and might limit my capacity to really learn from them about their lives. These concerns were further heightened as I began to learn more about the considerable skepticism and distrust directed toward the NGO by some villagers. Because I did not want to be in the middle or be seen as on one side or the other, the act of resituating myself relative to the NGO and the villagers came to feel like walking an ethical tightrope and meant that it took a bit longer to win the confidence of some villagers.

Although the preceding example may appear to be a mere misunderstanding, it demonstrates how unanticipated ethical dilemmas may emerge during fieldwork. In what follows, I draw on my own experiences as well as others', including those in this volume, to make two sets of observations about the when, where, how, and what of ethical dilemmas, beyond those that might be raised by following the prescriptions of your local IRB. These observations are meant to provide some tools during the research process for anticipating, recognizing, and deconstructing the dimensions and scope of an ethical dilemma. There usually is no easy answer at one point in time or a definitive answer over time, but more often than not, some sort of clarity can be gained through systematic reflection outside the field setting, either by physically removing yourself or by engaging in a dialogue with somewhat disinterested others who reside outside the field context.[18] My observations can be divided into two kinds: overarching contextual considerations and particular considerations relating to fieldwork, from choosing topic or site to publishing results.

Considering Overarching Contexts of Power

Whenever personal relationships are defined by differential access to resources, rights, entitlements, and obligations, then power structures emerge, and with them comes the possible emergence of conflicts of interest and justice concerns throughout a project. Anticipating and addressing these concerns require a disciplined reflectivity on the part of the researcher as well as openness, flexibility, and responsiveness. And, as Alma Gottlieb points out so eloquently in Chapter 3 of this volume, a hermeneutic approach to the emergence of a "problem" can also yield greater intellectual insight about the place and its people in the long run. Not only does it yield insights on those "others," but, Gottlieb notes, these moments also reveal a lot about oneself, one's comfort levels, and one's own issues of identity. Together, they inform the necessary, hermeneutic narrative about the research and its results.

There are two issue areas concerning contexts of power that I will highlight here: collaborations and funding. In the third part of this essay, I will also highlight a number of other moments in the fieldwork process when ethical dilemmas might arise.

Conflicts of interest arise when competing interests compromise obligations and responsibilities to respective parties within a relationship. Despite good intentions, we frequently face moments, under any circumstances, when our own interests may be at odds with the interests of those we are working or living with. Recognizing and then deconstructing the elements of a conflict of interest as it arises or just before it arises help minimize negative fallout. Conflicts of interest usually arise when we occupy several different positions of obligation, or put more colloquially, "wear many different hats." For example, a graduate student piggybacking a dissertation research project onto an ongoing larger project may simultaneously be a research project manager, a student, a teacher, and a grant recipient. At some times, a graduate student may have obligations to the project that shortchange the dissertation. Or dissertation research results may not be obviously independent of the larger project, calling into question concerns about authorship and rights to data.

Concerns about justice are related to conflicts of interest over adjudication of obligations, entitlements, and responsibilities. In addition, justice concerns may reach more broadly. For example, research may be taking place in contexts of severe exploitation or conflict where violence is being inflicted by some on others. Such conditions may warrant a response by the researcher quite independent of the narrowly defined ethical requirements laid out by the *Common Rule* or the IRB. Philippe Bourgois's thoughtful and provocative essay on this topic indicates a number of ways one can put ethical responses into perspective (Bourgois 1990). Justice issues also emerge when you consider the voices to privilege in ethnographic fieldwork or whom to sample from a population when you are conducting a survey. Of recent concern, especially in light of the controversies surrounding HIV/AIDS research in developing countries, are the justice issues surrounding researchers' obligations to improve the lives and well-being of the vulnerable and disadvantaged; the possibility that exploitation has contributed to disparities, creating interesting research on how studies may perpetuate inequality, especially as researchers from more advantaged countries take data and use information for their own country's interests; and the need to build research capacity, including research ethics adjudication capacity, among colleagues in research locales (Benatar 2002). A second growing justice concern has to do with research that identifies unique communities for research—singling them out because of particularly high incidences of any outcomes, but usually those identified with physical or social ills. Typically, research protocols look to individuals for consent to participate and are less likely to call for community consent. Considering community interests raises a whole host of concerns, including how a community is defined, how community representation is determined, whether community and individual interests can be reconciled, and how research benefits are to be distributed (Kaufman & Ramarao 2005).

Whether it is access to research sites, movement around a country, legitimacy, academic resources, getting one's foot in the door, gaining entrée into an archive, finding a place to live, having an office to go to, finding research assistance, getting medical help, or being introduced to important elites, collaborations will multiply during the process of fieldwork. Although one can think narrowly about collaborations as those among academic colleagues, many of the authors in this volume suggest a broader definition, which includes collaborative relations one develops. In that sense, the relationship is clearly defined as one of exchange and mutuality rather than a vague acquaintanceship. And as research approaches broaden to actively include participatory ones, the relationship between researchers on the one hand and subjects-informants-participants on the other becomes less distant and brings into relief the researchers' responsibilities and obligations toward those they interview and learn from. Defining relationships as collaborative also pushes a researcher to consider that simple cash payments may not constitute adequate or fair compensation and may even harm long-term access to assistance (see Chapter 3 in this volume for some good examples). Instead, collaborations may mean that a researcher offers in-kind services, builds capacities, or helps create networks of access for underserved populations. In some contexts, the power dynamics between researcher and subjects may be reversed, revealing the many preconceived notions about that relationship in other settings and challenging standard operating procedures. For example, Alan Benjamin describes how, during his dissertation research, his access to a religious community was proscribed by a legal contract that was drawn up by congregation leaders and ceded considerable control of written products to the congregation (Benjamin 1999). In the process of negotiating the contract, determining his own research questions, and working with his adviser, Benjamin ran up against considerable opposition to his contractual accession from his professional colleagues, who felt he had given up too many intellectual property rights and academic freedoms (see Fox 1999 and Estroff 1999, companion essays to Benjamin 1999).

A final concern with regard to contexts of power is the issue of money. As graduate students enter the field, their sources of money are universities, national and private scientific foundations, or some combination of all three. Typically, these funding sources have no separate, special interest in the particular outcomes of the research but instead require competency, reporting, and follow-through with the project. Michael Watts (Chapter 10) eloquently describes the obligations and responsibilities of graduate students concerning topic development and proposal preparation. But as research careers develop, funding sources may widen to include a broader array of sources, including corporate sponsors or government sponsors with special interests (e.g., Defense or National Security funding). During the 1960s and 1970s, the U.S. government funded Project Camelot in Latin America and similar projects in Southeast Asia, all of which came under particularly intense scrutiny because social scientists were funded by the U.S. Department of Defense to study and report on rural villages at risk of becoming places of communist insurgency. Wakin (1992) describes the angst of anthropologists in the United States over village-based research in Thailand supported by the U.S. Department of Defense during the Vietnam War. After the terrorist attacks of September 11, 2001, and with considerable growth in funding for research on terrorism and national security as it pertains to understanding human behavior, an increasing number of social scientists will probably revisit the ethical dilemmas of Project Camelot and Southeast Asian village-based studies. Behavioral research about health outcomes is also receiving more attention from the private sector. Barry Popkin has described his research team's ethical concerns with accepting money from corporate sponsors when studying breast feeding and infant nutrition issues (Popkin 1999). Popkin, in combination with the essays by Kopelman, Brandt, and Freidenfelds in the King, Henderson, and Stein volume (1999), delineates the full array of issues surrounding funders with special agendas. But a researcher's consideration of ethical concerns about funding should include those relating to the recipient as well as the funder. In fact, since researchers typically conduct their research in a country or community that is significantly less well off than their own, it is highly likely that they will begin to support a variety of individuals and activities within the community. In Chapter 3 of this volume, Gottlieb outlines several ways in which to consider money in the context of research. Downplaying or overplaying money runs its own risks. It is essential that a researcher be well prepared through background research and discussions with experienced researchers or language instructors or anyone well versed in cultural norms of the study area.

Considering Particular Conditions
for Emergent Ethical Dilemmas

The preceding discussions of conflicts of interest, justice, collaborations, and funding deserve their own special section because these considerations infuse most aspects of the research process. But that process requires a step-by-step approach, and ethical dilemmas may emerge at several other moments that deserve mention at this point.

As Watts and Gottlieb point out numerous times in their essays, there is no better way to be prepared for fieldwork than to have invested significant time in language training and cultural immersion. Language and cultural skills enhance access and build trust. Most important, decent language and cultural skills necessarily diminish opportunities for misunderstandings, a root cause of many ethical dilemmas.

Upon arrival in the field, it is critical to begin establishing perceptions, trust, and reliable collaborations. Taking one's time in gaining entrée can frequently minimize opportunities for ethical dilemmas. Learning the "lay of the land" and not jumping into research activities (like going door to door to conduct a household survey) or overstating plans or goals can give a researcher the space to figure out the best way to begin. In fact, time, like money, and in combination with money, is a resource that can create ethical dilemmas. Rushing to get through a project or basing a decision on expediency may yield long-term unintended consequences.

The process of doing research raises a host of issues. I list them here as questions. There are many resources to draw on for guidance in identifying some answers to these questions, including the essays in this volume by Schrank, Chapter 2; Gottlieb, Chapter 3; Giles-Vernick, Chapter 4; Short, Chapter 5; and Harrell, Chapter 8. But the best sources for answers are the experts with experience in the locale. Should you hire someone to help you? Who will you hire? How will you pay them? Will they be from the community or from outside the community? When interviewing your respondents, where is the best place to talk to them? Where will they be most comfortable? Under what circumstances can you have a conversation with an entire group? About which topics? How do you go about double-checking your informants' facts and stories? What do you do with competing information? What kind of gifts should you give your informants? If you are in the field for a long time, how likely are your respondents and now friends to forget that you are doing a research project? When should you remind them? How often? When you have collected your data, notes, pictures, or evidence and are ready to depart from the field, how do you say "thank you"? When should you return? Do you have an obligation to share your findings with those who gave their time to you?

It is also possible that unusual circumstances may occur that you can never prepare for. As Watts in Chapter 10 and many others in this volume observe, managing fieldwork is about being flexible and recognizing that you are not alone at that moment. Others are there to help you, and others have experienced something similar. The uncertainty, awkwardness, or discomfort is not yours alone to experience. As Schrank cautions in Chapter 12, do not panic and rush to judgment. Trust your intuition and learn from the moment.

The preceding thoughts brush the surface of the kinds of ethical questions and moments a researcher might confront. Again, these comments are not exhaustive but are meant to be evocative and prepare a researcher for the necessary reflective approach to the research process.

Conclusion

In conclusion, let me return to the broader ethical issue that Michael Watts introduces in Chapter 10 of this volume. This is the weak institutionalization of the most formative experiences in graduate training: dissertation and proposal writing. In reading Watts's essay, I immediately harked back to the one lecture on ethics I was required to attend during my graduate training. In that lecture, the speaker (unfortunately, I cannot remember who it was) argued that the hardest part about Ph.D. work was not the first part of the experience—the courses, the general exams, the short papers—but the latter half. This, he argued, is when ethical dilemmas are most likely to arise. Weak institutionalization of training, long periods with little contact with advisers, fatigue, money shortages, emotional limbo, and other factors can prompt shortcuts that might otherwise not be taken. And, as Watts points out, responsibilities and obligations lie with both the student and the institution. Watts carefully delineates all the responsibilities for graduate students and implies that academic institutions should formalize more training for independent research.

Nevertheless, throughout the essays in this volume, including this one, contributing authors have made remarks that bear repeating at this point because they are touchstones for social science. The first is an obligation to truth as best as one can discern it. The second is transparency in method and narrative. The third is reflection. And the fourth is frequent interaction and communication with knowledgeable others to enhance one's own accountability. These are not new messages, but they certainly resonate in the literature on the ethics of research practice.

Notes

1. I do not discuss in this essay epistemological issues surrounding norms in scientific practice among philosophers of science. For good examples, see Hardwig, J. R. (1991). "The Role of Trust in Knowledge." *Journal of Philosophy* 88(12), 693–708; Hauptman, R. (2002). "Dishonesty in the Academy." *Academe* Nov/Dec.; Mulkay, M. J. (1976). "Norms and Ideology in Science." *Social Science Information* 15(4–5), 637–656; and Merton, R. K. ([1942] 1973). "The Normative Structure of Science." In *The Sociology of Science*, edited by N. W. Storer. Chicago, IL: University of Chicago Press.

2. Publications based on this research include Entwisle et al. 1993, 1996, 1997; Rindfuss et al. 1996.

3. The precise citation is "Trials of War Criminals Before the Nuremberg Military Tribunals Under Control Council Law No. 10, Vol. 2, pp. 181–182. Washington, DC: U.S. Government Printing Office, 1949." Retrieved September 14, 2005, from onlineethics.org/reseth/nuremberg.html

4. For more information, readers can visit the Centers for Disease Control website, accessed September 14, 2005, at www.cdc.gov/nchstp/od/tuskegee/ or the University of Virginia's Medical Library archive, accessed September 14, 2005, at www.med.virginia.edu/hs-library/historical/apology/

5. For more information, visit the Stanford history page, accessed September 14, 2005, at www.stanford.edu/dept/DoR/hs/History/his06.html

6. Murphy, Timothy. (2004). *Case Studies in Biomedical Research Ethics.* Cambridge, MA: MIT Press.

7. Milgram, Stanley. (1974). *Obedience to Authority.* Cambridge, MA: MIT Press.

8. For a description and overview, see Philip Zimbardo's website, accessed September 14, 2005, at www.prisonexp.org/

9. Retrieved September 14, 2005, from ohsr.od.nih.gov/guidelines/belmont. html

10. Regulation retrieved September 14, 2005, from www.hhs.gov/ohrp/human subjects/guidance/45cfr46.htm

11. There are several very good reviews of the history of and debates about the current regulatory system. See, for example, Faden, Ruth R. and Tom L. Beauchamp (with Nancy King). (1986). *A History and Theory of Informed Consent.* New York: Oxford University Press.

12. Again, this approach to moral behavior derives from the European Enlightenment; moral principles and rules are enunciated and then logically related to moral behavior (even using mathematical calculations to determine the right behavior; King, Henderson, & Stein 1999, p. 8).

13. Often, incomplete disclosure is possible if disclosure threatens validity, that is, if incomplete disclosure is truly necessary to accomplish the goals of the research, if there are no undisclosed risks to subjects that are more than minimal, and if there is an adequate plan for debriefing subjects, when appropriate, and for disseminating the research results to them. Good examples of such a project are the increasingly popular audit studies that seek to uncover racism or sexism. See, for example, the

following: Massey, Douglas S. and Garvey Lundy. (2001). "Use of Black English and Racial Discrimination in Urban Housing Markets: New Methods and Findings." *Urban Affairs Review* 36(4), 452–469; Pager, Devah. (2003). "The Mark of a Criminal Record." *American Journal of Sociology* 108(5), 937–975; and South, Scott and Kyle D. Crowder. (1998). "Discrimination and Residential Mobility: Impacts for Blacks and Whites." *Population Policy and Research* 17(4), 369–387.

14. For example, sizable gifts in exchange for participating in a survey can overwhelm the possibility of voluntarism, especially in resource-poor environments.

15. See, for example, Bayer, Ronald. (1995). "AIDS, Ethics, and Activism: Institutional Encounters in the Epidemic's First Decade." Pp. 458–476 in *Society's Choices: Social and Ethical Decision Making in Biomedicine*, edited by Ruth Ellen Bulger, Elizabeth Meyer Bobby, and Harvey V. Fineberg; Resnik, David B. (1998). "The Ethics of HIV Research in Developing Nations." *Bioethics* 12(4), 286–333; and Specter, Michael. (2003). "The Vaccine." *The New Yorker*, February 3, pp. 54–65.

16. Although obtaining IRB approval from the place where you will do your research is not required, it is probably better to do so prior to obtaining IRB approval from your home institution. Interestingly, the proliferation of IRB panels in many institutions in developing countries has served to empower local researchers in important ways.

17. See, for example, The American Association of University Professors website, accessed September 15, 2005, at www.aaup.org/statements/Redbook/Rbethics.htm; the American Sociological Association website, accessed September 15, 2005, at www.asanet.org/page.ww?section=Ethics&name=Ethics; the American Psychological Association website, accessed September 15, 2005, at www.apa.org/ethics/homepage.html; the American Anthropological Association website, accessed September 15, 2005, at www.aaanet.org/committees/ethics/ethcode.htm; the American Historical Association website, accessed September 15, 2005, at www.historians.org/PUBS/free/professionalstandards.cfm; and the American Political Science Association website, accessed September 15, 2005, at www.apsanet.org/section_513.cfm. Economics and geography do not have codes of ethics, but the American Statistical Association has guidelines, accessed September 15, 2005, at www.amstat.org/profession/index.cfm?fuseaction=ethicalstatistics

18. By referring to "somewhat disinterested others," I am suggesting that colleagues not in the field—whether peers, advisers, or mentors—might be good sounding boards and reflectors for your situation. I do not preclude discussions with those "interested others" in the field with perspectives on the dilemma that will help illuminate the multiplicity of dimensions comprising the ethical dilemma.

Supplemental References

Entwisle, Barbara, Ronald R. Rindfuss, David K. Guilkey, Apichat Chamratrithirong, Sara R. Curran, and Yothin Sawangdee. (1993). "Social Networks and Contraceptive Choice in Thailand: Lessons Learned from a Focus Group Study in

Nang Rong District." In *Qualitative Methods for Population and Health Research*, edited by Bencha Yoddumnern-Attig and Associates. Salaya, Thailand: Institute for Population and Social Research, Mahidol University.

———. (1996). "Community and Contraceptive Choice in Rural Thailand: A Case Study of Nang Rong." *Demography* 33(1), 1–11.

Entwisle, Barbara, Ronald R. Rindfuss, Stephen J. Walsh, Tom P. Evans, and Sara R. Curran. (1997). "Geographic Information Systems, Spatial Network Analysis, and Contraceptive Choice." *Demography* 34, 171–187.

Rindfuss, Ronald R., David K. Guilkey, Barbara Entwisle, Apichat Chamratrithirong, and Yothin Sawangdee. (1996). "The Family Building Life Course and Contraceptive Use: Nang Rong, Thailand." *Population Research and Policy Review* 15, 341–368.

12

Maintaining
Perspective Is Essential

Bringing It All Back Home:
Personal Reflections on Friends,
Findings, and Fieldwork

Andrew Schrank

At the heart of the present volume lies an implied paradox: While the authors of the individual chapters have almost invariably described their own methods as "intuitive," "instinctual," and "idiosyncratic" (see, e.g., Chapter 6, Chapter 3, and the Part II overview), they would appear to believe that their approaches can be learned—or else they would not have wasted their time and energy contributing their individual stories to the collection. Is the portrait of the intuitive, instinctual field-worker compatible with the need for a guide to the process of fieldwork, and if so, how? I hope to answer the question by arguing that fieldwork is a craft and that, like craftspeople, field researchers would do well to study the efforts of their peers and predecessors *not* because they expect to find ready guidelines and recipes—the knowledge involved in craft production is inherently tacit and noncodifiable—but to immerse themselves in the cultures and customs of their communities; that is, *to understand a complicated ethos rather than to find a simple formula.*[1]

Seen in this light, a book like this one is perhaps different from most "methods" texts, for it is designed to offer an introduction to the craft of fieldwork rather than a guide to the—to my mind nonexistent—science of fieldwork. If it serves to demystify the craft of field-workers, to introduce a culture and community, and to translate and naturalize a language, then it will have achieved its goals.

I learned the craft of fieldwork the hard way—by making mistakes. I entered the field as a member of the first cohort of fellows of the Social Science Research Council's (SSRC's) International Predissertation Fellowship Program in 1992. I hoped to study what at the time seemed a fascinating empirical puzzle: the presence of a large community of Haitian migrants in the Dominican Republic, itself the source of an enormous outflow of migrants to the United States. I wanted to know how and why a small, low-income country like the Dominican Republic could simultaneously attract and disgorge migrant laborers. Why would Haitians migrate to a country so poor as to expel tens of thousands of its own citizens every year? And why would Dominicans employ immigrant Haitians rather than their own compatriots? I hoped to answer the question by drawing on theories of race, ethnicity, and labor market segmentation in plantation economies of the developing world.

Little did I know, however, that the question of Haitian immigration had already been addressed—and addressed in a very sophisticated manner—by scholars in the Dominican Republic. On arriving in Santo Domingo in early 1992, I scoured the local bookstores and libraries and found a number of compelling monographs and countless scholarly and popular articles on the subject—many of which I would later discover in my own university library (see, e.g., Báez Evertsz 1986; Moya Pons 1986; Lozano 1992). I simply had not known where or under what author and subject headings to look for them before entering the field, meeting local scholars, and talking to local librarians and booksellers.

Confronted by the potentially anachronistic nature of my research proposal, however, I faced a choice. I could either continue down the path I had set for myself and carry out yet another study of Haitian migrants in the Dominican Republic, or I could look for a new research question and reformulate my plans. Of course, the easy thing would have been to contact my advisers back in Wisconsin and ask their advice. But I was so embarrassed at having written—and, indeed, sold them on—what I now considered to be a "stupid" proposal that I was loathe to acknowledge what was going on. If this book had been available to me, I would have read Michael Watts's discussion of research proposals (see Chapter 10) and realized that "even the best-laid research plans cannot—and should never—be cast in stone" and that, in any event, I should have been in touch with my advisers all along. They would have welcomed periodic updates, not viewed them as a burden.

But I did not know this. I knew only that I could not in good conscience spend a year of my life and thousands of the SSRC's dollars essentially replicating somebody else's research and publishing it under my name. So, all but debilitated by "ethical angst" (see Chapter 11), I chose Plan B and spent the next few months looking for a new topic.

Fortunately for me, I found one rather quickly. In the early 1990s, the Dominican Republic was undergoing a profound and largely unanticipated socioeconomic transformation. On the one hand, the sugar plantations, which had traditionally constituted the backbone of the Dominican economy—as well as the chief locus of Haitian employment—were in crisis. North American soft drink producers were beginning to use artificial sweeteners. North American sugarcane and sugar beet farmers were beginning to demand protection. And the U.S. government had therefore decided to cut the Dominican sugar quota in half. On the other hand, the country's labor-intensive, export-oriented manufacturing sector was booming. Asian garment manufacturers had reached the limits of their export quotas to the United States. North American apparel firms and retailers were demanding new, more proximate sources of supply. And Washington was therefore encouraging the spread of export processing zones (EPZs) in—and foreign direct investment to—the Caribbean Basin.

Thus, I set out to investigate the social origins and consequences of export diversification in the Dominican Republic—that is, the underpinnings and impact of the country's rapid transformation from an exporter of bulk agricultural commodities in the so-called old international division of labor to an exporter of low-cost, labor intensive manufactured goods in the new international division of labor (see Fröbel, Heinrichs, & Kreye 1980). I hypothesized that the EPZ—a geographically circumscribed "free market island" (Schrank 2001)—would constitute the modern-day institutional equivalent of the plantation, and at first, the parallels seemed uncanny. EPZs not only required ready access to roads, ports, and large volumes of unskilled, easily repressed labor, like the plantations that had come beforehand, but were in many cases built on top of the old plantations themselves—for the Dominican government had deliberately transformed a number of the country's more vulnerable sugar estates into EPZs (see Safa 1999). Nor was I the only observer to note the uncanny parallels. Tom Brass and Henry Bernstein had recently outlined the similarities in the *Journal of Peasant Studies* (1992), and Michael Lind would eventually argue that "the EPZ is nothing new; it used to be called the plantation" (Lind 1995).

Thus, I returned to the United States and prepared to write a dissertation that would unpack the variegated ways in which the "banana republic," in Lind's words, was being replaced by the "sweatshop republic" as "national middle class capitalism" gave way to "global plantation capitalism" (Lind 1995). I took a host of methods classes, not only in sociology, my home discipline, but in statistics, geography, and urban planning as well. I read everything I could find on EPZs and labor-intensive, export-oriented manufacturing more generally. And I returned to the Dominican Republic to pursue exploratory fieldwork in the summer of 1996, armed with my newfound knowledge of theory and methods.

In a sense, my trip was a fruitful one. I carried out open-ended interviews with a number of public- and private-sector officials who had ties to the EPZs. I gained access to a treasure trove of primary documents on U.S. efforts to promote the export manufacturing sector in the 1980s and early 1990s. And I gathered valuable survey data from a number of government agencies. But the evidence contravened my hypothesis in at least three ways. First, while the EPZs were frequently located on or near old sugar plantations, they utilized a distinct labor force. The plantation labor force had been almost entirely male and largely immigrant. The EPZ labor force was disproportionately female and almost entirely native born. Second, while the EPZs were located near the old plantation ports, they almost invariably shipped their materials from the country's largest containerized port, in Santo Domingo. And finally, and perhaps most important, while a plurality of the country's EPZs were located in the traditional eastern sugar zone, the most successful EPZs—in terms of attracting and retaining investment, developing local linkages, and "upgrading" their production—were located in the traditional tobacco, coffee, and cocoa territory to the north. Thus, my empirical findings flew in the face of my theoretical expectations. The EPZs were not simply the modern incarnations of the old sugar plantations.

Furthermore, the north's achievements were particularly vexing, for tobacco, coffee, and cocoa had not been grown on plantations at all but had customarily been grown by commercialized family farmers and exported by large trading houses in the relatively prosperous interior city of Santiago. Why, given its remote location and relatively high factor costs, had Santiago come to dominate the low-cost export-manufacturing sector? On my return to the United States, I tried to ignore the question and to treat Santiago's success as nothing more than an anomaly—the sort of thing that goes in the error term of a multivariate equation—rather than to "incorporate the surprise" into a revised version of my hypothesis, as suggested by Michael Piore (Chapter 7).

As time went on and a return to the field—this time to complete my dissertation fieldwork—drew closer, however, my hypothesis grew less and less tenable, and alternatives came to seem more and more attractive. Why? On the one hand, I had by now taken enough mainstream methodology courses to be convinced of the merits of at least a moderate version of "falsificationism," and if ever a hypothesis had seemed falsified, it was my "sweatshop republic" idea. On the other hand, I had begun to notice a recurrent pattern in the comparative historical literature on secondary cities, that is, that secondary cities are often more dynamic than their primary counterparts (see, e.g., the various references in Hirschman 1968).

Therefore, I began to acknowledge Santiago for what it was: not an exception to be ignored or explained away but the basis for a new theory of export diversification. Perhaps, I reasoned, the residents of Santiago—a geographically and culturally remote secondary city—had little choice but to abandon agriculture for industry. While the public sector offered residents of the capital of Santo Domingo at least a modicum of prosperity and upward mobility, low factor costs guaranteed the flow of foreign investors to the southeastern sugar zone. Santiago had neither public-sector jobs to dole out nor the lure of particularly low-cost labor, however, and as its agrarian economy began to decline in the late 20th century, its relatively cohesive elite was all but forced to pursue export manufacturing with a vengeance. Hence, the success and domestication of the northern EPZs.

I therefore returned to the field once more in early 1998, hoping to explore the variety of agro-industrial transformations under way in the Dominican Republic: the EPZ as a modern-day plantation in the southeastern sugar zone and the EPZ as a potential stepping-stone toward sustainable industrial development in the northern coffee, tobacco, and cocoa zone. So far so good. But on my arrival, I was forced to confront a new—and literal—crisis. The EPZ sector was in turmoil, and firm after firm was closing up shop. The culprit, according to almost every factory owner I interviewed, was the North American Free Trade Agreement (NAFTA), which offered Mexico both tariff and factor cost advantages that the Caribbean Basin could not duplicate. My respondents carried on incessantly about the unfairness of it all, the inevitable disappearance of the Dominican Republic's new leading sector, and the likely arrival of "una pobreza espantosa" (a terrifying poverty) in short order.

Except for one. One elderly and experienced factory owner, when asked about the crisis, denied its very existence. "Have you looked at the aggregate export data?" he asked. "No," I replied, "but I've seen the bankruptcy figures." "Look at the aggregate export data," he advised. And so I did. And much to my surprise, the Dominican Republic's textile, clothing, and footwear exports—the chief products of the EPZs—had continued to grow in the wake of NAFTA's implementation in the mid-1990s. The rate of growth had diminished, of course, but the volume of exports had grown, and by 2000, the number of workers employed in the country's EPZs had grown by several thousand over the pre-NAFTA level.

What, then, was going on? A shakeout, my source suggested, induced not so much by NAFTA as by broader changes in the industry. I need not rehearse those changes at great length here. I have done so elsewhere, and I feel confident in my—and my source's—assessment (Schrank 2005). Suffice it to say, however, that I had stumbled onto a much more interesting story than the one I had gone looking for in 1992, 1996, or even 1998. And it gets more interesting as time goes on (see Chapter 2, on case studies).

What does this have to do with the craft of fieldwork? Well, I would like to think that in the course of getting my story straight and learning how to tell it—that is, how not only to understand but to explain the Dominican Republic's unanticipated and yet undeniable transformation—I also learned how to do fieldwork. But I did not do so as an individual or an isolate. The differences between my first visit to the field and my last included, not only the fact that I had taken courses back home and that I now had experiences from my previous trips to draw on, but also, and not least importantly, that I had had exposure to dozens of other scholars who had themselves undertaken fieldwork. When I first went to the Dominican Republic, I was a year out of college. Not only had I never been to the field, but almost none of my peers had either. I was not even an apprentice yet. I was a novice. By the time I reentered the field to undertake my dissertation research, however, almost all my peers had undertaken fieldwork, and we had spent countless hours discussing our experiences: our successes, our failures, and what we would do differently if we had it to do over again. I was, in other words, part of a community of craftspeople, and our craft was fieldwork.

This book is the product of such a community. It contains many of their stories, and I cannot help but think that if I had had it, or something like it, in 1992, I would have learned faster and perhaps more efficiently what I ultimately learned over a period of six years. I know that at the very least I would have learned what I ultimately learned with less "ethical angst" and fewer sleepless nights. For it most assuredly would have helped me deal with what I thought at the time was a unique situation but now realize is all but universal in our craft: the overwhelming sense of distress one feels when one reaches the field and realizes that one's project is either undoable, already done, or not worth doing: "I've invested all this time and energy, pulled up stakes, moved to a foreign country where I'm a complete stranger to everybody, and for one reason or another, my time here is going to be worthless."

What is the appropriate reaction to such a quandary? I think the chapters in this volume point to a few important lessons: First, don't panic. When I first went to the field and found that my project was anachronistic, I thought I was the only one ever to encounter the situation. When I encountered similar situations later on, however, I had a number of peers to turn to. One friend, in particular, had studied at Berkeley with Michael Watts. He told me that Watts had warned him that when he reached the field, he would inevitably find that his proposal was either undoable or undoable as planned; that he would need to make the necessary adjustments; and that the ability to do so was the mark of the true scholar—all points which, perhaps ironically, he reiterates in his contribution to this volume (see Chapter 10). Just knowing that there was a tenured professor out there at Berkeley who had not only gone through a similar situation but described it as normative or typical calmed me down, and I now realize—as Watts and a number of other contributors to this volume have underscored—that such unanticipated shocks are part of the normal course of events in our profession. It is how we deal with them that matters.[2]

And how do we deal with them? A second friend quoted his adviser, an American historian, as saying that a topic was not overstudied until it had generated as many books as Abraham Lincoln's life. The Library of Congress contains several hundred biographies of Lincoln, and I am not sure every problem requires so many. But the basic point remains: We tend to think that if a problem or phenomenon has been studied at all, it is no longer worth studying. Nothing could be further from the truth. Scholarly progress occurs when we study and restudy an old problem in order to garner new insights. And the best studies are often the latter ones—precisely because they engage and build on their predecessors.

Nevertheless, sometimes we really do encounter a problem that is not worth the effort. In my case, it was not simply that the issue of Haitian migration had been studied to death or that there was nothing new to say on the matter, although the former was close to the truth and the latter a distinct possibility. But many Dominican scholars had already staked their claims in the area, and out of ethical concerns like those discussed by Sara Curran in Chapter 11, I did not wish to encroach on their territory. I did not abandon the project, however, until I had found a more interesting—to me—area to move into. The lesson here, I believe, is not to abandon ship until you have found a reliable lifeboat.

Where are you likely to find such a lifeboat? In Chapter 10 of this volume, Michael Watts suggests a focus on empirical puzzles. Arthur Stinchcombe makes a similar point in his classic work on *Constructing Social Theories*

(1968). Historically, the great social scientists have been problem solvers, he argues. Marx, Weber, and Durkheim "did not work mainly at what we now call 'theory.' Instead, they worked out explanations of the growth of capitalism, or of class conflict, or of primitive religions" (Stinchcombe 1968, p. 3)— and thereafter used their findings to build more general theories. When they are good, according to Stinchcombe, scholars like de Tocqueville, Trotsky, and Smelser are doing the same thing: using history and empirical facts to build theory, not vice versa (Stinchcombe 1978, pp. 2–3).[3]

And finally, how do we know where the puzzles are—let alone how to solve them? Here, I would second the advice of Harrell, Gottlieb, Giles-Vernick, Piore, and Vitalis in this volume and say, at least in part, "Let your sources tell you." The sources may be living or dead, found in archives or on street corners, but they almost certainly know as much or more about their surroundings than you do, and by listening to them and trusting them, by treating them as your friends and guides, you will almost certainly make yourself a better field-worker.

That said, however, there is still no substitute for the actual practice of fieldwork. After all, Michael Piore (Chapter 7) and Charles Sabel note that skilled craftspeople require a wide array of expertise and ability; that the relevant knowledge is often tacit rather than codifiable; and that they are therefore unlikely to be adequately prepared by "book learning alone" (Piore & Sabel 1984, pp. 273–274). The same holds true of field-workers. While books like this can go a long way toward demystifying the process and opening the door for the novice, actual mastery demands entry into—and immersion in— a community of experienced scholars. As a number of the preceding chapters have argued, however, one need not wait to reach the field before beginning the initiation process. Most universities have archival resources worth perusing (Chapter 1). Many departments offer courses that foster practical experience in ethnography (Chapter 3). And almost all have statistical software and access to online survey data (Chapter 6). Thus, there is no obvious barrier to initiation. It simply takes the willingness to explore new approaches and to learn by doing. Better to begin sooner rather than later.

Notes

1. I would like to express my sincere gratitude to Michael Piore, who has not only taught me most everything I know about craft production and a good deal of what I know about fieldwork but has also served as a model of an intellectually acute, publicly engaged, and downright generous comparative social scientist—as well as a good friend. See Piore and Sabel (1984, especially pp. 273–275) on the training of craftspeople and craft workers in general.

2. Watts echoes these sentiments yet again in his discussion of the "necessary and inevitable risks and uncertainties of *doing* research" in Chapter 10 of this volume (p. 195).

3. Michael Piore (Chapter 7) describes a microlevel version of the same process: using individuals and their stories to build theories. As C. Wright Mills would have noted, the individuals and their stories scale up to constitute what we call "history."

Bibliography on Research Ethics and Other Essential Reading

1. Research Ethics

Overview of Ethical Research Practice

American Anthropological Society. (n.d.). "Final Report of the AAA El Dorado Task Force." Retrieved September 15, 2005, from www.aaanet.org/edtf/index.htm

American Association of University Professors staff. (2001). "Protecting Human Beings: Institutional Review Boards and Social Science Research." *Academe* 87(3), 55–57.

Brainard, Jeffrey. (2001). "The Wrong Rules for Social Science?" *Chronicle of Higher Education* 47(26), 26–27.

Brandt, Allan M. and Lara Freidenfelds. (1999). "Context and Community: Assessing the Ethics of Industry-Funded Research." Pp. 128–134 in *Beyond Regulations: Ethics in Human Subjects Research*, edited by Nancy M. King, Gail Henderson, and Jane Stein. Chapel Hill: University of North Carolina.

De Vaus, David A. (1996). *Surveys in Social Research*. London, UK: University College of London Press. See Chapter 19, "Ethics in Survey Research."

Faden, Ruth R. and Tom L. Beauchamp (with Nancy King). (1986). *A History and Theory of Informed Consent*. New York: Oxford University Press.

Feinstein, Alvan R. (1991). "Scientific Paradigms and Ethical Problems in Epidemiologic Research." *Journal of Clinical Epidemiology* 44, 119S–123S.

Fluehr-Lobban, Carolyn. (1994). "Informed Consent in Anthropological Research: We Are Not Exempt." *Human Organization* 53(1), 1–10.

Freed-Taylor, Marcia. (1994). "Ethical Considerations in European Cross-National Research." *International Social Science Journal* 142, 523–532. Retrieved September 15, 2005, from www.unesco.org/most/ethissj.htm

Johnson, Carole Gaar. (1982). "Risks in the Publication of Fieldwork." In *The Ethics of Social Research: Fieldwork, Regulation, and Publication*, edited by Joan Sieber. New York: Springer-Verlag.

Katz, Jay (with Alexander Morgan Capron and Eleanor Swift Glass). (1972). *Experimentation With Human Beings: The Authority of the Investigator, Subject, Professions, and State in the Human Experimentation Process*. New York: Russell Sage Foundation.

King, Nancy M., Gail Henderson, and Jane Stein. (1999). *Beyond Regulations: Ethics in Human Subjects Research*. Chapel Hill: University of North Carolina.

Kopelman, Loretta M. (1999). "Bias and Conflicts of Interest in Science: Controversial Industry Funding of Infant-Feeding Studies." Pp. 123–127 in *Beyond Regulations: Ethics in Human Subjects Research*, edited by Nancy M. King, Gail Henderson, and Jane Stein. Chapel Hill: University of North Carolina.

Lederman, Rena S. (2004). "Bureaucratic Oversight of Human Research and Disciplinary Diversity." *Anthropology News* (May).

Miles, Matthew B. and A. Michael Huberman. (1994). "Ethical Issues in Analysis." In *An Expanded Sourcebook: Qualitative Data Analysis*, 2d ed. Thousand Oaks, CA: Sage.

National Commission for the Protection of Human Subjects of Biomedical and Behavioral Research. (1979). "Belmont Report." Retrieved September 15, 2005, from www.hhs.gov/ohrp/humansubjects/guidance/belmont.htm

Pels, Peter. (1999). "Professions of Duplexity: A Prehistory of Ethical Codes in Anthropology." *Current Anthropology* 40(2), 101–136.

Popkin, Barry M. (1999). "Truth-in-Funding: Studying the Infant-Feeding Controversy With Industry Support." Pp. 113–122 in *Beyond Regulations: Ethics in Human Subjects Research*, edited by Nancy M. King, Gail Henderson, and Jane Stein. Chapel Hill: University of North Carolina.

Ruane, Janet. (2005). "Ethics: It's the Right Thing to Do." In *Essentials of Research Methods: A Guide to Social Science Research*, edited by M. A. Malden. Oxford, UK: Blackwell.

Sieber, Joan. (2001). "Privacy and Confidentiality: As Related to Human Research in Social and Behavioral Science." In *Ethical and Policy Issues in Research Involving Human Participants: Volume II*. Bethesda, MD: National Bioethics Advisory Commission.

Steneck, Nicholas H. (1994). "Research Universities and Scientific Misconduct: History, Policies, and the Future." *Journal of Higher Education* 65(3), 310–330.

U.S. Department of Health and Human Services. (2005). "Protection of Human Subjects." 45 C.F.R. 46. Retrieved September 15, 2005, from www.hhs.gov/ohrp/humansubjects/guidance/45cfr46.htm. This is known as the *Common Rule*.

Wakin, Eric. (1992). *Anthropology Goes to War: Professional Ethics and Counterinsurgency in Thailand*. Madison: University of Wisconsin, Center for Southeast Asian Studies.

Wax, Murray L. (1995). "Commentary: Informed Consent in Applied Research." *Human Organization* 54(3), 330–331.

Ziman, John. (1998). "Why Must Scientists Become More Ethically Sensitive Than They Used to Be?" *Science* 282(5395), 1813–1814.

Ethics and Fieldwork

Adams, Richard N. and Delmos J. Jones. (1971). "Responsibilities of the Foreign Scholar to the Local Scholarly Community." *Current Anthropology* 12(3), 335–356.

Adams, William M. and Charles McGraw. (1997). "Researchers and the Rural Poor: Asking Questions in the Third World." *Journal of Geography in Higher Education* 21(2), 215–220.

Allen, Charolette. (1997). "Spies Like Us: When Sociologists Deceive Their Subjects." *Lingua Franca* 7(9), 31–39.

Barnes, John A. (1979). *Who Should Know What? Social Science, Privacy and Ethics.* Cambridge, UK: Cambridge University Press.

Benjamin, Alan. (1999). "Contract and Covenant in Curaçao: Reciprocal Relationships in Scholarly Research." Pp. 49–66 in *Beyond Regulations: Ethics in Human Subjects Research*, edited by Nancy M. King, Gail Henderson, and Jane Stein. Chapel Hill: University of North Carolina.

Cassell, Joan and Sue-Ellen Jacobs, eds. (1987). *Handbook on Ethical Issues in Anthropology.* Special Publication of the American Anthropological Association #23. Washington, DC: American Anthropological Association.

Chilungu, Simeon W. (1976). "Issues in the Ethics of Research Method: An Interpretation of the Anglo-American Perspective." *Current Anthropology* 17(3), 457–481.

Coy, Patrick G. (2001). "Shared Risks and Research Dilemmas on a Peace Brigades International Team in Sri Lanka." *Journal of Contemporary Ethnography* 30(5), 575–606.

Craemer, Willy De. (1983). "A Cross-Cultural Perspective on Personhood." *Health and Society* 61(1), 19–34.

De Vaus, David A. (1996). *Surveys in Social Research.* London, UK: University College of London Press. See Chapter 19, "Ethics in Survey Research."

De Vita, Philip R., ed. (2000). *Stumbling Toward Truth: Anthropologists at Work.* Prospect Heights, IL: Waveland Press.

De Volo, Lorraine Bayard and Edward Schatz. (2004). "From the Inside Out: Ethnographic Methods in Political Research." *Political Science & Politics.* 37 (April): 267–271.

Emerson, Robert M., Rachel I. Fretz, and Linda Shaw. (1995). *Writing Ethnographic Fieldnotes.* Chicago, IL: University of Chicago Press.

Estroff, Sue. (1999). "The Gaze of Scholars and Subjects." Pp. 72–80 in *Beyond Regulations: Ethics in Human Subjects Research*, edited by Nancy M. King, Gail Henderson, and Jane Stein. Chapel Hill: University of North Carolina.

Eysenbach, Gunther and James Till. (2001). "Ethical Issues in Qualitative Research on Internet Communities." *British Medical Journal* 323(10), 1103–1105.

Fontes, Lisa Aronson. (1998). "Ethics in Family Violence Research: Cross-Cultural Issues." *Family Relations* 47(1), 53–61.

Fox, Renee. (1999). "Contract and Covenant in Ethnographic Research." Pp. 67–71 in *Beyond Regulations: Ethics in Human Subjects Research*, edited by Nancy M. King, Gail Henderson, and Jane Stein. Chapel Hill: University of North Carolina.

Giles, James E. (2001). "Ethics and Epistemology in the Twenty-first Century." *Cross Currents* 51(3), 399–404.

Herrera, C. D. (1999). "Two Arguments for 'Covert Methods' in Social Research." *The British Journal of Sociology* 50(2), 331–343.

King, Nancy M. P., Gail E. Henderson, and Jane Stein. (1999). "Relationships in Research: A New Paradigm." In *Beyond Regulations: Ethics in Human Subjects Research*, edited by Nancy M. King, Gail E. Henderson, and Jane Stein. Chapel Hill: University of North Carolina Press.

Lee, Raymond and Claire Renzetti, eds. (1993). *Doing Research on Sensitive Topics*. Newbury Park, CA: Sage. See Chapters 1–13.

Lee-Treweek, Geraldine and Stephanie Linkogle. (2000). *Danger in the Field: Risk and Ethics in Social Science*. London, UK: Routledge.

Morgan, George A., Robert J. Harmon, and Jeffrey A. Gliner. (2001). "Ethical Problems and Principles in Human Research." *Journal of the American Academy of Child and Adolescent Psychiatry* 40(10), 1231–1233.

Online Ethics Center. (2000). "Do the Ends Justify the Means? The Ethics of Deception in Social Science Research." *Online Ethics Center*, 11(June). Retrieved November 3, 2005, from onlineethics.org/reseth/appe/vol1/justify.html

Orkin, Mark. (1998). "The Politics and Problematics of Survey Research: Political Attitudes During the Transition to Democracy in South Africa." *American Behavioral Scientist* 42(2), 201–222.

Partridge, William. (1979). "Ethical Dilemmas." In *The Craft of Community Study: Fieldwork Dialogues*, edited by William L. Partridge and Solon T. Kimball. Gainesville: University Press of Florida.

Punch, Maurice. (1986). *The Politics and Ethics of Fieldwork*. Beverly Hills, CA: Sage.

Rynkiewich, Michael and James P. Spradley, eds. (1976). *Ethics and Anthropology: Dilemmas in Fieldwork*. New York: Wiley.

Shea, Christopher. (2000). "Don't Talk to the Humans: The Crackdown on Social Science Research." *Linguafranca* 10(6), 26–34.

Shrag, Brian. (2001). "Commentary on Crossing Cultural Barriers: Informed Consent in Developing Countries." *Online Ethics Center*, 5. Retrieved November 3, 2005, from onlineethics.org/reseth/appe/vol5/culturalc1.html

Tisdale, Kit. (2004). "Being Vulnerable and Being Ethical With/in Research." In *Foundations for Research: Methods of Inquiry in Education and the Social Sciences*, edited by Kathleen DeMarais and Stephen D. Lapan. Mahwah, NJ: L. Erlbaum Associates.

Ethics of Research Collaborations and Dissemination

Adams, Richard N. and Delmos J. Jones. (1971). "Responsibilities of the Foreign Scholar to the Local Scholarly Community." *Current Anthropology* 12(3), 335–356.

Barrett, Christopher and Jeffrey W. Cason. (1997). *Overseas Research: A Practical Guide*. Baltimore, MD: Johns Hopkins University Press.

Benatar, Solomon. (2001). "Commentary: Justice and Medical Research: A Global Perspective." *Bioethics* 15(4), 333–340.

————. (2002). "Reflections and Recommendations on Research Ethics in Developing Countries." *Social Science and Medicine* 54, 1131–1141.

Benatar, Solomon and Peter Singer. (2000). "A New Look at International Research Ethics." *British Medical Journal* 321(7264), 824–826. Retrieved September 15, 2005, through www.bmj.com

Bourgois, Philippe. (1990). "Confronting Anthropological Ethics: Ethnographic Lessons from Central America." *Journal of Peace Research* 27(1): 43–54.

Canagarajah, A. Suresh. (1996). "Non-Discursive Requirements in Academic Publishing, Material Resources of Periphery Scholars, and the Politics of Knowledge Production." *Written Communication* 13(4), 435–472.

Carey, David. (2003). "Symbiotic Research: A Case for Ethical Scholarship." *NEA Education Journal* (Summer), 99–114.

Cassell, Joan, ed. (1987). *Children in the Field*. Philadelphia, PA: Temple University Press.

DaVita, Philip, ed. (1990). *The Humbled Anthropologist: Tales From the Pacific*. Belmont, CA: Wadsworth.

Dumont, Jean-Paul. (1978). *The Headman and I: Ambiguity and Ambivalence in the Fieldworking Experience*. Austin: University of Texas Press.

"Ethics of Clinical Research in the Third World" (editorial). (1997). *New England Journal of Medicine* 337(12), 847–849.

Golde, Peggy, ed. (1986). *Women in the Field: Anthropological Experiences*, 2d ed. Berkeley: University of California Press.

Gottlieb, Alma and Philip Graham. (1994). *Parallel Worlds: An Anthropologist and a Writer Encounter Africa*. New York: Crown Publishers.

Gregory, James. (1984). "The Myth of the Male Ethnographer and the Woman's World." *American Anthropologist* 86(2), 316–327.

Jones, Todd. (1998). "Interpretive Social Science and the 'Native's Point of View': A Closer Look." *Philosophy of Social Sciences* 28(1), 32–68.

Kaufman, Charles E. and Saumya Ramarao. (2005). "Community Confidentiality, Consent, and the Individual Research Process: Implications for Demographic Research." *Population Research and Policy Review* 24, 149–173.

Lee, Raymond and Claire Renzetti, eds. (1993). *Doing Research on Sensitive Topics*. Newbury Park, CA: Sage. See Chapters 14–16.

Mitchell, William. "A Goy in the Ghetto: Gentile-Jewish Communication in Fieldwork Research." In *Anthropology for the Nineties: Introductory Readings*, edited by Johnetta Cole. New York: Free Press.

Rabinow, Paul. (1977). *Reflections on Fieldwork in Morocco*. Berkeley: University of California Press.

Romm, Norma R. A. (2001). *Accountability in Social Research: Issues and Debates*. New York: Kluwer Academic/Plenum Publishers.

Salzano, Francisco M., John E. Ferling, and A. Magdalena Hurtado, eds. (2003). *Lost Paradises and the Ethics of Research and Publication*. New York: Oxford University Press. Contributes to the debate over the work of Napoleon Chagnon and James Neel among the Yanomamö.

White, Catherine and Cathy Bailey. (2004). "Feminist Knowledge and Ethical Concerns: Towards a Geography of Situated Ethics." *Espace, Populations, Societes* 1,131–141.

Wolfe, Alan. (2003). "Invented Names, Hidden Distortions in Social Science." *Chronicle of Higher Education* 30(May), B13–14.

2. Other Essential Reading

Abbott, Andrew. (1988). "Transcending General Linear Reality." *Sociological Theory* 6(2), 169–186.

Adams, Julia, Elisabeth Clemens, and Ann Shola Orloff. (2005). "Social Theory, Modernity, and the Three Waves of Historical Sociology." In *Remaking Modernity: Politics, History and Sociology*, edited by Julia Adams, Elisabeth Clemens, and Ann Shola Orloff. Durham, NC: Duke University Press.

Asad, Talal. (1973). *Anthropology and the Colonial Encounter*. New York: Humanities Press.

Báez Evertsz, Franc. (1986). *Los braceros haitianos*. Santo Domingo, Dominican Republic: Taller.

Barnett, Michael. (1990). "High Politics Is Low Politics: The Domestic and Systemic Sources of Israeli Security Policy, 1967–1977." *World Politics* 42(4), 529–562.

Barrett, Richard and Martin King Whyte. (1982). "Dependency Theory and Taiwan: Analysis of a Deviant Case." *American Journal of Sociology* 87(5), 1064–1089.

Becker, Howard. (1986). *Writing for Social Scientists*. Chicago, IL: University of Chicago Press. This reference pertains to the writing up of research, as opposed to the conduct of research.

———. (1998). *Tricks of the Trade*. Chicago, IL: University of Chicago Press. This reference pertains to the writing up of research, as opposed to the conduct of research.

Bernard, H. Russell. (2002). *Research Methods in Anthropology: Qualitative and Quantitative Approaches*, 3d ed. New York: AltaMira Press.

Bhagwati, Jagdish. (1986). "Rethinking Trade Strategy." In *Development Strategies Reconsidered*, edited by John Lewis and Valeriana Kallab. New Brunswick, NJ: Transaction Books.

Blok, Anton. (1974). *The Mafia of a Sicilian Village*. Oxford, UK: Blackwell.

Booth, Wayne, Gregory Colomb, and Joseph Williams. (1995). *The Craft of Research*. Chicago, IL: University of Chicago Press. This reference pertains to the writing up of research, as opposed to the conduct of research.

Bowen, Elenore Smith [Laura Bohannan]. (1964). *Return to Laughter*. New York: Doubleday. Written pseudonymously by Laura Bohannan as a novel but grounded in actual fieldwork among the Tiv of Nigeria.

Bowen, William and Neil Rudenstein. (1992). *In Pursuit of the Ph.D.* Princeton, NJ: Princeton University Press.

Brass, Tom and Henry Bernstein. (1992). "Introduction: Proletarianisation and Deproletarianisation on the Colonial Plantation." *Journal of Peasant Studies* 19(3/4), 1–39.

Brenneis, Donald. (1994). "Discourse and Discipline at the National Research Council: A Bureaucratic Bildungsroman." *Cultural Anthropology* 9(1), 23–36.

Burawoy, Michael, Joshua Blum, Sheba George, Zsuzsa Gille, Teresa Gowan, Lynne Haney, Maren Klawiter, Steve Lopez, Sean O'Riain, and Millie Thayer. (2001). *Global Ethnography.* Berkeley: University of California Press.

Burawoy, Michael, Alice Burton, Ann Ferguson, Kathryn Fox, Joshua Gamsun, Nadien Gartrell, Leslie Hurst, Charles Kurzman, Leslie Salzinger, Josepha Schiffman, and Shiori Ui. (1991). *Ethnography Unbound.* Berkeley: University of California Press.

Burgess, Robert, ed. (1982). *Field Research.* London, UK: Allen and Unwin.

Campbell, Donald. (1975). "'Degrees of Freedom' and the Case Study." *Comparative Political Studies* 8(2), 178–193.

Campbell, Donald and Julian Stanley. (1966). *Experimental and Quasi-Experimental Designs for Research.* Chicago, IL: Rand McNally and Company. See Campbell (1975) for critique of Campbell and Stanley 1966.

Cantor, Nancy. (2000). "Statement From University of Michigan Provost Nancy Cantor on the Book, 'Darkness in El Dorado,' by Patrick Tierney, Published by W.W. Norton & Co." Retrieved September 15, 2005, from www.umich.edu/~urel/darkness.html

Chagnon, Napoleon. (1974). *Studying the Yanomamö.* New York: Holt, Rinehart and Winston.

——. ([1968] 1983). *Yanomamö: The Fierce People*, 3d ed. New York: Holt, Rinehart and Winston.

Clifford, James. (1988). "On Ethnographic Authority." In *The Predicament of Culture*, edited by James Clifford. Cambridge, MA: Harvard University Press.

Clifford, James and George Marcus, eds. (1986). *Writing Culture.* Berkeley: University of California Press.

Consortium on Qualitative Research Methods. This organization promotes case-based social scientific inquiry and maintains an essential website and a Listserv that cover developments in the field (accessed September 15, 2005, at www.asu.edu/clas/polisci/cqrm/).

Deleuze, Gilles. (1993). *Critical and Clinical.* Paris: Editions de Minuit.

Dion, Douglas. (1998). "Evidence and Inference in the Comparative Case Study." *Comparative Politics* 30(2), 127–145.

Dumont, Jean-Paul. (1978). *The Headman and I: Ambiguity and Ambivalence in the Fieldworking Experience.* Austin: University of Texas Press.

Durkheim, Emile. ([1897] 1997). *Suicide.* Glencoe, IL: Free Press.

Ellen, Roy F. (1984). *Ethnographic Research.* London, UK: Academic Press.

Emigh, Rebecca Jean. (1997). "The Power of Negative Thinking: The Use of Negative Case Methodology in the Development of Sociological Theory." *Theory & Society* 26(5), 605–740.

——. (1998). "The Mystery of the Missing Middle Tenants: The 'Negative' Case of Fixed-Term Leasing and Agricultural Investment in Fifteenth-Century Tuscany." *Theory & Society* 27(3), 351–375.

Evans-Pritchard, Edward E. (1940). *The Nuer*. Oxford, UK: Clarendon Press.

Feagin, Joe, Anthony Orum, and Gideon Sjoberg. (1991). *A Case for the Case Study*. Chapel Hill: University of North Carolina Press.

Firth, Raymond. (1936). *We, the Tikopia*. London, UK: Allen and Unwin.

Freeman, Derek. (1996). *Margaret Mead and Samoa*. Ringwood, Victoria, Australia: Penguin Books.

Fröbel, Folker, Jürgen Heinrichs, and Otto Kreye. (1980). *The New International Division of Labour: Structural Unemployment in Industrialised Countries and Industrialisation in Developing Countries*. Cambridge, UK: Cambridge University Press.

Geertz, Clifford. (1973). *Interpretation of Cultures*. New York: Basic Books.

———. (1988). *Works and Lives: The Anthropologist as Author*. Stanford, CA: Stanford University Press.

Geever, Jane and Patricia McNeill. (1997). *A Proposal-Writing Short-Course, Excerpt from the Foundation Center's Guide to Proposal-Writing*. New York: Foundation Center.

Geis, Gilbert. (1991). "The Case Study Method in Sociological Criminology." In *A Case for the Case Study*, edited by Joe Feagin, Anthony Orum, and Gideon Sjoberg. Chapel Hill: University of North Carolina Press.

Gilsenan, Michael. (1990). *Recognizing Islam*. London, UK: Tauris.

Hamilton, Nora. (1982). *The Limits of State Autonomy: Post-Revolutionary Mexico*. Princeton, NJ: Princeton University Press.

Hirschman, Albert. (1968). "The Political Economy of Import-Substituting Industrialization in Latin America." *Quarterly Journal of Economics* 82(1), 1–32.

Hoddinot, John and Stephen Devereux, eds. (1992). *Fieldwork in Developing Countries*. London, UK: Harvester Wheatsheaf.

Honingman, John J. (1982). "Sampling in Ethnographic Fieldwork." In *Field Research*, edited by Robert Burgess. London: Allen and Unwin.

Johnson, Allen and Orna Johnson. (1990). "Quality into Quantity: On the Measurement Potential of Ethnographic Fieldnotes." In *Fieldnotes: The Makings of Anthropology*, edited by Roger Sanjek. Ithaca, NY: Cornell University Press.

Johnson, Chalmers. (1982). *MITI and the Japanese Miracle: The Growth of Industrial Policy, 1925–1975*. Stanford, CA: Stanford University Press.

King, Gary, Robert O. Keohane, and Sidney Verba. (1994). *Designing Social Inquiry: Scientific Inference in Qualitative Research*. Princeton, NJ: Princeton University Press. For debate inspired by this book, see "Symposium on a Qualitative-Quantitative Disputation." (1995). *American Political Science Review* 89(2), 454–481.

Krathwohl, David. (1988). *How to Prepare a Research Proposal: Guidelines for Funding and Dissertations in the Social and Behavioral Sciences*. Syracuse, NY: Syracuse University Press. See especially Chapter 8, "A Checklist for Critiquing Proposals." (This reference pertains to the writing up of research, as opposed to the conduct of research.)

Kurtz, Marcus and Andrew Barnes. (2002). "The Political Foundations of Post-Communist Regimes: Marketization, Agrarian Legacies, or International Influences?" *Comparative Political Studies* 35(5), 524–553.

Latour, Bruno. (1987). *Science in Action*. Cambridge, MA: Harvard University Press.

Levi, Margaret. (2000). "Making a Case for Case Studies." *APSA-CP* 11, 19–21.

Lieberson, Stanley. (1985). *Making It Count: The Improvement of Social Research and Theory*. Berkeley: University of California Press.

———. (1991). "Small N's and Big Conclusions: An Examination of the Reasoning in Comparative Studies Based on a Small Number of Cases." *Social Forces* 70(2), 307–320.

Lijphart, Arend. (1971). "Comparative Politics and the Comparative Method." *American Political Science Review* 65(3), 682–693.

Lind, Michael. (1995). "To Have and to Have Not." *Harper's Magazine*, June, 35–39.

Lipset, Seymour. (1950). *Agrarian Socialism: A Study in Political Sociology*. Berkeley: University of California Press.

Lozano, Wilfredo. (1992). *La cuestion haitiana en Santo Domingo*. Santo Domingo, Dominican Republic: FLACSO.

Lubeck, Paul. (1987). *Islam and Urban Labor in Northern Nigeria*. Cambridge, UK: Cambridge University Press.

Lubeck, Paul and Robert Alford. (1985). "Epistemology and Social Science." University of California, Santa Cruz. Unpublished manuscript.

Malinowski, Bronislaw. ([1922] 1984). *Argonauts of the Western Pacific*. Prospect Heights, IL: Waveland Press.

March, James, Lee Sproull, and Michal Tamuz. (1991). "Learning From Samples of One or Fewer." *Organization Science* 2(1), 1–13.

Marcus, George and Michael Fischer. (1986). *Anthropology as Cultural Critique: An Experimental Moment in the Human Sciences*. Chicago, IL: University of Chicago Press.

Marx, Karl. (2001). *The 18th Brumaire of Louis Bonaparte*. London, UK: Electric Books.

Mead, Margaret. (1928). *Coming of Age in Samoa*. New York: William Morrow.

———. (1975). *Blackberry Winter*. New York: Washington Square Press. See especially chapters on fieldwork.

Moya Pons, Frank. (1986). *El batey: Estudio socioeconómico de los bateyes del Consejo Estatal del Azúcar*. Santo Domingo, Dominican Republic: Fondo para el avance de las ciencias sociales.

O'Donnell, Guillermo. (1973). *Modernization and Bureaucratic Authoritarianism: Studies in South American Politics*. Berkeley: Institute of International Studies, University of California.

Paige, Jeffery. (1975). *Agrarian Revolution: Social Movements and Export Agriculture in the Underdeveloped World*. New York: Free Press.

———. (1999). "Conjuncture, Comparison, and Conditional Theory in Macrosocial Inquiry." *American Journal of Sociology* 105(3), 781–800.

Pelto, Pertti and Gretel Pelto. (1978). *Anthropological Research: The Structure of Inquiry*, 2d ed. Cambridge, UK: Cambridge University Press.

Piore, Michael and Charles Sabel. (1984). *The Second Industrial Divide: Possibilities for Prosperity.* New York: Basic.

Pryke, Michael, Gillian Rose, and Sarah Whatmore. (2003). *Using Social Theory.* Thousand Oaks, CA: Sage.

Przeworski, Adam and Frank Salomon. (1995). *The Art of Writing Proposals: Some Candid Suggestions for Applicants to Social Science Research Council Competitions.* New York: Social Science Research Council. This reference pertains to the writing of research proposals, as opposed to the conduct of research.

Przeworksi, Adam and Henry Teune. (1970). *Logic of Comparative Social Inquiry.* New York: John Wiley and Sons.

Ragin, Charles C. (1987). *The Comparative Method: Moving Beyond Qualitative and Quantitative Strategies.* Berkeley: University of California Press.

———. (1994). *Constructing Social Research: The Unity and Diversity of Method.* Thousand Oaks, CA: Pine Forge Press. See especially Chapter 4.

———. (2000). *Fuzzy Set Social Science.* Chicago, IL: University of Chicago Press.

Ragin, Charles C. and Howard Becker, eds. (2000). *What Is a Case? Exploring the Foundations of Social Inquiry.* Cambridge, UK: Cambridge University Press.

Reno, William. (1995). *Corruption and State Politics in Sierra Leone.* Cambridge, UK: Cambridge University Press.

Romer, Paul. (1993). "Two Strategies for Economic Development: Using Ideas and Producing Ideas." *World Bank Economic Review* March, 63–91 [Supplement]. Proceedings of the World Bank Annual Conference on Development Economics 1992.

Rosaldo, Michelle and Louise Lamphere. (1974). *Woman, Culture, and Society.* Stanford, CA: Stanford University Press.

Rosaldo, Renato. (1986). "From the Door of His Tent." In *Writing Culture,* edited by James Clifford and George Marcus. Berkeley: University of California Press.

Royal Anthropological Institute of Great Britain and Ireland. (1951). *Notes and Queries on Anthropology,* 6th ed. London, UK: Routledge and K. Paul.

Safa, Helen. (1999). "Women Coping With Crisis: Social Consequences of Export-Led Industrialization in the Dominican Republic." *North-South Agenda* 36(April), 1–22.

Sanjek, Roger, ed. (1990). *Fieldnotes: The Makings of Anthropology.* Ithaca, NY: Cornell University Press.

Sayer, Andrew. (1992). *Method in Social Science,* 2d ed. London, UK: Routledge.

Schensul, Jean and Margaret LeCompte, eds (1999). *Ethnographer's Toolkit* (7 volumes). Walnut Creek, CA: AltaMira Press.

Schoepfle, Werner. (1987). *Systematic Fieldwork: Ethnographic Analysis and Data Management.* Newbury Park, CA: Sage.

Schrank, Andrew. (2001). "Export Processing Zones: Free Market Islands or Bridges to Structural Transformation?" *Development Policy Review* 19(2), 223–242.

———. (2003). "Luring, Learning, and Lobbying: The Limits to Capital Mobility in the Dominican Republic." *Studies in Comparative International Development* 37(Winter), 89–116.

———. (2005). "Entrepreneurship, Export Diversification, and Economic Reform: The Birth of a 'Developmental Community' in the Dominican Republic." *Comparative Politics* 38(October).

Skocpol, Theda. (1976). "A Structural Analysis of Social Revolutions." *Comparative Studies in Society and History* 18(2), 175–210.

Skocpol, Theda and Margaret Somers. (1980). "The Uses of Comparative History in Macrosocial Inquiry." *Comparative Studies in Society and History* 22(2), 174–197.

Spradley, James. (1979). *The Ethnographic Interview*. New York: Holt, Rinehart, Winston.

———. (1980). *Participant Observation*. New York: Holt, Rinehard, Winston.

Srinivasan, T. N. and Jagdish Bhagwati. (2001). "Outward Orientation and Development: Are Revisionists Right?" In *Trade, Development and Political Economy: Essays in Honour of Anne Krueger*, edited by Deepak Lal and Richard Shape. London, UK: Palgrave.

Stinchcombe, Arthur. (1968). *Constructing Social Theories*. New York: Harcourt, Brace and World.

———. (1978). *Theoretical Methods in Social History*. New York: Academic Press.

Stoll, David. (2001). "Science Attacks Amazon Tribe." *The New Republic,* March, p. 34.

Tierney, Patrick. (2002). *Darkness in El Dorado: How Scientists and Journalists Devastated the Amazon*. New York: Norton.

Tilly, Charles. (1964). *The Vendée: A Sociological Account of the Counter-Revolution of 1793*. Cambridge, MA: Harvard University Press.

Walton, John. (1992). "Making the Theoretical Case." In *What Is a Case? Exploring the Foundations of Social Inquiry*, edited by Charles Ragin and Howard Becker. Cambridge, UK: Cambridge University Press.

White, Luise. (1990). *The Comforts of Home*. Chicago, IL: University of Chicago Press.

Whitehead, Tony Larry and Mary Ellen Conaway, eds. (1986). *Self, Sex and Gender in Cross-Cultural Fieldwork*. Urbana: University of Illinois Press.

Zerubavel, Eviatar. (1999). *The Clockwork Muse*. Cambridge, MA: Harvard University Press.

All issues of the 1982 *American Anthropologist.*

The review symposium in the 1995 *American Political Science Review* 89(June).

Various issues of the American Political Science Association Organized Section in Comparative Politics newsletter, accessed September 15, 2005, at www.nd.edu/~apsacp/

American Political Science Association's new Organized Section on Qualitative Methods provides a useful newsletter on qualitative methods (visit its website: http://www.asu.edu/clas/polisci/cqrm/).

Author Index

Subject Index

African history, oral history in, 85–86, 87–88
American Historical Association, 88–89
American Political Science Association's Qualitative Methods Section, 173
Anthropology, critique of, 165–166
Anthropology and the Colonial Encounter (Asad), 165–166
Anthropology as Cultural Critique (Marcus & Fischer), 166
Archives, 5–20
    familiarizing oneself with, 15
    political economy research in, 8–9
    primary sources in, 6
    record keeping needs, 7, 15
    skills needed for research in, 7–8
    use to assess internal validity, 11

Beard, Charles, 6–7, 16 (n8)
Belmont Report, 201
Beng people, 49, 54
Bias
    gender bias, 165, 207
    in case study research, 172
    in fieldwork, 163, 165–166
    in surveys/survey data, 120, 121, 125, 126, 131, 146, 190
    reporting bias, 120
    See also Ethical considerations
Bunche, Ralph, 16 (n8)

Case-based research, 21–45
    concept formation in, 22–23
    data collection/analysis, 33–35

democratic transitions case study, 25–29
industrial downgrading in garment trade, 29–31
industrial policy case study, 23–25
large-n research, 22
small-n research, 22–23
Case study
    causal mechanisms in, 31–33
    defining, 21–22, 169–170
    Mill's method of difference/ agreement, 171–172 (tab)
    one-shot, 171
    prevailing view of, 171
    variables in, 170, 171–172 (table)
    when to use, 173
Causal theory, variables in, 190, 192
Census, definition of, 119
Central America, democratic transitions case study on, 25–29
Charting, of social networks, 55–56
Coffee and Power (Paige), 23, 27
Coming of Age in Samoa (Mead), 167
Common Rule, 201, 202
Confidentiality, in focus group interview, 111–112
Consortium on Qualitative Research Methods, 173
Construct validity, in focus group research, 104
Costa Rica, democratic transitions case study on, 25–29
Côte d'Ivoire, 49, 54, 61
Curve fitting, 29